Counseling at the Workplace

Norman C. Hill

Exxon Corporation

McGraw-Hill Book Company

New York   St. Louis   San Francisco   Aukland   Bogotá   Düsseldorf
Johannesburg   London   Madrid   Mexico   Montreal   New Delhi   Panama
Paris   São Paulo   Singapore   Sydney   Tokyo   Toronto

Library of Congress Cataloging in Publication Data

Hill, Norman C   1951-
   Counseling at the workplace.

   Bibliography: p.
   Includes index.
   1. Employee counseling.   I. Title.
HF5549.5.C8H54   658.3'85   80-21769
ISBN 0-07-028785-6

COUNSELING AT THE WORKPLACE

1 2 3 4 5 6 7 8 9 0 DODO 8 9 8 7 6 5 4 3 2 1

This book was set in century by Toledo Typesetting. The editor was James J. Walsh, the production supervisor was Marie Birdsall, the copy editor was Joni Capuano, and the designer was William Dippel.

R.R. Donnelley & Sons Company was printer and binder.

Acknowledgements

I am grateful for the help and assistance of many people in the preparation of this manuscript. This book is a composite of many of my own experiences as well as of others with whom I have come in contact—many while I have been employed at Exxon. Although I alone am responsible for this book, and it does not necessarily reflect the philosophy or endorsement of Exxon, my employment experience with the managers and Employee Relations professionals who are a part of this company is both gratifying and challenging. Moreover, I have felt challenged by the work of many others, particularly the authors who are cited in the pages of this book. Gene Dalton, Paul Thompson, Edgar Schein, George Vaillant, William Glasser, Ernst Beier, and others have had a significant influence on my own thinking and my attempt to express those thoughts here.

Bill Kane of McGraw-Hill first suggested I write a book on counseling and has continually provided encouragement and support. Marie Birdsall and Jim Walsh, also of McGraw-Hill, have provided support and advice. Don Cherry of Exxon, Gary Jewkes of Tektronix, and Barbara Humphreys of Connecticut General all read the entire manuscript and provided many helpful suggestions. Some useful ideas were provided by Don Carpenter and Bill Wiggleworth who read several chapters. I appreciate as well the patience and efforts of Lisa Walsh and Peggy Jensen who typed and retyped several drafts of the chapters and vignettes.

I am deeply indebted to my family for their help and support. Raelene not only listened to my thoughts and offered suggestions, but also conducted role playing situations with me and critiqued both the process and content of them. Ryan and Kristen, though of less direct help, still cheered me on in their own way. I am also grateful to my extended family for their indirect participation in this project.

Preface

There is a growing concern, particularly in the United States, about productivity and how it can be improved. This is not to suggest that productivity has not always been a major concern. Clearly, such is not the case. The emphasis today, however, is more widespread than it has ever been in the past. Where productivity was once a topic primarily in the boardroom, now it is mentioned in the speeches of presidents and prime ministers and is the subject of television news specials. As a topic, it has reached a popular audience and become an everyday word.

Despite the concern about productivity, there still seems to be much disagreement about its definition, let alone its improvement. What factors should be used to evaluate it and what should be excluded? This is a simple enough question which, unfortunately, has many complex answers.

This book does not attempt to provide a definitive answer to that question. It is, instead, aimed only at a specific component of it. The focus of this book revolves around improving the competence of people at work; that is what counseling is really all about. Whether or not these same people will also be productive depends on the uses to which their competence is put.

Developing a sense of competence in others is not an easy task. It is a task made more difficult by the reward systems utilized in most organizations. Peter Drucker illustrated this concept with his observation that unfortunately in most organizations

"Getting ahead" is seen as the exclusive criterion of success. But inevitably only a minority can advance, only a minority of workers can become foremen, only a minority of foremen can become superintendents. If, as is the case in our society, advancement is seen as the only social goal, if every other satisfaction is regarded as subsidiary, the majority must necessarily feel dissatisfied.[1]

There are several alternatives to the kinds of outcomes Drucker describes, many of which are being applied in business and nonprofit organizations today. Workers on the board of directors, self-managed work teams, and participatory management efforts are all designed, implicitly, to reduce the alienation that is a consequence of traditional organizational structures and processes.

Changes in the formal structure are not the solution to the problem. Attempts to reorganize along different lines may make some organizations more egalitarian, but will not necessarily make them more productive. Productive goals require capable leaders who can inspire others to reach them. What is needed to improve overall productivity is a monetary and nonmonetary reward system to compensate those who are competent. Recognizing and using nonmonetary rewards will help shift the focus from a zero sum reward system where only a few benefit to a system where many can feel generously compensated. This is the real productivity challenge: to motivate those who feel no compelling reason to do well. Counseling employees at the workplace can assist in meeting that challenge.

Every organization has its "stars", those people with talent who will undoubtedly make it to the top. And respectively, every organization also has its "doughboys," those with less talent who quietly do their work and don't particularly care if they ever run the enterprise. The ability to tap the capabilities of this latter group is the productivity challenge in most organizations.

What Eric Hoffer, the philosopher-longshoreman, has said about the fabric of society also applies to the daily productivity of every organization.

It has often been stated that a social order is likely to be stable so long as it gives scope to talent. Actually, it is the ability to give scope to the untalented that is most vital in maintaining social stability. For not only are the untalented

---

[1] Peter Drucker, *The Concept of the Corporation* (New York: The John Day Company, Inc., 1972).

more numerous but, since they cannot transmute their grievances into creative effort, their dissatisfaction will be more pronounced and explosive. Thus the most troublesome problem which confronts social engineering is how to provide for the untalented...[2]

Any organization that is reasonably well-run provides numerable incentives for those who are talented and committed. This sector is given opportunities both for advancement and for creative expression of their talents. What about the others, the majority? In *The Concept of the Corporation*, Peter Drucker presented an idea for dealing with this very problem. Although rather general, his suggestion does indicate the direction one should follow in search of productivity improvement.

The problem of dignity and fulfillment—of status and function—is real...The problem cannot be solved alone by more or better opportunities for advancement or greater economic rewards...It is even likely that the lack of dignity and fulfillment which is so obviously the major problem of industrial society may only be aggravated by emphasizing economic opportunites and rewards. It is an oversimplification—but not altogether a falsification—that dignity and individual fulfillment are so difficult to achieve in industrial society because of its exclusive concern with economic advancement.[3]

Although status and dignity may seem like vague solutions to a pragmatic problem, they are the elements needed to develop the competence of people in organizations. The development of status and dignity need not remain vague abstractions. Nor are they simply "pie in the sky" or prologues for a new human relations gimmick that stresses "being nice to employees". Ideas and suggestions for enhancing personal worth and developing individual capabilities are outlined in this book. They are practical. They work. If they are carefully studied and consistently applied, they can improve the competence of people in dealing with work-related problems and thereby improve their personal productivity. Nothing less than aiding people in solving their individual problems holds as much

---

[2] Eric Hoffer, *In Our Time* (New York: Harper and Row, 1976).

[3] Peter Drucker, *The Concept of the Corporation* (New York: The John Day Company, Inc., 1972).

potential for performance improvement as this approach. Counseling is worth the effort because everyone benefits.

COUNSELING: AN ORIENTATION

Charles Reich in *The Greening of America*, a popular book on American society written in the early 1970s, described a dismal picture of life at work as he believed most people experienced it.

> The majority of adults in this country *hate their work.* Whether it is a factory job, a white collar job, or, with some exceptions, a professional job, or the role of being a housewife, they hate their work as much as young people who rebel at the prospect of similar work; indeed it is the parents' feelings that are a principal source of the children's feelings. The middle class also resents the authority that is imposed by work—the boss and the system—and they feel that they lack power over their own lives.[4]

Most people may not agree completely with Reich, but still feel some of the frustrations and restrictions to which he alludes. We dislike the drudgery and the repetition of our jobs. We resent the "bureaucrats" and the "apple polishers" who make our organizational lives difficult by their preoccupations with rules or themselves. We feel anxious about our place in the pecking order and our prospects for advancement. Our jobs are important to us, and if we find them dissatisfying it may be because we are dissatisfied with ourselves. Who we think we are and what we think we are capable of doing affects our satisfaction with our work. Job satisfaction and personal satisfaction are a two way street. If we feel trapped or powerless in our job, this may be the *result* of other actions and attitudes on our own part. Certainly, the converse may also be true. People who are capable of doing more or better do get locked into circumstances. Yet challenging work and feeling in control of our lives is not necessarily achieved through job enrichment or participatory management. People as well as circumstances must change for satisfaction and competence to be improved.

Organizations, like people, vary: how rigid, how flexible, how considerate, how ruthless. The relationship people have with the type of

---

[4] Charles A. Reich, *The Greening of America* (New York: Random House, 1970).

organization that employs them also varies. It is true that organizations are similarly structured in that people entering them find defined roles, prescribed relations between these roles, established norms and values, and the like. But their interaction is with other people. Roles and role relations are adaptable and subject to personal and group negotiation and redefinition. One does not relate to an organization but to other people who collectively make it up. There is no such thing as an organization per se. People act on their environment. They can change aspects of it. In fact, that is usually what they are paid for doing. We argue, advise, instruct and recommend in order to perform our jobs more efficiently. We act on our environment and it acts on us. The result is our satisfaction with our jobs and ourselves.

Focus of This Book

There are several basic reasons why this book was written. First and foremost was my own experience as a personnel and human resource development specialist. Over the last few years, I have increasingly been asked to counsel with people who had problems. For example, line managers have asked for help in correcting employees who had specific performance deficiencies such as excessive absenteeism or poor work habits. At other times, I have been called upon to coach someone whom a supervisor thought could perform much better with a little direction. I have also been asked by managers, and by employees directly, for assistance in defining and resolving concerns over pay, advancement, interpersonal relations, and career development. I have struggled to be a resource, to be helpful, and to facilitate the personal development of the person who sought me out. I have not always been successful. But I have not been satisfied with merely trying hard. I wanted to be effective.

I have read much on the topic of counseling. While there are many good books on mental health counseling, there is little that has been written about the process of counseling employees. Although there are some similarities, there are also some differences. As a minimum, there are three principal differences between the counseling process described here and mental health counseling:

Employee counseling is specific and task oriented. This means that the goal of employee counseling is usually related to a specific concern or problem. This does not mean that someone counseling an employee must accept the problem as given. Since many people disguise what may be troubling them until they are certain a prospective counselor is really going to listen, the most basic principle of counseling is to "listen with a third ear." This phrase suggests reading between the lines to understand what someone may *want* to say. It means discerning what may be problem symptoms, what may be problem causes and what may be simply "static" that must be cleared before the real message can be accurately relayed. Importantly, however, employee counseling attempts to deal with a *single* concern and leaves deep-seated neuroses to the mental health professional. Effective counselors learn to recognize their limits and abilities and refer people whose problems are beyond their capabilities to others.

Employee counseling is interactive and facilitative. Generally, both counselor and employee know one another and each has access to information pertinent to the employee's concerns. Whether the counselor is manager, trainer, or human resource development specialist, he or she has information that may assist in problem definitions or solutions that may be more useful than any the employee could develop with a complete outsider. Because of their position or their ability to be influential in the organization, counselors may be able to directly contribute to solving an employee's concern.

Employee counseling is both remedial and developmental. The focus of mental health counseling is usually aimed at fixing something that has gone wrong. Employee counseling may, however, be aimed at helping others cope with a specific aspect of their workaday lives, altering an interpersonal relationship, capturing an opportunity, or developing their skills. These problems require unique approaches that are explored in the pages of this book. Fritz Roethlisberger is credited with saying that the role of the behavioral sciences is to provide people with walking sticks. These walking sticks are simplified models and maps of essential life issues that will help people to better understand their personal world and make knowledgeable decisions when walking along life's path. The intent of this volume is to identify some markers that signal decision points in every day work life and provide walking sticks that will aid employees and counselors alike in appreciating the various implications of common work related issues.

This book is intended to appeal to a wide range of managers, trainers, and personnel specialists. The initial chapter is an introduction and an overview of the counseling process and describes some fundamental reasons why on-the-job counseling is important and what objectives it can be expected to achieve. The second chapter presents some important concepts and operational principles about people. Understanding the way people work is essential to understanding the counseling process. Key concepts about people which can be put to use in counseling are presented and described. This chapter does not present all there is to know about people, but does present some concepts describing some basic reasons why most of us act, believe, and feel as we do based on experiences we have had in our lives.

The third chapter presents some of the major concerns people experience: disappointment, anxiety, conflict, resentment, frustration. How these concerns develop and general ways for dealing with them are presented. In addition, hazards encountered in counseling are outlined. This chapter points out some ways to deal with dependency, superficiality, and intellectualizing. The chapter illustrates the timeliness of nondirective and facilitative approaches in comparison to more directive approaches.

Chapter 4 includes procedures for correcting, coaching, and consulting—the three basic types of counseling. It describes specific "how to's" for dealing with these basic approaches. This chapter is the essential link between what follows and what precedes it. It translates the general principles or theories presented in the earlier chapters into practical procedures. In addition, it provides a framework for the applications section that follows.

The applications section is more than a chapter. It is divided into nine units with each unit composed of three to five vignettes. The title of each vignette is written in dialogue form and represents the underlying reason for the counseling session. Examples are derived from a variety of work contexts: plant and office, private sector and public sector, manager and wage earner. Each of these examples is introduced with a brief description of the situation, is composed of a counselor-employee dialogue, and is followed by a critique highlighting the main counseling principles utilized and including relevant caveats to the method recommended. The names used in the dialogues are hypothetical and do not represent people known to me.

The intent of the vignettes or examples in the applications section is to illustrate how to apply concepts and principles discussed in the first four chapters.

There are two primary reasons for including so many examples and having almost two-thirds of the book composed of specific incidences. The first reason is that most people learn new concepts by initial exposure to specific, concrete events either personally or vicariously. We develop decision rules for ourselves by experiencing specific events and then generalizing because of them. For instance, an employee may have a single experience ("When I sent that letter out with a typographical error, did I ever hear about it!") which he or she doesn't think much about until he or she is able to create a category for such events ("Everything which goes out of this office must be carefully checked.") Only by being aware of and analyzing this generalization can accurate decision rules be made for determining how and when to abide by this conclusion ("Everything which goes out of this office must be carefully checked; but if the engineering manager discovers a mistake, I can easily be forgiven because he likes me and I can bluff the operations manager most of the time."). As individuals we learn, change our minds, or develop new attitudes when we react to a specific situation, examine the conclusions we reach (or have reached in the past), and decide what decision rules to consider. We accept new ideas or new ways of doing things by moving from the simple to the complex, from the concrete to the abstract. Each of the vignettes in the applications section is constructed in this manner.

The second basic reason for having most of this book composed of specific incidences is so it may more easily serve as a resource book. Organization according to commonly-voiced problems or concerns permits the reader to quickly locate ideas or methods that may fit a particular situation he or she faces.

The examples included in the applications section can be used in several ways. Managers can read a particular vignette when they face a specific situation and orient a discussion according to the pattern presented. Personnel and training specialists can use them as the focus of training programs on the various topics included or on the counseling process itself.

The final chapter of the book is a summary and a postscript. It presents some useful ways for creating and maintaining both personal and organizational change and includes a list of pertinent resources (books, films etc.) that may be useful in applying principles presented in the applications section.

For the sake of simplicity throughout this book, when referring to the person who is counseling, I will use the terms "counselor" or "manager" interchangeably. I do this because I think the process is basically the same whether or not one is a manager, trainer or personnel specialist. When referring to the person being counseled, I have used either "employee" or "the other person." Since these are basically neutral terms, they all seemed appropriate to use when discussing various principles and practices of counseling.

This book is the result of my experiences; it is based on my reading, my observations, and my counseling. It is my firm belief that the development of new skills is dependent upon the combined utilitization of each of these activities. It is my hope that those who read this book might be encouraged and directed to read, observe and counsel.

Counseling is something that most of us do on an everyday basis though we don't always think of it as such. Counseling does not require a formal setting or a set-aside time. It can be done in the hallway, the shop floor, on the bus, or in an office. What sets it apart from an ordinary discussion or a casual conversation is the element of *problem-solving*. When one person has a problem that he or she decides to discuss with someone, that someone becomes a counselor. Whether or not the role is performed well and whether or not the implicit contract of assistance is fulfilled is the matter with which this book attempts to deal.

Table
of Contents

Section II
Counseling: Applications

Unit 1

Pay, Promotions and Appraisals

Unit 2

Career Counseling

Unit 3

Male/Female Issues

Section I

Counseling: Approaches and Methods

Chapter 1

Employee Counseling: An Overview

Counseling is problem-solving with people. It is not so much a skill as it is a set of skills, being composed of such things as listening, communicating, understanding, clarifying, thinking, helping, assisting, advising, sharing and more. Counseling is not a passive function. It is more than "talking things over", although it is *not* a complicated set of procedures that must be followed correctly to avoid dire consequences. Counseling is a perspective that maintains that people often think best when they can think outloud with someone else who will test their ideas and help them be rigorous in their approach. Such reality testing, it has been found empirically, does improve the quality of problem-solving.[1]

Counseling is assisting people in the process of problem-solving. It includes helping people decide. It is not deciding for people, but rather aiding people in *how* they go about deciding. Rather than telling people what they should do, a counselor points out assumptions which may be questionable, constraints which may be self-imposed, problem definitions which may be restrictive, alternatives which may be incomplete, and solutions which may not fit the problem at hand. These activities, performed in a way that encourages people to

[1] Norman R. F. Maier, *Problem-solving Discussions and Conferences*, (New York: McGraw-Hill, 1963).

1

generate valid conclusions during each of these distinct phases, are a reflection of the skills needed to be effective in counseling.

A Counseling Perspective

Since this is a book on counseling, it is primarily a book on interpersonal problem-solving. It must be this way if it is to accomplish its purpose as a resource and guide to practicing managers and training specialists. It cannot simply be a book on "helping," or "listening," or "understanding." All these terms are commonly associated with counseling and are useful ways to think about a *portion* of the counseling process. Instead, if the material on these pages is to actually be applied and not simply read, it must emphasize interpersonal problem-solving.

It must describe ways and means to resolve conflicts, overcome resistance to change, utilize information, plan careers, make decisions and give advice. Yes—*give advice.* Some problems will never be solved unless advice is given. Listening, paraphrasing, and seeking to understand another's point of view is *necessary* in all counseling situations, but alone is not *sufficient* in many of them. Giving advice, providing direction, or explaining a personal perspective is important if counseling discussions are actually going to resolve the problem at hand.

This emphasis on giving advice in counseling is not universally held. Examples from pioneer works on counseling employees in organizations[2] to popular manuals on leadership training[3] could be cited which advise managers, trainers, counselors and others to avoid giving advice. The basic reason for this perspective is that many professional counselors have noticed that people who are depressed, worried, anxious or upset already possess answers to the questions they are bringing to the counselor. Consequently, counselors have avoided looking for answers that troubled people can easily formulate themselves with a little help.

Thus, the role of someone counseling has often been seen as one of calming down the person who is troubled, acting as a mirror reflecting back to that person feelings and thoughts, and allowing the person to come to their own conclusions about what should be done next.

[2] William J. Dickson and Fritz Roethlisberger, *Counseling in an Organization: A Sequel to the Hawthorne Researches,* (Cambridge: Harvard University Press, 1966).

[3] Thomas Gordon, *Leadership Effectiveness Training: The No-Lose Way to Release the Productive Potential of People,* (Chicago: Wyden, 1978).

This is a simplification of the nondirective approach to counseling which certainly contains a lot of merit.[4] Listening is important. Understanding the emotional baggage people pack into the words they use does make a difference. Knowing when someone just wants a "sounding board" needs to be discerned. But this is not enough in many employee counseling situations. Why? Because the reasons people seek out (or need) counseling in a work situation are often different from the reasons someone meets with a mental health counselor. In some cases, employees are troubled and can develop solutions to their own problems through a nondirective approach. In other cases, however, the basis of an employee problem is not an internal emotional conflict, but the results of frustration with company policy, uncertainty over role requirements, or insecurity about skills and abilities. In such cases, the information and advice (the counsel) sought or needed could not be developed by the employee continuously having his or her thoughts and feelings paraphrased and restated. As an old adage goes, "You can't draw water from an empty well." Good information, including the experience of others in similar situations, is needed.

Good information is a scarce resource in many organizations. Although computers have enabled managers to collect tremendous quantities of data and even experience "information overload", information on how things "really" work remains difficult to retrieve and disseminate. Whether the labels describe the informal system or the politics of the organization, the fact remains that few people in most organizations have the information they need to effectively plan their careers, fully develop their skills and abilities, and appropriately match their interests with organizational goals. When this information isn't appropriately relayed in counseling discussions, both the individual and the organization suffer. Besides dissatisfaction and lethargy on the job, the effects also can be manifest in increased turnover and reduced productivity.

COUNSELING IS

Counseling at the workplace is, and must remain, different from counseling in a therapeutic setting. The goal of therapy is to help people feel good—or, at least, feel better. During therapy, the in-

[4] For a more complete discussion of the nondirective approach, see Carl Rogers, *On Becoming A Person* (New York: Houghton Mifflin, 1961).

dividual withdraws and refocuses energy and attention to his or her internal world. When successful, the outcome is increased awareness and sharpened self-insight.[5]

There is a necessary and important role for such therapy, but there is also a danger in assuming that it can be successfully applied at the workplace. Aside from the hazard of having lay people attempting to utilize techniques that require professional and judicious use, there is also the danger of emphasizing goals and roles that are not in the best interests of the person's organizational life. Feeling good is a different goal and may suggest different roles than the need for competence, which is critical if both people and the organizations in which they work are to be successful.

Developing competence is, and must remain, the goal of counseling at the workplace. The development of such competence by on-the-job counselors requires that therapeutic notions of counseling cannot simply be translated into ordinary language and practiced effectively. They must instead be altered, or, in some cases, ignored. Minimally, recognition must be given to the fact that the roles of therapeutic counselors and counselors at the workplace are different in some very fundamental ways.

The goals we possess affect what we do. The distinction in goals between therapy and organizational counseling is a simple but important one. It makes a difference in how the counseling role is defined and what methods are selected when attempting to resolve various problems. Since the focus of employee counseling is the development of competency, the outcome of such discussions should be an increased ability to cope with life in the organization as people experience it. Rollo May pointed to the importance of this process rather eloquently:

> No matter how great the forces victimizing the human being, man has the capacity to know that he is being victimized and thus to influence in some way how he will relate to his fate.[6]

Coping, adapting, or changing are important processes in developing competence. They are processes that can be learned and communicated during counseling discussions. While a professor at the Harvard Business School, Gene Dalton, did a comprehensive review

---

[5] See for example, Gerald F. Corey, *Theory and Practice of Counseling and Psychotherapy* (Monterey, California: Brooks-Cole, 1977) and Barbara Okun *Effective Helping: Interviewing and Counseling Techniques.* (Belmont, California: Wadsworth Press, 1976).

[6] Rollo May, *Existential Psychology,* (New York: Random House, 1961).

of successful personal and organizational change projects and highlighted some of the conditions under which planned changes would realize their intended objectives.[7] Dalton's conclusions suggest some general conditions that will facilitate the development of competence in counseling. He noted that change was most likely to occur when:

- there was a strongly-felt need for wanting to do things differently, often brought about due to a discrepancy between current conditions and desired conditions;
- someone assisted in the change process who was highly regarded by the person or people involved in changing;
- general feelings about a situation were channeled into operational goals and specific plans;
- an external motive for changing was replaced by an internal one;
- new social ties were created or old ones reformulated so that peers were essentially enlisted in supporting and maintaining the changes; and,
- the people who were changing felt better about their abilities to manage their own world.

Each of these characteristics describe appropriate aspects of the counseling process. They underscore the fact that such counseling must be action-oriented. They all illustrate the importance of counselors developing an appropriate counseling *perspective* in addition to learning counseling *skills*. This counseling perspective suggests a focus on resolving individual problems and not overhauling employees' personalities. At the workplace, the role of the counselor is more akin to an eye specialist than a painter: instead of creating a scene that represents reality, he or she widens and broadens perspectives so that reality can be seen more clearly.

It is imperative that the person doing counseling, as in the case of doctors and lawyers, be respected and well regarded by those who receive his or her advice. Although the importance of trust and credibility is often stressed, there is little written material available on how this perspective can be demonstrated. Sidney Jourard is a notable exception to this trend. At one point in his book, *The Transparent Self,* he describes how one can develop openness and cultivate confidence during a counseling discussion. Jourard says

[7] Gene W. Dalton, "Influence and Organizational Change" in *Changing Organizational Behavior* (Englewood Cliffs, New Jersey: Prentice-Hall 1973).

that he does things quite differently now than he did when he first began in the counseling field:

> I reflect feelings and content as I always did but only when I want the (other person) to know that I really heard what he had to say. But now I find myself sometimes giving advice, lecturing, becoming angry, interrupting...[8]

Jourard's point is that no one is interested in being counseled by someone who hides behind a sterile mask of objectivity. Who, after all, wants to be treated as an object? We want to interact with others who can show their humanity and demonstrate that they understand our problems. We are relieved when people we regard show their humanity. We are more likely to drop our defenses and openly explore options to a problem when we are not constrained by objectivity. Jourard is suggesting that a person wanting to do counseling unfortunately only gets invited to a discussion of the real problem when he or she gets subjectively involved. The counselor may free the other person up to explore options that may require the alteration of a typical habit pattern.

The issue surrounding subjectivity is not whether, but when. How does a person doing counseling know when to give advice and when to listen? How can one tell when advising will be interpreted as browbeating instead of path defining? Who can be sure that getting angry won't further complicate an already tense situation? Besides having clear answers to questions such as these, a counselor must be able to resolve such dilemmas as being able to:

- give advice without creating dependency,
- contribute to the development of options without being parental and forcing strictly personal views on another,
- point to the likely consequences of various courses of action without being condescending and,
- assist in decision-making without being superficial.

These are important and cannot be resolved easily or abstractly; much of what is appropriate depends on the situation. Having said that, I intend to explore such questions and dilemmas in Chapter 3. Basic principles and concepts involved in counseling will then be discussed in the applications section through the use of specific vignettes and specific examples. At this point, my purpose is simply

[8] Sidney Jourard, *The Transparent Self,* (New York: Van Nostrand Reinhold, 1971).

to point to some of the possible pitfalls and dilemmas encountered in counseling. It is not sufficient that someone wants to be an effective counselor. It is necessary to know *how* to be effective in a way that comes across as *being* effective.

As noted previously, counseling is many things: resolving conflicts, implementing changes, making decisions. It is not a delicate process and does not have to be done carefully. In some situations, being bold may be the most important thing to do.[9] Counseling is a perspective, a way of doing things, as well as a set of skills. Like the proverbial horse and carriage, they go together. Just as there are some ways to think about what counseling is, there are some ways to contrast what it is not. The following table summarizes the counseling perspective and compares it to its antithesis.

Counseling Is	Counseling Is Not
1. Counseling is thinking *with* another person.	1. Counseling is not thinking *for* another person.
2. Counseling is a process for resolving problems.	2. Counseling is not repeating adages and cliches about what someone else ought to do.
3. Counseling is accepting another person's feelings as relevant data bearing on the problem at hand.	3. Counseling is not simply being sympathetic toward another's feelings.
4. Counseling is understanding human nature and realizing that people are alike in some ways and unique in others.	4. Counseling is not merely the application of techniques.
5. Counseling is often done best when the counselor believes he or she is doing the least.	5. Counseling is not an ego trip for the counselor.
6. Counseling is assisting in changing things and developing competence.	6. Counseling is not being arbitrary or manipulative.
7. Counseling is building self reliance by aiding someone else in making decisions and fulfilling commitments.	7. Counseling is not just talking things over.

[9] Research for this perspective is reported in Norman C. Hill and J.B. Ritchie, "The Effect of Self-Esteem on Leadership and Achievement: A Paradigm and a Review," *Group and Organization Studies* (December 1977), pp. 491-503.

ROLES OF A COUNSELOR

Anyone who assists in interpersonal problem-solving is a counselor. Before, during, and after such discussions with someone else, a counselor performs one of several distinct roles. Recognizing the range of possible roles can make counseling a more effective process than it otherwise would be. Roles of a counselor include being the following.[10]

Teacher	This role includes providing information, giving direction, and the like. It is asking questions and summarizing points so that they are not overlooked in addition to pointing out what has worked for others. A teacher is prepared to explain *why* particular approaches were successful.
Educator	People learn through the reflective examination of their own experience as much as they do from gaining new information. Another aspect of counseling is helping people learn how to learn. Counseling involves pointing out to people how they have coded and filed their past experiences and how they can better adapt to life not only by responding to the content of their lives but also by changing their previously held points of view.
Detective	Counseling may involve uncovering evidence and fitting it together. It may include noticing details that are meaningless except when they are considered as part of a pattern.
Barbarian	It can be painful to some people to have a counselor disrupt their perceived view of reality. At times, a counselor must confront the accepted ("civilized") ritual and point out its inappropriateness.
Clock	With scheduled or periodic follow-up, a counselor can cause another person to prepare for the deadline (i.e., think about goals, take action, do a self-critique, etc.)
Monitor	A counselor can provide someone else with an independent view of performance and evaluate efforts being made to increase competence.

[10] These roles are adapted from Fritz Steele's *Consulting for Organizational Change* (Boston: University of Massachusetts Press, 1975).

Catalyst   Through counseling, people can get started on
objectives that they would have been unlikely to
initiate on their own. Many times discussing specific
problems leaves people feeling profoundly different.
Counselors do not often know the degree or extent of
their influence. It is possible that even advice that is
not immediately taken may create enough internal
reaction to cause people to examine their approaches
to problems differently.

People do not always know what they want or the costs associated
with getting it. Yet, although they may be unclear about their goals
and values, they may still have a vague sense that they are not
keeping up with everyone else. We all know that we do not want to
be left out or left behind when it comes to getting the rewards
available through the organization that employs us. We want to be
considered normal, of course, to be accepted; but we do not want to
be considered average. In fact, one survey of employees in a large
multinational company revealed that nearly 80% of the employees
considered themselves to be among the top performers in the
company.[11] Reconciling aspirations with organizational options,
managing disappointment, clarifying values, specifying goals—all of
these demands and others require that the effective counselor
perform a variety of different roles. Doing this while keeping
employees continuously engaged and productive is all part of the
balancing act and synthesizing role of the counselor.

WHY COUNSEL

Counseling is an effective means of providing for the growth and
development of people. Since management is essentially utilizing the
abilities and capacities of people to get things done, it also seems
apparent that managers and trainers must develop the potential of
employees if they are to utilize them effectively.

One study of the effectiveness of counseling has been reported by
Walter Mahler and William Wrightnour.[12] They studied the practices

[11] Herbert Meyer, "The Pay for Performance Dilemma," *Organizational Dynamics* (Fall, 1975),
pp. 39-50.

[12] Walter R Mahler and William F. Wrightnour, *Executive Continuity: How to Build and Retain an
Effective Management Team* (Homewood, Illinois: Dow Jones-Irwin, 1973).

of 210 managers in three different organizations: a manufacturing company, a supermarket chain, and a public utility. The results suggest that when managers and others spend a portion of their time counseling employees either by formal, systematic interviews, or informal sessions, the employees:

1. feel more satisfied with their work,
2. believe their managers supervise them adequately, and
3. report that they like the way their bosses motivate them.

Counseling can provide a service to both the organization and to individuals within it who have particular problems. Counseling can provide a release for the frustrations that are an inevitable part of human interaction in an organization. Since counseling provides a forum for expressing personal frustrations, it also provides the promise of defusing and managing them. The alternative to promoting and encouraging such counseling is described by Frederick Herzberg:

> Implicit in the psychological contract between a manager and his subordinates is the clause, "If you work for me, I'm going to have to frustrate you sometimes," Any time you manage people you have to frustrate them—it's the name of the game and no amount of agonizing is going to negate this reality. However, the danger to the organization lies in extending this tacit contract to include the statement, "When I do frustrate you don't you dare express your hostility to me—I am the boss. Go home and kick your dog or go eat your heart out—that is, turn the hostility back on yourself."[13]

A work situation where frustrations arise and opportunities for expressing and dissipating concerns are not provided experiences both high personal and organizational costs.

Counseling can also increase employee identification with the organization that employs them. It can reduce the feelings of estrangement that are especially prevalent in many large organizations. The fact is that there are typically only feeble attempts at

[13] Frederick Herzberg, *The Management Choice: To Be Efficient and To Be Human*, (Homewood, Illinois: Dow Jones-Irwin, 1976).

mutual employer-employee problem-solving in most organizations. Few attempts are made to re-organize discouraged people or recycle bored workers. So conflicts exist in an uneasy détente, frustrations continue unchecked, and unconscious conspiracies develop that suggest "Don't get too close, I don't want to get too involved." Knowing how and when to utilize appropriate counseling skills can counter such trends. With knowledge and skills, the manager or trainer need not shy away from dealing with emotions—anger or tears or resentment. One's own fears about competence can thus be dealt with more easily.

The changing nature of today's workforce, a phenomenon that has been extensively documented,[14] provides another reason to integrate counseling into organizational practices. Sunshine laws and privacy legislation reflect the desires of a workforce who want to know the what and why of policies that affect them. They want to have a dialogue on matters that were once left to management discretion. Personnel policies and practices are on the verge of becoming transparent.

TYPES OF COUNSELING

There are a variety of approaches that are available to someone who is engaged in doing counseling. It is possible to categorize these approaches into one of three general types: correcting, coaching and consulting. The degree of directiveness and the nature of the problem are the most important factors to consider in deciding which type and which approach to utilize.

Correcting: This type of counseling is the most directive. It results from a mistake or a missed opportunity. In addition to pointing out errors, such counseling should also indicate how the person can both learn from the error and learn how to detect such errors. Such disciplinary action is not necessarily punitive in nature. It is, however, an enforcement of work rules or performance standards.

[14] Daniel Yankelovick, "Work, Values, and the New Breed" in Clark Kerr and Jerome Rosow, *Work in America: The Decade Ahead*, (New York: Van Nostrand Reinhold, 1974).

Coaching: This type of counseling is aimed at specific performance improvement. The emphasis is on listening and understanding, but the counselor shares in the task of deciding on a course of action and a plan to achieve it. It is aimed at achieving a specific objective or developing specific skills and abilities. It is often associated with annual performance reviews and periodic performance improvement discussions.

Consulting: This type of counseling is distinguished from the other two primarily by the locus of the problem. In correcting and coaching, the counselor notices a deficiency or sees a need for improvement. When the counselor initiates a discussion on a topic of his or her own selection, it is the counselor who has a problem, not the employee. The employee may have a deficiency or latent potential, but it is the counselor who wants the situation to change. This need to alter, to resolve, to have something done differently, is all on the part of the counselor. This is not simply a semantic exercise but an important distinction. The motivation for change is all with the counselor prior to the discussion. The intent of the discussion is to develop a commitment in the employee for "joint ownership" of it.

In consulting, the focus of the problem is with the employee. It is the employee who feels a need or has an incentive for changing things. Sometimes employees initiate discussions that fall into this category hoping the supervisor will assume responsibility for the problem they have. Sometimes would-be counselors invite such discussion and don't know how to allow the employee to retain primary responsibility for his or her problem.

Each of these types of counseling is oriented toward problem-solving and has as an intended outcome the development of competence. This means competence in fulfilling task requirements, competence in fully utilizing abilities and capabilities, competence in coping with frustrations and disappointments. Recognizing when to do a particular type of counseling and being familiar with approaches and techniques appropriate to each will increase the likelihood of counseling effectiveness.

SUMMARY

Counseling is a general term that involves specific processes. It is a perspective as well as a set of skills. It is an approach to problem-solving as well as a container of specific methods for doing so. It is a set of personal rules of thumb, practice theories, and techniques in addition to being a way to view the development of competence in people. It can be either remedial, developmental, or motivational. And it can work.

Counseling includes listening to and understanding someone else's point of view. It also includes giving advice. But there are some do's and don'ts for giving advice. It is not as easy as it may appear to give good advice. Some of these do's and don'ts of advice-giving are:

DO	DON'T
• clarify the nature of a problem	• impose personal values
• test perceived constraints	• judge the other person's motives
• contribute to options	• tell the person what he or she should do
• challenge fears and anxieties	• take sides
• disclose potential relevant information	
• test commitment to a position	
• point out shortcomings of a solution	

It is not necessary for a counselor to completely understand another person's problem in order to be an effective resource. There may be aspects the other person does not feel comfortable explaining or cannot articulate very well. This is not necessarily a limitation. Questioning techniques used by a counselor may be able to help a person express beliefs, sentiments, or values that might otherwise lie dormant. Most of the time we fail to define what bothers us or what we would like to do about it until we talk it over with someone else. Such focused discussions when they develop competence are the warp and woof of employee counseling.

There is a great deal of talk today about giving people pride and a sense of importance or achievement in their work. But pride and accomplishment cannot be given. People cannot be made to "feel" important. They are either valued, or they are not valued; and they, in turn, either see their work as being valuable or unimportant. Service pins and other forms of recognition have meaning only when they represent some inner accomplishment. That's what counselors need to do something about: the opportunities for people at all ability levels to achieve and to accomplish at all levels in the organization.

Motivation is often thought of as some kind of personality trait which people either do or don't have. Often, poor performance is attributed to a person's lack of motivation. Despite its use in this way, it seems that motivation is more the result of work conditions which allow employees to be responsible. Thus, motivation is something which simply takes the right combination of keys to unlock and release.

It is not necessary to understand complex theories of how people's personalities work to improve motivation and productivity. People are complex and different, but they are also very similar in some very basic ways. These similarities and how they affect what people do should be the focus of improvement. Similarities are what make the difference. Some of these differences and similarities are explored and discussed in the following chapter.

Chapter 2

Understanding People: Prerequisites for Counseling

What is it that makes people tick? Why are we the way we are? —Heredity? Environment? Childhood experiences? Major emotional events? When we attempt to generalize regarding what causes people to act the way they do, we come up with various contradictions. We are *all* influenced by many different things in many different ways.

Despite the fact that we are all different and unique in our own way, we also possess similarities. Although we may react to various events differently, there are still some generalizations that can be made about how people think, feel, and behave. These generalizations may not explain all there is to know about human nature, but they do describe some basic operating principles that can be utilized in the counseling process.

PURPOSE

People do things for reasons even though their reasons may be difficult for them to identify. Sometimes we do things that we are hardly aware of, but our actions are still purposeful. We try to impose order and predictability in our world and do things to create this order. For instance, when a woman angrily confronts her husband about the time he spends at the office and he angrily responds that the house is a mess, both are offering predictable responses. They are more interested in expressing and releasing their pent-up feelings than they are in working through their differences. Expressed anger, like the expression of other strong emotions, is an attention getter. Strongly worded statements are attempts to achieve certain ends, to get predictable reactions, and are seldom purposeless. The usual intent of sarcasm is to put someone else "in their place." Its purpose is to establish dominance. But if this purpose is confronted directly by the person who is the target, they are likely to be accused of being overly sensitive or "thin skinned."

Although most of what we do is purposeful, it is not always well thought out or the result of rational deliberation. There are non-rational aspects of our behavior which are the results of being impulsive. Thus, we react to a specific event like a numbered ball on a billiards table instead of deciding for ourselves what is best for us. We are influenced by external events: we strive for good grades in school so we may be accepted; we choose an occupation in order to gain status or prestige; we are frustrated and resentful because others do not recognize our abilities. Recognizing that we do things for reasons does not mean those reasons are always good or rational ones, or reasons that are the result of self-deliberation.

Purposeful behavior implies that we do things to reach some goal or relieve some tension. We want things. We want to feel in control of what happens to us. We want to manage the ambiguity and uncertainty that surround us. We want to be able to adapt and cope with events and opportunities that come our way. The purpose of counseling is to assist people in achieving these objectives.

ADJUSTMENT

Formally, we think of adjustment as trying to bring about a balance between our personal goals and external events and opportunities. Good adjustment involves achieving our goals at a satisfactory level. Adjustment can be thought of as the process of reacting to circumstances and deciding how they will affect us. It involves coping with problems and learning how to improve our own problem-solving abilities with the specific problems we face. The well-adjusted person is one who holds a realistic and accepting attitude toward himself or herself and is aware of personal values, beliefs, and feelings. The more we *understand* ourselves, including typical reactions and our parental and cultural heritage, the better we are able to *decide* who we are and how we will act. If we think in terms of personal adjustment, then beliefs and actions which produce excessive anxiety, lower efficiency, or prevent us from coping with changes are counterproductive. If we intend to improve our competency, we must be attuned to factors and conditions which prevent us from doing so.

Understanding people in organizations means knowing about some common difficulties we all have in maintaining our self-image and adequately adjusting to daily tensions and pressures. In some respects, just the makeup of organizations and groups puts pressure on individuals. The tension created by the ubiquitous presence of authoritative figures who are required to make personal evaluations and thereby distribute merit increases, promotions, and work assignments creates its own anxiety. Thus, subordinates often worry about whether they are pleasing their bosses as much as they worry about performing well.

Worry occurs when a person constantly goes over his or her troubles without ever coming any closer to a solution. Sometimes the worrier continually rehashes past events, emotionally whipping himself or herself with "If only I had...". Such introspection is debilitating rather than rejuvenating. There is no analysis, only regret; thus, there is no learning or growth or self-insight.

Worry is partially an individual reaction. People who are insecure and who lack self-confidence are worriers. Organizational settings can also contribute to insecurity. An organization's emphasis on results is sometimes so concentrated that people believe they are nothing more than a "pair of hands" to the organization. In fact, the greater the emphasis on results, the more likely people are to withhold information, lie, blame others for things they share responsibility for and the like. In organizations where mistakes are not tolerated and results are all that matters, people do all kinds of things that reduce the overall productive functioning of the organization. Two examples reported in the *Wall Street Journal* illustrate this tendency:

The president of a manufacturing company ordered work to begin on a new type of photocopying machine. Although those with direct responsibility believed the machine would take two years to build, they cooperated in forecasting that it could be developed in a matter of months. Working furiously, they managed to complete a prototype to meet their deadline. The president inspected it and left the test room with assurances that it was ready for production. Shortly after leaving the lab, however, the machine burst into flames and was destroyed.

In one electronics firm, shipments were being predated and papers falsified to meet sales targets. Sales representatives had accepted the targets rather than complain for fear that they would be labeled as uncommitted. It took months before upper-level managers realized what was happening.[1]

It is not easy to adjust to the constant ebb and flow of pressures and tensions in an organization. Some people adjust well and seem to be unaffected by the conditions they face on the job. However, the high rate of alcoholism, ulcers, hypertension, and migraine headaches—to name a few—are evidence that many people face problems that they have not adjusted to in their work.

The counseling process can do much to aid in the process of adjustment. Through ordinary counseling, people can learn to better identify the source of their concerns and more accurately problem solve to resolve them. The emphasis of such counseling, however, must go beyond listening to and understanding the other person's point of view. As important as that activity is, it is not enough. What is needed is to help others achieve better problem solving and thereby increase their ability to cope with the circumstances they face.* Such a focus results in more than helping people feel good about themselves. Counseling is needed not only to fulfill the humanistic urges we often feel to help people. By increasing the problem-solving abilities of employees, the organization can expect to profit in several ways:

1. people will be better adjusted to work demands and thus absenteeism will be lower due to such stress-related illnesses as colds, flu, and general nausea;

[1] John and Arnold Mack, "The Manager's Journal," *The Wall Street Journal* (June 5, 1979), p. 5.

* A good example showing how counseling can aid in the process of adjustment is found in the situation entitled "I'm not sure I can handle moving again," which is in Unit 9, "Personal/Work Problems."

2. performance and satisfaction will be enhanced as a result of employees' feeling more in control of their workaday and everyday lives;

3. anxiety about making mistakes and pressures of "looking good" can be minimized with the result that people will be more intent on solving problems than on blaming others for them; and,

4. those who improve their overall problem-solving abilities can be expected to improve their ability to solve work-related problems.

DEFENSE MECHANISMS

One way to think of human behavior is that it can go in three different directions: toward resolving problems, toward avoiding their examination, and toward substituting some defensive reaction for problem solving. Some people feel they are solving problems by getting angry. Others say they don't care about a particular matter or that it's not important to them and deny that a problem exists. By giving excuses for failure or rationalizing, we sometimes believe what we want to believe or, like Walter Mitty, we try to escape from reality by day-dreaming. Generally, these defensive reactions stem from our fear of what the consequences might be if our solution to a problem doesn't work (i.e., loss of approval, rejection, etc.).

A common defense mechanism used to cover up for some weakness is projection. Someone who is being corrected for not meeting performance standards may respond by saying, "No one else works any harder than I do. I work as hard as the rest." This is projection. Many times people feel that they are honestly working as hard as they can and this fact is simply not being recognized by their supervisor or others. Those who do not advance as quickly or as often as they desire, may blame it on the system or say, "It's politics that determines who gets ahead—not what you know."

Erving Goffman, a noted student of human behavior, has described ways in which disappointments in career ambitions and analogous situations give rise to the use of defensive reactions. Goffman points out that people come to develop their careers in terms of a sequence of legitimate expectations and to base their self-conceptions on the assumption that in due course they will realize their ambitions. They define themselves as possessing a certain set of qualities and then discover (or have pointed out to them) that they do not, or at least, others cannot discern them. That moment of truth is awful. Assumption had become presumption and then to loss of opportunity is added loss of face. When this occurs, people will develop rationalizations to explain what has happened to protect their self-image and to keep from losing face.[2]

Recognizing these processes of rationalization, projection, blaming, and denial is necessary in order to begin dealing with them. More will be said in the next chapter about dealing with anxiety, disappointment and frustration. Specific techniques will be outlined. However, there is a general process for assisting someone in realizing the unproductive nature of resorting to defensive reactions. This process has the counselor:

1. *encouraging* the full expression of the other person's defensive reaction. Emotions cannot be purged until they are fully expressed.
2. *examining* the person's motives, what he or she really wants. Value clarification results only when we examine our actions and feelings in light of our own beliefs.
3. *highlighting* ways we prevent ourselves from achieving, ways we contradict ourselves, and undercut our own efforts. We may say we want something, but not mean it. If we do something that keeps producing outcomes which we claim we don't want, it may be that that is precisely what we do want. It represents a workable compromise which allows us to say we want one thing, not get it, and complain to others about it.
4. *helping* the person set goals that are consistent with his or her personal values and beliefs and within the person's control. One of the most common ways we prevent ourselves from achieving is to strive for goals that others can determine the outcomes of. There is a difference between striving to be competent in a skill and striving to win the Nobel Prize. Few people can win Nobel Prizes, even when they are the best in their field. There is a vast difference between focusing on skills rather than rewards. One is competence-oriented; the other is approval-oriented. This process is well illustrated in "Why was I passed over for a promotion?" located in Unit 1, "Pay, Promotions and Appraisals."

[2] Erving Goffman, *Presentation of Self in Everyday Life,* (Doubleday, 1959)

NEEDS OR SENTIMENTS

Much has been written and discussed about the *basic* characteristics of human beings. Attempts to define human behavior by identifying needs that are common to all of us have been advanced by several social scientists. Perhaps the most widely known of these is the work of Abraham Maslow. Maslow has proposed a hierarchy of needs that is the same for everyone. Physical needs occupy the lowest rung, followed in ascending order by safety needs (to be protected, to be free from danger), social needs (to be liked, to belong), esteem needs (to be respected, to obtain recognition and status) and at the top of the hierarchy, self-actualization needs. Maslow defines self-actualization as "the desire to become everything that one is capable of becoming."

Unfortunately, a number of researchers have compiled evidence that this simple hierarchy does not exist as universally as Maslow says it should. People are much more complex than that. Human behavior is simply more complex and diverse than some have considered. People cannot be reduced to a short system of pulleys and levers. Pull this one or that one and this or that will happen. People in organizations simply have different values and orientations —often these are internally conflicting. We neither have the same values, drives, and aspirations as others, nor do we always want just the things that are consistent with our values and aspirations. We want many things at once and usually all that we can get.

It is only when we sit down and think about it that we realize that the costs (time, energy, commitment, risk, etc.) of some things we desire are more than we are willing to pay. When we reflect upon it, we realize that some things are more important to us than others. However, what we value may be unimportant to someone else. Our valuations are not the same. The needs and aspirations of people cannot be classified into a simple hierarchy. We are not the same; in fact, instead of falling along a hierarchy, human needs can better be thought of as existing like the jumbled contents of a grocery bag. We want and aspire to many things at once. It is only when we begin to examine our wants and aspirations, that we begin to establish order. Thus, we create our own individual hierachy of needs.

Another way of viewing the makeup of people that provides a systematic method of examination without forcing all of us into prepackaged parcels has been proposed by William F. Whyte and

George C. Homans.[3] Their model presents an approach for dealing with the subjective aspects of human behavior. They note that we not only interact with other people and carry on various activities, but we also have feelings about what we are doing, about the people with whom we are associating, and about the world we encounter on a day-to-day basis. Sentiments are those feelings that are of particular concern to us. Sentiments are composed of an idea or belief about something or somebody, and emotional content or feelings that accompany it. Sentiments are our personal frame of reference through which we perceive, interpret, and evaluate the world around us and our place in it. Based on our individual perception of ourselves, we make decisions about what we want and its importance to us. People in organizations are continually evaluating the adequacy of their positions and the nature of their relationship with others—especially those in authority—by estimating the value of the rewards they are receiving (pay, advancement, recognition, friendship, etc.) with the investments they have made to gain these outcomes (worked late, attended night school, made frequent attempts to be cordial, etc.) If people feel they are investing more than they are receiving from their work and work relations, they will feel dissatisfied, resentful and used. They may express concern about getting a better job, blame the system for being unfair, or reduce the effort they put into their jobs in order to achieve a better balance. Those who see their rewards as equal to or greater than their efforts will feel satisfaction and loyalty toward the organization.

This notion of distributive justice is a common theme expressed by many employees. Sometimes they are right. Some have been the recipients of favoritism. However, this issue of justice is sometimes raised by employees and used as a rationalization to protect their own self-image and explain why their ambitions have not materialized. Without detailed knowledge of the person and the organization, it is difficult to determine which is the case. Regardless of the true nature of the situation, an effective counselor can help clarify the nature of the person's perceived reward-investment balance and develop personal strategies for improving the situation. "You guys want more work but you're not willing to pay more money" in Unit 6 "Performance Problems", shows how a supervisor counseled an employee who perceived an imbalance between his investments and his rewards.

[3] William Foote Whyte, *Organizational Behavior: Theory and Application*, (Homewood, Illinois: Irwin-Dorsey, 1969) and George C. Homans, *Social Behavior: Its Elementary Forms* (New York: Harcourt, 1974).

PAYOFF AND GAMES

People in organizations do not exist in isolation. Organizations exist to combine the know-how and abilities of people to achieve particular objectives. Likewise, as individuals, we strive to achieve our own objectives and realize the rewards or payoff that achievement brings. Whenever someone achieves a particular goal, he or she achieves payoff.

A concept of human behavior that has been popularized by Eric Berne in his bestselling book, *Games People Play,* is the recognition that we have interpersonal objectives and strive to realize payoffs through our interaction with others.[4] Although Berne identified positive interpersonal games that people participated in, the notion of games has come to be associated with the achievement of negative payoffs. Games are characterized by the following elements:

- there is a predictable outcome or payoff,
- two or more people are required to "play,"
- the words, gestures, and tone of voice have a different meaning than they would in a different context (that is, they have a special meaning to at least one of the players),
- there are at least two roles being played (victim and rescuer) with a third role (persecutor) implied or waiting for a chance to appear.

Games are played for many different reasons. They may be played to get attention or sympathy, to appear superior, or to justify stereotypes and preconceived ideas, to name a few. The underlying reason the game is played, is to achieve payoff. Games may sometimes provide considerable psychological satisfaction to the players. Why else would they persist in playing them? But they also consume vast quantities of time and energy that if redirected could be used more constructively. ["There's so much stress in this job" in Unit 8, "Coping with Job Demands", shows how managers as counselors can become involved in game playing.]

Games are played between supervisors and subordinates, coworkers in the same work group or in different departments, and

---

[4] Eric Berne, *Games People Play* (New York: Grove Press, 1964) and *What Do You Say After You Say "Hello?"* (New York: Bantam, 1975).

between counselors and the persons who have sought counseling. The essence of games is that people are not taking responsibility for their part of a problem or their ability to solve it. Counselors are particularly susceptible to game playing when they accept too much responsibility for helping someone else with his or her problem. Counseling is helping others see the responsibility they have for solving their own problems while facilitating the problem-solving *process*. Counselors who accept responsibility for developing solutions to problems people bring are probably "spinning their wheels." They are like a car with the engine running, but still in neutral.

People who go to counselors may be looking for sympathy. A counselor who exhibits understanding may satisfy this desire, but prevent the person from improving his or her own competency. Here are some rules of thumb for detecting and reducing game playing.

1. Assess the other person's willingness to identify the contributing factors to a problem—especially the part he or she contributes. Responsibility for most problems is usually shared by several people. Is the person willing to examine his or her contribution on the reason why a problem exists?
2. Be aware of payoff. In looking at the payoff, the procedures for playing the game can be detected. This awareness allows a counselor to stop the game and point out to the person more constructive alternatives for getting what he or she wants.
3. Communicate without requiring agreement. Many games are reduced when people give up the desire to have others completely agree with them. Communication involves being understood. When we give up the desire to be right, we are more likely to improve understanding.
4. Refuse to take sides. Refusing to take sides helps to extinguish the person's normal expectation and leads them to accept responsibility for personal feelings.
5. Give an unexpected response. Games continue because at least one game player is getting a predictable payoff. When pushing a button fails to elicit the response a person is looking for, it avails the person with the opportunity to look for other options. Games only exist because they work; by giving an unexpected response, the predictability is disrupted and a person is more likely to attempt realistic problem-solving.

SELF-ESTEEM

Any individual can be thought of as a diverse set of "social selves" that are organized around a basic self-image or self-concept. If the individual feels good about who he or she is, self-esteem is usually high. Similarly, if the individual has a low opinion, low aspirations, or a self-conception that suggests he or she is unimportant, self-esteem is low. Everyone has a basic temperament, intelligence factor and psychological defenses that are chronic and enduring. But people also have learned ways of coping with situational pressures that basically determine their self-image and the set of social selves the person will construct to deal with his or her environment.

Self-esteem is an evaluation we make about ourselves that is continually changing. It is based on our beliefs about our competence in each of the roles we adopt (i.e., parent, spouse, friend, citizen, employee, etc.). How we determine our role in each of the situations we face and how capably we think we fulfill the role requirements powerfully influences our behavior. Better understanding our roles, their requirements, and our behavior in them can help us to be more effective in achieving our desired outcomes. This concept of constructed social selves is one that has been employed by a variety of theorists and researchers including Mead, Goffman, and Schein.[5] This theory of how people think, feel, and behave is a product of past interactions and present expectations. This perspective does not deny the existence of basic personality traits, but it maintains that personality traits tell little about how a person acts or reacts in various situations. For example, someone may have a personality structure that revolves around the repression of strong agressive impulses, may be temperamentally easily frustrated, and may rely upon denial as a common defense mechanism whenever backed into a corner. These characteristics may describe the person's basic personality, but they say little about that person's self-image, how he or she behaves in occupational or social roles, how he or she interacts with others, and the like.

Focusing on someone's constructed self, on the other hand, shows how he or she interacts with others and the impact this interaction has on how that person thinks, feels, and behaves. Even people with

---

[5] George H. Mead, *Mind, Self and Society: From the Standpoint of a Social Behaviorist,* (Chicago: University of Chicago Press, 1967); Erving Goffman, *op.cit.;* Edgar H. Schein, *Career Dynamics: Matching Individual and Organizational Needs,* (Reading, Massachusetts: Addison-Wesley, 1978).

the same kind of personality structure might enter into similar interactive situations quite differently. In other words, if a manager or someone else is interested in improving someone's motivation to work, the manager should take note of the person's constructed self in various interaction situations as a key place to begin working with that individual. A major implication of this approach is that an employee cannot remain lazy or unmotivated; cannot have poor work habits; and must be willing to take initiative without the interactional support of others. People are unmotivated only to the extent that their interaction patterns with others reinforce this perspective. To change someone, a manager must alter that person's view of himself or herself—a view that is only constant to the extent that interaction patterns remain unchanged. [See "He's always testing the limits" in Unit 5, "Boss/Subordinate Relations", for an example of how this can be done through counseling.]

All of our past interaction patterns become a part of us. We catalogue them and reuse them in new situations if they apply. They give us the predictability and control we desire. To a large extent, we are not conscious of the almost instantaneous choices we make among possible options as we compose ourselves on encountering a new situation. The changes which occur in us during the course of our careers are changes in the nature of these constructed selves. It is unlikely that we will substantially change our basic personality structure, but we can and do drastically change our constructed selves in that we develop new attitudes and values, adopt new images of ourselves, acquire new competencies, and create new ways of thinking, feeling and behaving. This process of developing people is one that every manager and human resource professional should be familiar with in order to tap the potential of employees at work.

Self-Esteem and Productive Functioning

Research from a variety of sources verifies that increasing the self-esteem of individuals is the key to their improved performance. Consider the following:

1. The work of Richard Hackman[6] (Yale) has illustrated the fact that people will not take advantage of enriched jobs if

---

[6] J. Richard Hackman, "Work Design" in J. R. Hackman and J. L. Suttle (eds), *Improving Life at Work: Behavioral Science Approaches to Organizational Change,* (Santa Monica, California: Goodyear Publishing Co., 1977).

they do not possess a certain high self-esteem level. The key to improved motivation, Hackman has found, lies both in job characteristics and individual self-esteem.

2. Paul Lawrence's[7] (Harvard) research on conditions that affect job satisfaction maintains that a high correlation exists between job satisfaction and individual self-esteem.

3. George Strauss[8] (California-Berkeley) completed an extensive review on the tools and technology of Organization Development and concluded that what made OD work was changes in the self-esteem of participants. Unsuccessful OD efforts could be identified by the lack of attention paid to this factor.

4. Abraham Korman[9] (Michigan) has provided much evidence to support a theory of motivation that centers on one's beliefs about one's self. Korman maintains that (a) people attempt to behave in a manner consistent with their own self-image; (b) if employees see themselves as failures on the job, they will not put forth much effort, their performance will be poor, and a self-reinforcing cycle will be set in motion; and consequently (c) the most successful managerial strategy to improve performance will focus on enhancing employees' self-images.

5. The successful work of David McClelland[10] (Harvard) and of most Management By Objectives (MBO) strategies is aimed at altering individual aspiration levels. By establishing high performance expectations, employees will work out the details of getting there. All they need is a target to shoot for that stretches them.

6. Gene Dalton's[11] (Brigham Young University) comprehensive review on how people and organizations change emphasizes that successful efforts are predicated on an increase in self-esteem. Without this foreseeable outcome, any new attempts at doing things will be unlikely.

[7] Cited in Raymond A. Katzell, et al. *Work, Productivity and Job Satisfaction*, (New York: Harcourt, Brace, Jovanovich, 1975).

[8] George Strauss, *Organizational Behavior*, (Belmont, California: Wadsworth Press, 1976).

[9] Abraham Korman, *Industrial and Organizational Psychology*, (Englewood Cliffs, New Jersey: Prentice-Hall, 1971).

[10] David G. McClelland, "Achievement Motivation Can Be Developed," *Harvard Business Review* (Mar-Apr, 1965), pp. 6-24.

[12] H.H. Kelley, "The Warm-Cold Variable in First Impressions of People," *Journal Of Personality*, V. 18, (1950), pp. 431-439.

It could be argued that any attempt to enhance the competency of one's self or others is an attempt to improve self-esteem. Unfortunately, many instructional programs fail because they do not provide activities or events that enhance this. There is an old French proverb that maintains, "To teach French to Tommy one must not only know French, but also Tommy." It isn't enough for an instructor to be familiar with a particular subject matter; he or she must be knowledgeable about the students. Likewise, a manager who is interested in performance improvement through counseling must possess some understanding of each employee as well as the counseling process itself.

Years ago management training programs in industry stressed the importance of managerial self-insight. Awareness was viewed as the key to managerial performance. How managers reacted to power, conflict, dependency and other issues was the focus of seminars and schools. But this approach seemed less practical and pragmatic than was needed for the busy manager. Something more hard-hitting and everydayish appeared to be more appropriate, so training programs began emphasizing this approach of enumerating pragmatic techniques for managing.

Although every training program must be based on predetermined needs identified at the time, training seminars ought to take note of both of these factors. Importantly, timing and sequencing can make all the difference in the world. Self-insight sets the stage for skills-building. One must become aware of inadequacies or opportunities before being interested in developing skills for doing things differently.

Those who manage organizations and are interested in improving the performance of people they supervise must know how to develop their own self-esteem as well as that of others. If we understand the kind of person we are in general, our roots, and where we are headed, we will present ourselves as capable and competent in interaction situations. Others will pick up on this self-confidence as well, and it will become self-reinforcing. Self-esteem is neither arrogance nor ignorance. It is an evaluation which we all make and customarily maintain of ourselves. It expresses our belief at the moment in our capabilities.

By reflecting on the causes, correlates, and consequences of self-esteem, we gain important benefits. By explicitly analyzing the nature and dimensions of individual self-esteem, we begin to objectify and see self-esteem as it truly is. We see it as a developmental process that can be enhanced or degraded. We see it as something that can be influenced. Knowing that, we can begin to lay the groundwork for a rational plan of intervention and change.

The Self-Esteem Process

How people regard themselves is a product of a very distinct process. Recognizing the various aspects of this process provides intervention points for taking action. The flowchart shown in Table 2-1 represents the basic process by which people develop their own self-image and shows ways in which self-regard can be enhanced.

Table 2-1

HOW SELF-ESTEEM WORKS

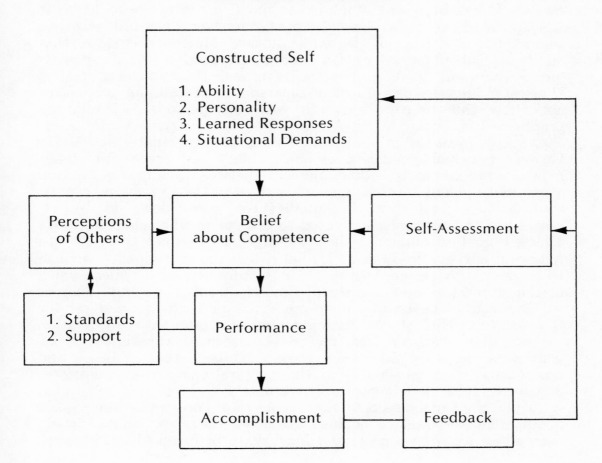

In providing this overview, it is clear that individually we exert some control on how we will perform, but we are also influenced by the perceptions of others. The expectations of others can act as self-fulfilling prophecies which may powerfully influence us.

INTRAPERSONAL SELF-FULFILLING PROPHECIES

How we regard ourselves affects our performance. This is the basic conclusion of a group of popular writers who have been successful salespeople and entrepreneurs. Their collective thesis is that through the power of positive thinking, one can become whatever he or she is capable of becoming. The popularity of their books attests to both the value of their ideas and the pervasiveness of the Horatio Alger ethic in America. Although this basic thesis is directionally correct, it has been oversimplified in most of the books in which it has appeared. What we believe about ourselves does influence our competence, but it is not the *only* influence. Moreover, exaggerating our beliefs about ourselves can produce frustration and disappointment when our goals prove to be unrealistic and unattainable. Understanding the *process* of intrapersonal self-fulfilling prophecies (and how this process interacts with interpersonal self-fulfilling prophecies) is vital.

A study initiated in 1922 established an important relationship between personal evaluation of one's ability and successful performance. Approximately 1400 adolescents between the ages of ten and eleven with genius level IQ's (placing them in the top one percent of the nation's population in intelligence) were identified by researchers. These scientists wanted to determine what characteristics affected goal attainment when intelligence was not a factor. In follow-up surveys in 1940 and 1950 (when the participants were in their peak productive years), three factors were identified which distinguished the most successful from the least successful. (Success was defined in terms of career goals the participants had set for themselves.) The three distinguishing factors were integration toward goals, perseverance, and self-confidence. Apparently, those who were the most successful recognized both their abilities and limitations, were reasonable in their aspirations and expectations, and were undaunted in pursuing them.

People are goal-directed. Sometimes we consciously set goals about what we want to achieve. At other times, we unconsciously decide how we want a particular incident to be resolved and attempt to influence matters so that our desired result will be achieved. Much of what is involved in interpersonal relations can be viewed as attempts to achieve our own goals and to impose some sort of order and predictability in our world. For instance, when a supervisor angrily says to an employee, "Can't you do anything right?", he or she is not asking a question, but making a statement that is expected to produce meekness and penitence on the employee's part. If the employee gives an angry retort, the supervisor will probably then feel even more justified in rebuking the employee. Either reaction on the employee's part is what the supervisor might expect.

Desire for certainty and predictability is the underlying reason why self-fulfilling prophecies exist. Most of us don't like surprises. We want to know what is going on. This is a natural feeling which is illustrated by the following example: A high school principal tested the validity of this phenomenon. Throughout the school year as substitutes were needed in various classrooms, he would distribute biographies of the new teacher prior to the teacher's arrival. The biographies were identical except that half described the substitute as a "warm, concerned, supportive" person and half described the substitute as a "cold, rigid, demanding" person. Substantial differences resulted in the students' evaluation of the teacher an in their interaction patterns with him or her. The students who expected the substitute to be warm rated him or her higher as an effective teacher, while those who were told that the substitute was cold, had less to do with this teacher and rated him or her poorly.[12]

Our own subjective evaluation of a situation affects how we approach it and how capable we presume we'll be in successfully completing any required tasks. Based on prior advancements and failures, we develop a subjective probability of success that acts as an intrapersonal self-fulfilling prophecy. We cannot simply *think* ourselves into doing better in such situations, but we can more realistically *evaluate* ourselves and our experiences in order to improve our belief about our competence.

Chapters 3 and 4 describe this developmental process in detail. At this point, it is sufficient to describe the nature of the relationship between personal beliefs and competence. Let's now examine the relationship between the beliefs of others and our own beliefs about our competence.

[12] H.H. Kelly, "The Warm-Cold Variable in First Impressions of People," *Journal of Personality* V. 18 (1950) pp. 431-439.

INTERPERSONAL SELF-FULFILLING PROPHECIES

In everything we do or fail to do, we communicate attitudes and values which others take as cues to their own behavior. How much and to what extent the positions we project are picked up by others, however, depends largely on the confidence people sense we have in ourselves and in our point of view. Our communicated attitudes and expectations act as self-fulfilling prophecies when we really believe in them.

This notion of a self-fulfilling prophecy based on attitudes and expectations has long been recognized by behavioral scientists, therapists and doctors. The existing evidence for the effects of these interpersonal self-fulfilling prophecies is almost overwhelming. Yet, their findings have not been widely communicated nor implications for action generally understood.

What other people (e.g., family, friends, co-workers and supervisors) believe about a person powerfully affects that person's image of himself or herself. Since supervisors and managers have the authority to alter a person's status at the workplace, they can dramatically affect his or her self-image. Rare is the person who can be productive and feel good about himself or herself when treated poorly by supervisors and others at work; and, of course, the reverse holds true also. Praise and high expectations of other people enhance one's desire to do better and then some.

This was the point George Bernard Shaw was trying to make when he wrote the play *Pygmalion,* the basis for the musical hit, *My Fair Lady.* In the play, Shaw describes how Professor Higgins, an expert in languages and dialects, takes a London flower girl out of poverty and within a matter of months passes her off as a princess at a celebrity ball. Near the conclusion of the story, the girl, Eliza Doolittle, explains to Higgins' mother the reason for her development. It was not the result of the professor's teaching ability, but of Mrs. Higgins' belief in Eliza. Eliza explained it this way:

"You see, really and truly, apart from the things anyone can pick up, the dressing and the proper way of speaking, and so on; the difference between a lady and a flower girl is not how she behaves, but how she's treated. I shall always be a flower girl to Professor Higgins, because he always treats me as a flower girl, and always will; but I know I can be a lady to you, because you always treat me as a lady and always will."

Self-fulfilling prophecy, (or Pygmalion effect as it is sometimes call-ed) is based on expectations, and the subsequent treatment of others goes in both directions. That is, people tend to fulfill the expecta-tions of others regardless of whether they are positive or negative.

Every organization, every manager provides people with a sense of what is expected of them. If the expectations are sparse or lax, then people will exert little effort. If the expectations are negative, then people will be submissive, but act out what they think is "really" expected of them. However, if much is expected of employees in an organization, then chances are people will expect much of themselves. It is possible to create an atmosphere that encourages effort, striving and vigorous performance, a climate in which people want to fulfill the expectations of those who guide and direct them.

SUMMARY

The organizational imperative is to insure that work is accomplish-ed well and on time. To do that, supervisors are increasingly being called upon to counsel fellow employees. Since productivity in many jobs depends largely on how much a worker is willing to produce, a supervisor's or employee relations professional's ability to correct, coach, and consult has become an important means of improving productivity. To put the issue in terms of how influential a super-visor is in a given situation is to put the issue in perspective. Both individual employees and the organizations that employ them benefit from managers and others who are skilled counselors.

Managers and supervisors are facing a situation that is unique in the history of industry. Some are even calling it a crisis that few are prepared to deal with adequately. What is it? Simply this: Recent legislative and court actions make it difficult to terminate the un-satisfactorily performing employee and traditional incentives seem unable to significantly affect the rest. Moreover, new employees, bet-ter educated and with higher expectations than their predecessors, are taking their places in both the blue- and white-collar ranks and demanding more from their jobs than a paycheck. Management isn't the same as it was fifteen or twenty years ago, and those who manage must realize that the new situation calls for a new way of managing.

To be effective, today's manager must be vitally concerned about the performance of each person he or she supervises and involved in structuring their activities so that each one will be motivated to perform well. Motivation is not a personality trait which an employee either does or doesn't have, but is instead a product of the situation in which a person finds himself or herself. Most of the inputs which go into the making of motivation in an employee are within a manager's control. The trouble is, managers are not as adept at using them to improve employee output as they are in using raw materials and machines to improve material outputs. This chapter has provided some perspectives on understanding people, a beginning place for recognizing why counseling is important and how it can best be done.

Chapter 3

A Practical Approach to Counseling

There are a wide variety of general approaches and specific techniques to counseling people. Like the seven blind men who felt different parts of an elephant and consequently had different opinions on what an elephant was like, so counseling theorists have had different types of experiences and concluded that their individual approaches were the most appropriate in effectively counseling others. Moreover, both the seven blind men and counseling approaches could benefit by pooling, comparing and combining information in a unified way. In this chapter, eight basic approaches to counseling will be briefly described and compared. Some general objectives of counseling at the workplace will be noted and a variety of specific techniques, including their uses and limitations, will be explained. These techniques will be drawn from research on group and individual problem-solving in addition to the eight basic approaches previously described. In introducing and explaining counseling techniques, the emphasis will be on describing what works and why, rather than on consistency with some particular philosophical approach. Finally, some pitfalls and hazards in counseling will be described. In essence, a practical approach to counseling will be discussed.

APPROACHES TO COUNSELING

Over the years, professional counselors and others have formulated different approaches to counseling. These approaches differ as much as anything else on the assumptions made about human nature. Many managers and management observers are familiar with Douglas MacGregor's Theory X-Theory Y and Abraham Maslow's Hierarchy of Needs, both of which postulated basic assumptions of human nature, so approaches based on assumptions about what people are like should not seem unfamiliar. Table 3-1 summarizes seven prevalent counseling approaches and lists their distinguishing features.

There are three basic channels to note in listening to and influencing others in a counseling situation: a person's thoughts, feelings, and behavior. In counseling, there are alternative ways of responding to messages being sent by each of these channels. Moreover, it is important to realize that when and how one responds to messages in each of these channels will significantly affect what the other person may continue to reveal.

Generally, early in a counseling discussion it is important to respond in some manner to the feelings being expressed by the other person. Such feelings are typically disguised early in the discussion until the troubled person is able to determine what kinds of things the counselor is willing to listen to. Once a counselor conveys that he or she "hears" the feelings being expressed, it is necessary to make some decisions. What is the nature of the problem? Does the person *feel* upset, angry, frustrated? Are the person's *thoughts* confused, disoriented, unrealistic? Does the person *do* things that are inappropriate, self-defeating, unintentionally negative? How a counselor answers these questions and responds in the discussion will influence both the direction and outcome of the interview.

It is important to respond to that portion of what the person thinks, feels, or does that is *most* related to the person's problem. However, this comes with practice in noting the types of reaction that various responses elicit.

Since counseling is concerned with problem-solving and not just talking a problem over, it is important for the counselor to constantly be aware of ways to assist the other person in resolving the particular problem being discussed. This may require changes in the person or in the situation or both, but it does suggest that change must occur somewhere.

Table 3-1   BASIC APPROACHES

Psychoanalytic Approach	Human beings are basically determined by early experiences. Unconscious motives and conflicts are central in present behavior. Irrational forces are strong; the person is driven by aggressive impulses. Early development is of critical importance, for later personality orientations have roots in childhood conflicts.
Humanistic Approach	The central focus is on the nature of the human condition, which includes capacity for self-awareness, freedom of choice to decide one's fate, responsibility and freedom. Anxiety is a basic element in life. Self-actualization is a basic goal of everyone.
Gestalt Approach	The person strives for wholeness and integration of thinking, feeling, and behaving. The view is antideterministic, in that the person is seen to have the capacity to recognize how earlier influences are related to present difficulties.
Transactional Analysis Approach	The person has potential for choice. What was once decided can be redecided. Although the person may be a victim of early decisions and interpersonal game playing, self-defeating aspects can be changed with awareness.
Behavior Therapy	Humans are shaped and determined by environmental conditioning. Behavior is a product of learning and conditioning and is controlled through identifying and providing appropriate rewards.
Rational-Emotive Approach	Humans are born with potential for rational thinking but with tendencies towards crooked thinking. They tend to fall victim to irrational beliefs and to reindoctrinate themselves with these beliefs. Counseling approach stresses thinking, judging, analyzing, doing and redeciding.
Reality Therapy	The person has a need for identity and can develop either a "success identity" or a "failure identity." The approach is based on growth motivation and stresses the importance of accepting responsibility.

Knowing how to induce personal and organizational change is necessary to counsel effectively. Besides such general goals as assisting in problem-solving and creating change, counseling objectives include enabling someone else to do the following:

1. become more aware of personal goals and values;
2. accept responsibility for who he or she is and avoid blaming others or situations for existing conditions;
3. accept personal strengths as well as weaknesses, avoid playing helpless, and develop the necessary competence to manage one's own world;
4. learn to take risks that will open new doors while accepting and dealing with the ambiguity and uncertainty that such risk-taking implies;
5. develop techniques for coping with situational conditions that cannot be readily altered; and
6. make choices based on good information and implement those decisions with resolve and a willingness to work through their consequences.

These objectives do not suggest that people are completely self-determined and uninfluenced by their environment. Situations do affect us, but they pose options instead of one-way streets. It is true that an accumulation of choices affected and reinforced by our environment may make it difficult to change. But since we do have the capacity to choose our environment (at least within some limits) it seems obvious that we have the power to control who we are and how we will respond to cues in our environment.

The following chapter will present step-by-step procedures for dealing with three types of counseling situations: correcting, coaching, and consulting. In this chapter, techniques will be presented that may be appropriate in any counseling situation. Techniques for dealing with various kinds of emotion, developing individual responsibility, re-orienting thinking, making commitments, and giving praise are described. Specific techniques are presented along with some of their uses and limitations.

DEALING WITH EMOTIONS

Many people are uncomfortable in dealing with emotions and tend to deny or repress strong feelings. Encouraging people to ventilate their emotions when they feel strongly about something can be a cathartic event. In some counseling situations, being listened to is all a person seeks and needs. The effects of empathetic listening are documented in an interesting experiment attempted by a university professor. At the beginning of the semester in an undergraduate course in psychology, the professor stated that each student would be required to make weekly visits to the terminally ill ward of the local hospital. The students were told that they could stay as long as they wanted and discuss anything they wished. The professor had previously instructed the patients to simply listen if the students discussed their personal problems and try to understand the nature of the student's concern. At the end of the semester, the students reported that they had received a better understanding of life and help with their personal problems from these patients, while those who were actually visited assured the professor that substantive input by them was avoided.[1]

Developing Openness.   An initial challenge faced in counseling is knowing how to help someone openly express their feelings and concerns. Explicitly stating at the beginning of a discussion that all decisions reside with the employee is one technique. This removes any anxiety on the employee's part about pressure being brought upon accepting a particular solution. This also reinforces the person's sense of being in control, and makes it possible to explore a specific problem with someone with whom trust is being developed.

Another technique for developing openness is to seek understanding when another person begins to describe a situation. A natural tendency when someone is talking about a particular topic is to express approval or disapproval. For instance, if an employee says, "I don't think there's much of a future in this place," a natural response is to agree or disagree. Thus, we are inclined to say something like,"Oh, I think there's plenty of opportunity for people who work hard," or "I think it is quite difficult to get ahead in your particular department." Since both of these are "taking sides" responses, they signal to the other person a readiness to judge, to evaluate, to criticize. They do not suggest a readiness to understand.

There are some specific techniques which can be used to avoid this tendency to make a quick evaluation. As a group, they are called active listening skills because they allow the listener to actively participate in the communication process.

---

[1] Cited in Mildred Newman and Bernard Berkowitz, *How to Be Your Own Best Friend*, (New York: Random House, 1971).

One active listening tool is paraphrasing. Paraphrasing occurs when managers restate in their own words what they believe another person has just said. This ensures the understanding of the *intent* and the individual words of the speaker. It is a solution to the feeling expressed by this oft-repeated phrase: "I know you believe you understand what you think I said, but I am not sure you realize that what you heard is not what I meant."

Paraphrasing is not parroting. Rather, it is restating the intent of another person's ideas or feelings. Some phrases to use in paraphrasing include the following:

- "What I hear you saying is..."
- "Sounds like you feel..."
- "You believe that..."
- "Are you saying that..."
- "What happened was..."
- "You're concerned that..."

These are trigger phrases that can get speakers to clarify their original intent or express their feelings more completely. Just imagine what would happen if this tool were used regularly in everyday business activities. Frequently-heard phrases such as, "How did she get that from what I said?" and "I thought I told you not to.." would certainly be spoken less often and may even disappear altogether.

Another active listening technique that can promote better interpersonal communication is termed "door openers."[2] This is a tool that can get someone else to say more about a problem or a frustrating experience. Some door openers include:

- "Uh-huh"
- "Really?"
- "I see."
- "Oh."
- "How's that?"
- "Interesting."

They stimulate communication because they encourage another person to say more. Too often managers assume that they must have an answer to every question or defend the status quo whenever an

[2] Thomas Gordon, *Leadership Effectiveness Training*, (Chicago: Wyden, 1978).

employee describes a problem. In turn, employees feel that there is no point in talking with these managers because they never listen, they simply reply with a pat answer. [These methods are used often in the Applications Section. Note in particular, "I don't want to work for a woman" in Unit 3, "Male/Female Issues."]

Sometimes people just want and need to be heard. They want to blow off steam. Much of human communication asks for contact as much as content. Thus, phrases such as "You have no reason to feel that way" or "If you'd look at things from my position once in a while" or "Everybody knows that..." prevent communication rather than facilitate it.

In developing or maintaining openness, doing things that reduce status differences and emphasize equality can also be helpful. By doing things which suggest a person with a problem is "one down," a would-be counselor limits his or her own effectiveness. The following actions may convey this "one down" attitude:

Changing the subject without explanation. This is often done to avoid dealing with the strong emotions someone else may be conveying. The implicit message being sent to someone else when this is done is that such feelings aren't worth discussing.

Generalizing. Generalizations such as "Everyone has problems like that" or "We all feel that way at one time or another" deny feelings. They suggest that someone's problems are not unique and that the person is not being considered as an individual.

Agreeing vigorously. Head-bobbing, ready agreement, and the like bind a person to a position when he or she may only be "testing the water."

Obligating. Many people have great difficulty in counseling because they feel the need to defend themselves or their institutions. They obligate emotionally with such statements as "She has always spoken favorably of you," "Most people, however, think the policy is fair" or other statements which imply that the person should not feel as he or she does.

Uses. Techniques for developing openness can be especially useful at the beginning of a counseling discussion. They can convey a counselor's willingness to understand the other person's point of view. They suggest that evaluation will be limited to reviewing the problem at hand and its impact rather than judging personalities. They demonstrate that the counselor will not decide what is to be done, but rather contribute to the problem-solving process. They convey acceptance and can thereby free the person enough to talk about his or her real concerns rather than the superficial ones typically expressed at the beginning of a counseling discussion. In short, they can be very effective in getting to the root of a problem and positioning the other person as the ultimate decision-maker regarding any future action steps.

Limitations.   Using only techniques that develop openness may reduce the possibility of the employee being able to generalize aspects of the counseling relationship to other relationships. It is unlikely that other people will respond with such nondirective statements, and thus the person may come to believe that other people don't understand him or her. That is, the person may become so preoccupied with himself or herself that other relationships deteriorate. Moreover, although developing openness is a necessary step in counseling, in most cases it is only the beginning of the process. For some people, the release of pent-up emotions is all that is necessary; for others, it is not a sufficient goal.

Handling Anger and Frustration.   Frustration occurs when someone feels blocked from realizing a particular goal or achieving a certain objective. The goal or objective may be clearly or only vaguely defined and of central causal importance. Anger results when frustration is not dissipated and the block seems immovable. Anger is an intense form of frustration.

Several kinds of obstacles can cause frustration. Most of them can be classified as stemming from either interpersonal difficulties or personal aspirations. For instance, people may feel frustrated when:

- others do not agree with their ideas;
- others do not provide the information, time, or other resources needed to complete a project on time;
- opportunities for advancement appear limited; and
- personal contributions are not recognized.

Allowing another person to express anger or frustration is the first step in channeling such feelings into a productive mode. Expression has the effect of unburdening a person so new possibilities may be considered. If, however, angry or frustrated feelings are not affirmed, they will most likely intensify. One method for encouraging such expression is the empty chair technique. In this procedure, a counselor encourages an employee to "tell off" the person who is the source of frustration as if that person were sitting next to the employee in an empty chair. This technique avoids talking about generalized other ("they") in some nebulous form. It also encourages an employee to speak forth rightly instead of indirectly about his or her feelings.

Besides encouraging expression of the resentment a person feels, the dialogue with the empty chair can also help examine the consequences of such action. An extension of this technique is the role playing method. In performing a role play, an employee first describes the person who is blocking the fulfillment of a particular objective. Then, the counselor adopts the perspective of that person and a dialogue ensues. Following the dialogue, the interaction is reviewed and discussed with likely consequences of statements made by the employee highlighted by the counselor. In other words, the counselor puts himself or herself in the position of the person who is blocking the employee and states how he or she would likely act in such a situation. See "I don't think they like working for a woman" in Unit 3, "Male/Female Issues", for an example of how this method is applied in a specific situation.

When frustration results from the unfulfillment of personal aspirations, other techniques may be necessary. The unrealized aspirations of many people are a function of not counting the costs and developing an appropriate plan in order to achieve the intended goal. There are exceptions, of course: people who want to be musicians who are functionally tone deaf or those who want to possess technical expertise in some discipline but lack the necessary intelligence. But more often than not we want things that we are not prepared to sacrifice to achieve or know how to get if we were inclined toward such sacrifice.

The lack of fit between what individuals like to do and want out of their jobs and actual work requirements is another cause of frustration. Personal ambitions and the promise of monetary rewards may lure some people into accepting a job or an assignment for which they are not well suited. Ed Schein's work on career dynamics has shown that a "technically anchored" person will see the natural interpersonal process in organizational life, such as bargaining with other work units, facing departmental conflicts, and overcoming senior manager resistance to change, as "damn politics getting in the way." Yet, another person whose career anchor is in "managerial competence" will experience these same events positively. Such a person sees opportunities and challenges instead of frustration and roadblocks.[3]

An initial step in getting a handle on unfulfilled personal aspirations is to develop a goal statement that reflects as much individual control as possible. The more a person chooses goals that other people largely control, such as a goal to become vice-president of XYZ Company, the more likely that person is to be frustrated. People free themselves and avoid frustration when they explicitly select goals over which they themselves have primary control.

Another key factor in mastering such disappointments is to become aware of one's own emotional reaction to them.[4] For instance, is the frustration evoked at work handled by displacing it at home with one's spouse or children? Or do things build up until a tolerance level is surpassed? Becoming aware of how one reacts to frustrations is a key to their mastery. Counseling can be especially useful in such cases by directing this personal energy into productive activities such as assessment and goal-setting instead of displacement and disappointment. [Unit 2, "Career Counseling", illustrates through several different vignettes how frustration and disappointment develop and how to deal with it.]

Confronting Anxiety.   People attempt to use work to accomplish many personal needs and aspirations. Employment is a primary source of identity and both shapes and satisfies (or frustrates) these needs. Who we are and how we regard ourselves is largely a function of our experiences at work. What a person wants out of life, is capable of achieving, and what he or she is willing to do, are functions of both personal needs and work experiences.

The interrelatedness of personal needs and work experiences has been widely noted in recent books and articles on career development.[5] The personal concerns or anxieties which are a product of this interaction, however, are not new. In fact, perhaps the most famous investigation of the behavior of people at work, the Hawthorne studies, noted that people are often concerned and anxious about being able to develop individual abilities as well as satisfy organizational expectations while on the job.[6] The Hawthorne

[3] Edgar H. Schein, *Career Dynamics* (Reading, Massachusetts: Addison-Wesley, 1978).

[4] Abraham Zaleznick, "Management of Disappointment," *Harvard Business Review* (Nov-Dec., 1967).

[5] Douglas T. Hall, *Careers in Organizations*, (Santa Monica, California: Goodyear Publishing Co., 1976).

[6] William J. Dickson and Fritz Roethliesberger, *Counseling In An Organization* (Cambridge, Massachusetts: Harvard University Press, 1966).

researchers, proposed a typology of employee concerns that seems just as relevant today as when it was first proposed. These concerns interact with one another and are not entirely separable, but can be represented as shown in the following diagram:

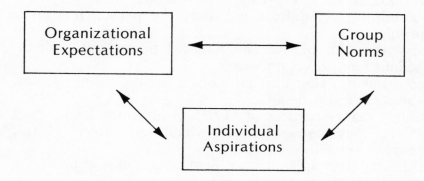

Anxieties at work arise out of a feeling that one cannot meet the demands imposed by one or more of these sources. When organization expectations seem too high, opportunities for group inclusion impossible, or individual aspirations unattainable, people become anxious. Frustration results when someone feels that someone or something else is preventing or blocking the attainment of a desired goal. Anxiety, on the other hand, is the result of a belief that particular goals are unrealizable to the individual. Anxiety is unattempted effort; frustration is blocked effort.

Anxieties about one's own possibilities and capabilities often result from changes at the workplace. A promotion or a new boss can create anxieties about measuring up. Automation or economic downturns can produce anxieties about job security. Transfers of coworkers or recruitment of new talent can produce concerns over fitting in and being accepted. Passage through various life and career stages can promote anxiety over meeting personal goals and ambitions. Almost any change creates anxiety of some kind regardless of whether or not the change is externally imposed or internally decided upon.

Since anxieties originate in our beliefs about things, in assisting others in overcoming their anxieties, and feeling competent enough to deal with their world, a useful beginning point is to focus on how such concerns can be appropriately confronted. Albert Ellis, the father of Rational-Emotive Therapy, has suggested some ways ordinary people can assist others in appropriately dealing with the anxieties that arise out of everyday life. Ellis' approach can basically be described as an educative process that focuses on self-understanding and personal change. Ellis[7] suggests this can be done by:

1. zeroing in on one problem at a time,
2. examining self-defeating beliefs the person has about the problem,
3. showing him or her the magical power with which such beliefs have been endowed,
4. confronting the implicit, often wrong, assumptions that support these beliefs,
5. doing reality-testing of such assumptions and beliefs and their likely consequences (which are often self-fulfilling prophecies), and
6. thinking through the problem in a more systematic, less emotional, more logical way.

Ellis maintains that by following this procedure, people can be assisted in thinking more rationally and thereby deal with anxieties more realistically. He emphasizes, as well, that the counselor should continuously be confronting another person's beliefs by asking:

- What is the worst thing that could happen if you did (did not) do that?
- How would that be so bad?

These two questions and their answers lead to self-examination and ultimately the ability to confront one's anxieties.

An especially useful technique in confronting anxiety is the combination of two related ideas: desensitization and behavorial rehearsal. In applying this technique, the employee is first encouraged to detach himself or herself from the problem after it has been identified. The employee is then encouraged, in this detached and more relaxed condition, to construct a series of statements that describe actual experiences where he or she was unsure about how to deal with a situation. Then, the person is encouraged to say what he or she would do not, upon reflection, and to identify the likely consequences of such courses of action. The person is then asked to do

[7] Albert Ellis, *Executive Leadership: A Rational Approach*, (Secaucus, New Jersey: Citadel Press, 1968)

"forward thinking" by applying this same analysis and rehearsing various options to identified situations. This technique desensitizes a person to past anxiety-provoking situations through their rational analysis and equips the person to deal with future situations by actually rehearsing them. [This method can be useful in dealing with career concerns, felt injustices, or perceived discrimination. See "Just because I work in the plant they think I'm here for something else besides the job" in Unit 3, "Male/Female Issues", for an illustration.]

It is natural for people to experience some anxiety at work. As individuals, we want to do well and be accepted. This desire for the approval of others is a basic source of anxiety for many people. Such day-to-day anxieties, if dissipated, however, can prevent the kind of accumulation that may lead to more severe tensions and strains. In this regard, an observation made by Aristotle provides a technique that a counselor may find useful in helping someone cope with ordinary anxieties. Aristotle noted that watching a tragic play performed "purged the soul" by creating and then exhausting pity and fear. Viewers drained off their anxieties and then became free from their effects. A friend, who is an executive with a major corporation, noted his own relief from some personal anxieties in connection with a major policy statement he had been working on for weeks after seeing *A Chorus Line* on Broadway. Viewing that performance had opened a tension relief valve for him.

Sorting Out Confusion. It is often assumed that people know what they want and that problems are the result of an inability to obtain desired outcomes. More often than not, however, people are confused about what they really want—especially from their work—or they want many different and conflicting things. Simply exhorting them to decide what is important to them, in such cases, is less than helpful. It is negatively self-reinforcing. People are not, as some psychologists have suggested, composed of a simple hierarchy of stable and orderly needs. They are instead, a polyglot of many things. Human needs can more appropriately be thought of as similar to the contents of a grocery bag—strewn, with no particular order. It is natural, then, to expect people to be unclear about what their real needs and wants are and how they can best be met.

It is not unusual for some employees to have a vague dissatisfaction with the organization that employs them. Ambitious employees, who want to excel and achieve, are often characterized by ill-defined goals except their most grandiose ones. The essence of ambition is simply a dissatisfaction with the way things are. Personal confusion, moreover, can also be the result of deliberately ambiguous lines of authority or organizational policies. In fact, organization uncertainties are so widespread that at least one organizational observer believes the most basic task of anyone in any organization is the task of coping with ambiguity.[8]

Confusion, moreover, can be its own reward. One can avoid taking responsibility for anything simply by resorting to this panacea. Responsibility for career planning can be placed on the organization; responsibility for ethical decisions can be passed up the pyramid; responsibility for the development of others can be neglected or seen as resting completely with the individual; all this and more can be done simply by being innocent and avoiding data gathering and decision that would dissipate confusion. Saying, "I'm not sure what I want," or "I didn't know I was supposed to do anything about it" or "I figured other people higher up in the organization had better information so I didn't question the decision," can be wonderfully self-satisfying to say the least.

Confusion can have many different sources, but ultimately it stems from indecision. Making decisions and choices about what is important and worth doing can dissipate the confusion that characterizes many lives. Moreover, recognizing that most decisions can be changed and modified can ease the burden of making choices. An important function of counseling is to help someone else see that nearly all decisions can be reversed, altered, or modified. Many times people are unwilling to make decisions because of their fear of being wrong. They lock themselves to their choices, hide behind them, or fail to make them. But few decisions, in fact, are irreversible or unalterable. Decisions can be re-made or situations can be altered. Moreover, making choices clarifies a position because it allows us to test our thinking and only, thereby, determine if the choice was good. Knowing that a decision was good is usually an afterthought.

There are several published tests available that can provide personal insight into one's primary values, and thereby help someone make decisions and sort out confusion. Both *The Study of Values* by Gordon W. Allport, Phillip E. Vernon, and Gardner Lindzey and *The Work Values Inventory* by Donald E. Super are distributed by Houghton Mifflin (Boston, Massachusetts) and are excellent. Thomas J. DeLong has developed a well-done work values questionnaire based on a concept of career and developmental anchors[9].

[8] J. B. Ritchie, personal correspondence.

[9] Thomas J. DeLong, unpublished dissertation, (Purdue University).

Developing a work or personal values inventory can be very useful not only in sorting out what one wants to *be*, but more importantly what one wants to *do*. Too often in looking at issues in career development or personal values counselors have sought to help a person answer the age old question "What do you want to be when you grow up?" This is the wrong question and approach. Attempts to answer it will likely only promote more confusion or frustration. Why? Several reasons. First of all, such a question views people as static entities, which we are not. The implicit message in the question is, "You are inadequate. You don't even know what you want to be." Secondly, attempts to answer such a question can create expectations that are unrealistic or unattainable. But most important of all, the question tends to shift a person's attention away from examining what he or she *likes to do* and instead focuses attention on his or her *outcomes* and the *rewards*. This focus on the destination instead of the journey is the cause of much confusion and frustration. [Unit 2, "Career Counseling", deals with personal confusion in most of the vignettes.]

And what if the destination is reached? In his autobiographical writing, John Stuart Mill described the nature of a particular personal depression. He was reflecting on his life and ambitions and asked himself this question: "Suppose that all your objects in life were realized; that all the changes in institutions and opinions which you were looking forward to could be completely effected at this instant: would this be a great joy and happiness to you?"[10] His answer was negative. Attaining goals brings less satisfaction than working toward them and enjoying the process.

A useful approach in sorting out personal confusion or internal conflicts is to focus on what the person *enjoys doing*. In this way, internal outcomes and personal satisfaction can be highlighted as the reward structure. In working through confusion, this counseling approach suggests that aid should be given to those seeking answers to such questions as:

- What kind of person am I?
- How do I react in pressure situations?
- What are the pluses that I have going for me?
- What can I learn about myself from noting how I relate to strangers, casual acquaintances, and friends?
- What recent experiences have I had that gave me a great deal of personal satisfaction?

[10] John Stuart Mill, *Autobiography* (New York: The American Library of World Literature, 1964).

This process approach to identifying values can be more helpful than outcome approaches which only focus on "end states." Such an approach which aids someone else in clarifying what he or she enjoys doing also recognizes the dynamic nature of human beings. Moreover, it is not a "one shot, once and forever" approach, but rather a method which notes the necessity of frequently assessing such interests and orientations and making decisions about them.

Managing Disappointment. Almost everyone experiences disappointment from time to time. We have goals, ambitions, and aspirations that go unrealized. Someone else gets the promotion we wanted. A salary increase is smaller than we had hoped. Recognition goes to friends and acquaintances and escapes us. Some form of disappointment is experienced by all of us at various times in our lives. People who want to achieve or excel or seek creative expression are periodically confronted with situations in which they are not as adequate or capable as they wish. They fail to perform and are disappointed. Disappointment, however, far from being the prelude to failure, may actually provide incentive that spurs accelerated personal growth and be the beginning of truly outstanding performance in some endeavor.

Perhaps many people can identify with the feelings of disappointment and inadequacy expressed by Harold Nicolson, a Parliamentry secretary under Winston Churchill, even though the events Nicolson describes are different from their own. After being asked to step down and submitting his resignation, Nicolson records the following in his diary:

> But I mind more than I thought I should mind. It is mainly, I suppose, a sense of failure. I quite see that if the Labour leaders have been pressing to have my post, there is good cause why they should have it. But if I had more power and drive, I should have been offered Rab Butler's job at the Foreign Office, which I should dearly have loved. As it is, I come back to the bench below the gangway having had my chance and failed to profit by it. Ever since I have been in the House I have been looked on as a might-be. Now I shall be a might-have-been. Always up till now I have been buoyed up by the hope of writing some good book or achieving a position of influence in politics. I know now that I shall never write a book better than I have written already, and that my political career is at an end. I shall merely get balder and fatter and more deaf as the years go by. This is an irritating thing. Suc-

cess should come late in life in order to compensate for the loss of youth; I had youth and success together, and now I have old age and failure.[11]

Although we may not all aspire to such positions of power and prominence, the feelings of unfulfilled expectations and personal goals are no doubt common to us all. The feeling of being passed over for a promotion affects people in a similar manner regardless of their employment level. A passed-over vice-president and a passed-over clerk may both feel the same degree of disappointment. They can both have the same doubts about their abilities, the same feelings of failure. The differences in status, level, and income may not affect the way they feel. Given this commonality, how does one effectively cope with disappointment?

First of all, it is important to realize that disappointment can be a catalytic experience that encourages personal growth and development. In fact, personal change hinges on such experiences that cause someone to re-examine goals and ambitions. Development is not a logical stair-step of positive experiences. Rather, growth and development are forged out of coping with crises, pain, and disappointment. We grow by overcoming. James Baldwin poignantly described this process when he wrote:

> Any real change implies the breakup of the world as one has always known it, the loss of all that gave one identity, the end of safety . . . it is only when man is able without bitterness or self-pity to surrender a dream he has long cherished or a privilege he has long possessed that he is set free, that he has set himself free for higher dreams, for greater privileges.[12]

Disappointment can be the beginning of growth. But, how? How can the process of experiencing disappointment be self-regenerating instead of debilitating? How can the counseling process be utilized to assist someone else in managing disappointment? The key to accepting disappointment and coming to grips with its implications is well-illustrated by Elizabeth Kubler-Ross, whose work with terminally ill patients is well known. From her time spent with such patients and others, Kubler-Ross has written:

[11] Harold Nicolson, *The War Years 1939-1945* (New York: Atheneum Publishers, 1967).

[12] James Baldwin, *Nobody Knows My Name* (New York: Dial, 1961).

I have worked with dying patients for 15 years, and I am very impressed with the fact that they are going through the same stages as anyone else who is in the process of losing something very important. These stages are connected with the experience of losing something that is very important to one's ego.[13]

The stages that Kubler-Ross has identified, which are common to both death and disappointment, are the following:

1. Denial
2. Anger
3. Bargaining
4. Grief and mourning
5. Acceptance

In order to assist someone's growth from disappointment, a counselor should recognize these stages and help the other person work through them. Most of us need to talk through disappointments if we are to learn from them. Without expressing ourselves on such matters, we are likely to turn inward and resort to self-blame and self-deprecation. Disappointment becomes destructive instead of constructive in such instances.

Some reflections on the process of working through one's own disappointments are provided in George Vaillant's *Adaptation to Life*.[14] This volume is a record of the lives of more than 200 young men from their college days through their mature years and is an attempt to generalize about ways people cope (or fail to cope) with their lives and their ambitions. Vaillant notes that one of the greatest advances of modern surgery was to recognize that nothing could be done to hasten wound healing except to understand it well enough to learn to stay out of its way. The process of inflammation is a healthy sign of healing. Purging infection and providing protection were about all that could be done by a doctor (or anyone else) to promote healing. So it is with depression and disappointment, Vaillant maintains. It is important to understand the process of healthy inflammation so that the wound can be protected enough for it to eventually heal itself.

[13] Elizabeth Kubler-Ross, *Questions and Answers on Death and Dying* (New York: Macmillan, 1974).

[14] George Vaillant, *Adaption to Life* (Boston: Little, Brown, and Co., 1979).

In counseling, then, when disappointment is the problem, it is useful to allow the other person to deny his or her disappointment. Instead of expressing skepticism over such denial—or worse, expressing sympathy over the concealed disappointment—it is necessary to just let the person talk. Feelings of anger or frustration are likely to follow along with such bargaining strategies as "Do you think that if I would have done . . . , I would have been more successful?" or "If only I would have . . . , this wouldn't have happened." A counselor should avoid participating in moralizing at this point and allow the expression of grief to occur. It is important not to short circuit this process. Only when the equivalent of mourning has occurred will the person be able or willing to face the future—instead of the past—and begin to problem-solve. Acceptance of the situation follows the experience of each of the other stages. A counselor's role, in such situations, is as a pilot in helping a person navigate through these five stages.

In helping others work through major disappointments, a counselor should recognize that the most important decision the disappointed person must make is the decision to say "goodbye." Acceptance comes when the person either sets new goals or otherwise makes some decision that a particular opportunity is gone, at least for now.

In the case of a manager or professional who has plateaued, it is particularly important that the person come to terms with his or her place in the organization. Fernando Bartolomé, who has extensively studied the professional and private lives of people in both the United States and Europe, has described what appears to be four ways of adapting to this condition.[15]

The first is to change one's job or career, to find an area of work which gives more satisfaction and fulfillment. This may, however, be difficult since the change for a higher level manager quite likely entails a cut in salary or a decrease in status. The second is to adopt a resigned instrumental orientation to work. The third is to adapt with a compensatory orientation, where energy is reinvested in private life. This is more likely to happen when the person plateaus at an early age, where his or her family, children and leisure habits are still in a developmental stage. The fourth is a particularly constructive type of compensation where professional energy is rechanneled into paraprofessional activities, generating a new sense of

[15] Paul A. L. Evans and Fernando Bartolomé, "Professional and Private Life: Three Stages in the Lives of Managers," *Organization Dynamics* (Sprint, 1979).

purpose to life. Rather than becoming resigned to a dissatisfying job, the person redirects his or her efforts toward professional associations or community activities. In his book, *The Executive in Crisis,* Eugene Jennings shows how individuals resolve a deep career crisis by reordering their lives around advising organizations that range from charity to education, religion, and politics.[16]

DEVELOPING INDIVIDUAL RESPONSIBILITY

An important, but often neglected, aspect of counseling is to build self-reliance in the person seeking assistance. The debilitating effects of a material dole system have been well documented by many sources. It breeds dependency and insecurity. Likewise, counseling can prevent a person from solving his or her own problems if the necessity of developing self-reliance is not incorporated in the counseling process. William Glasser, in particular, has emphasized the importance of each individual accepting and exercising responsibility and has incorporated it into a counseling approach known as reality therapy.[17]

According to Glasser, people develop and display both a *success* identity and a *failure* identity. Specific events and recent experiences will cause one of these two identities to predominate, but both are latent and intrinsic to mankind. Furthermore, Glasser stresses the importance of each person accepting responsibility for the way he or she is and the conditions that currently confront him or her. In this context, reality is defined as "the ability to fulfill one's needs, and to do so in a way that does not deprive others of the ability to fulfill their own needs." Responsibility is a learned process. It is also a process that recognizes one cannot be responsible without also being capable. Responsibility requires competence as well as a willingness to accept things the way they are and go from there.

This aspect of counseling emphasizes the importance of evaluating behavior. This does not mean the counselor acts as a moralist. Instead of judging the actions of someone else, a counselor teaches

---

[16] Eugene E. Jennings, *The Executive in Crisis,* (New York: McGraw-Hill, 1965).

[17] William Glasser, *Reality Therapy* (New York: Harper and Row, 1975).

responsibility by helping the other person evaluate his or her own actions. [See "Sometimes I feel like their token" in Unit 3, "Male/Female Issues", for an example of a counselor who helped an employee accept individual responsibility.]

Self-evaluation is the key to self-examination. The function of self-evaluation is to lay the groundwork for personal insight, without which change and development cannot occur. Insights (real, unfiltered glimpses of ourselves as we really are) are often reached only with great difficulty. There are many different views on how such self-insight is obtained. The passive body notions of zen, yoga, and TM, among others, suggest that such insight is gained by reflection. The active body approaches of biorhythms, jogging, and outward bound programs stress that insight results from a combination of strenuous physical and emotional efforts. Do such approaches produce insight? When accompanied by reflective self-examination they do. But they must be purposeful, aimed at evaluating where one is and how he or she feels about that condition. More importantly, examining experiences and determining what can be learned about ourselves from them is the way most of us obtain insights.

Consider this analogy: our minds are like the mail slots at the local post office. Categories are labeled so the right piece of mail will be put in the correct spot. Our minds too are composed of compartments and categories. Based on our experiences, we have labeled these slots so that we can process new experiences and fit them into reality as we already know it. Only when we examine the make-up of these categories in our minds—and not simply put new information into them—do we truly grow and develop. Learning responsibility means learning to cope with the changing reality that is all around us and testing the appropriateness of the categories we have created for defining our experiences.

In assisting someone else in this process of self-examination, the following procedures may be useful:

1. Get a clear definition of the problem or concern the person has.
2. Focus on what the implications of the situation are and ignore looking for the reasons things failed to turn out as expected.
3. Confront anxieties and unrealistic fears.
4. Accept no excuses. Deal with reality as the person is currently experiencing it. Stay in the "here and now" and avoid looking at previous mistakes or problems.

5. Set goals and establish a plan for taking action. Do not leave the discussion in the "talking things over" realm—make commitments, take action, and problem-solve.

Taking responsibility is a continual process. Most of us, at times, attempt to blame others or circumstances for our inability to perform as well as we ought. We can examine both our abilities and our expectations to more effectively learn from our experiences.

DEFINING THE SITUATION

There are a number of well-known situations that are excellent examples of how the definition of a problem affects the solutions considered. Perhaps two will suffice. One is the classic story of the truck that was stuck in an underpass. Various onlookers tried to be helpful by suggesting ways to free the truck. However, each suggestion involved considerable damage either to the truck or to the underpass. Then a little boy came along and suggested letting air out of the tires. Apparently, the little boy's perspective led to a definition of the problem different from the adults' and ultimately to a more acceptable solution.

Another well-known example is found in Mark Twain's *Tom Sawyer*. At one point, Tom had been assigned to whitewash the picket fence that surrounded his aunt's house. There was no way to avoid the task. Tom, however, has a flash of inspiration when a neighbor boy happens along, and the following dialogue ensues:

"Hello, old chap, you got work, hey?"

"Why, it's you, Ben! I warn't noticing."

"Say—I'm going a-swimming, I am. Don't you wish you could? But of course you'd druther work—wouldn't you? Course you would."

Tom contemplated the boy a bit, and said, "What do you call work?"

"Why, ain't that work?"

Tom resumed his whitewashing and answered carelessly, "Well, maybe it is, and maybe it ain't. All I know is, it suits Tom Sawyer."

"Oh come now, you don't mean to let on that you like it?"

The brush continued to move.

"Like it? Well I don't see why I oughtn't to like it. Does a boy get a chance to whitewash a fence every day?"

That put the thing in a new light. Ben stopped nibbling his apple. Tom swept his brush daintily back and forth—stepped back to note the effect—added a touch here and there—criticized the effect again—Ben watching every move and getting more and more interested, more and more absorbed.

Presently he said, "Say, Tom, let me whitewash a little."

Soon Tom has others joining in the task of whitewashing, even having them pay for the privilege. Tom succeeded in defining work as play, and his friends accepted this new definition of the situation.

These two examples illustrate the importance of defining a problem wisely and well. In doing so, it is vital to suspend judgment and try to get a clear picture of the nature of the problem before jumping to a conclusion. An experiment by the noted educator Jerome Bruner serves to illustrate this point. Bruner projected color slides of familiar objects on a large screen and asked people to try to identify them while they were still out of focus. He gradually improved the focus and called for reidentification at various times. His startling finding was this: If an individual wrongly identifies an object while it is still greatly out of focus, that person will generally be unable to correctly identify it when it is clearer. On the other hand, another person who has not seen the blurred image can easily identify it.[18] What this experiment seems to demonstrate is that more evidence is required to overcome an incorrect definition than is required to establish a correct one. A person who jumps to conclusions is less likely to see any other definition of a problem.

[18] Jerome S. Bruner, *Beyond The Information Given: Studies in the Psychology of Knowing* (New York: Norton, 1973).

One way to avoid jumping to conclusions and to define problems more accurately is to practice "reframing."[19] Reframing is trying to look for the obscure, trying to go beyond the apparent, in defining a problem. The term "reframing" is used because the person is attempting to change the frame of reference. Successful reframing does not include changing the facts, but it does include changing the way the facts are viewed. Thus, Tom Sawyer did not change the facts of whitewashing the fence, but instead redefined work thus reframing the situation. Likewise, the little boy did not change the facts in the case of the truck in the underpass, but redefined the critical elements that needed changing to remedy the problem.

Defining a problem is not a simple step. Effectively defining a problem may mean carefully redefining it several times if it appears that particular definitions lead nowhere. However, it is important to conscientiously test each problem definition, both those that appear at first glance to be accurate and those that appear to lead nowhere. It may be necessary in counseling to help someone reframe a situation in order to help them effectively solve a problem. [Reframing examples are scattered throughout the vignettes included in the Applications Section. Whenever a person says "I had not looked at it that way before", reframing has occurred. "The Company's gone overboard on this EEO thing" in Unit 4, "EEO Problems", has a good reframing example.]

RECOGNIZING CONSTRAINTS

Our beliefs about what can be done about a particular problem are often limited by constraints that either we or the situation impose. Recognizing constraints imposed by a situation are important. Without doing so, we might overlook aspects that dramatically affect any solutions. Time, resources, and implementation methods always constrain the effectiveness of any solution (although their influence is often overlooked). Self-imposed constraints can also significantly influence any potential solution we may devise or decide to implement. Through the counseling process, it is possible to help others see the constraints they are unnecessarily imposing on a situation and thereby help them consider a wider range of possible solutions to a particular problem.

[19] Paul Watzlewick, John H. Weakland, and Richard Fisch, *Change: Principles of Problem Formation and Problem Resolution* (New York: Norton, 1974).

Ernst Beier, a noted psychologist, believes that a counselor can help others see the self-imposed constraints they are placing on a situation by giving what he calls an "unexpected response."[20] Beier believes that people crave certainty and will go to great lengths to make their world as predictable as possible. For instance, if a woman says to a man, "I never want to see you again" what she may really intend is that she wants him to do what he always does when he is chastised. Thus, to help someone through counseling, it is necessary to look beyond the words spoken and instead decipher the response that the person is seeking to elicit in others. This is an important key to their personal objectives. Giving an unexpected response helps the other person consider other objectives and other solutions besides the predictable ones. An unexpected response refocuses someone's thinking, motivates their problem-solving, and helps their problem-solving search to be both more creative and realistic.

Although the following example is not taken from a counseling situation, it illustrates the effect an unexpected response can have in reorienting someone's thinking. According to a newspaper account, a young man went into a grocery store, pulled out a gun, and demanded that the elderly woman who was minding the store hand over all the money. The woman smiled and in a kindly voice asked, "How much do you really need, son?" Lowering the gun he replied "$5 ma'am." She opened her purse and gave him $5 from it. He promptly left.

The usual options that are considered in cases like this are either compliance or resistance. In this particular case, an unexpected response changed the eventual outcome of the situation. In counseling, giving an unexpected response can highlight the self-imposed constraints that can be dropped once we become aware of them. Sometimes a verbal message is not necessary to give an unexpected response.

Advice is often ineffective in counseling simply because the advice given is an extension of a cliché or superficial response. Without personal investment by a counselor in someone else's problem, advice means nothing. What makes advice effective is when it's least expected—like the marriage counselor who asks couples why they haven't already gotten a divorce. Such a counselor is effective because few couples expect such a question. The question helps them to begin to look at self-imposed constraints.

[20] Ernst Beier, *People Reading* (New York: Doubleday, 1976).

ACHIEVING CLOSURE

Considering resources that can be used to implement a solution is another important aspect of problem-solving. Implementation can make the difference between an effective and an ineffective solution to a problem. Since counseling is problem-oriented and aimed at assisting someone in their personal decision-making, it is imperative to reach a sense of closure in the discussion. Without closure, there has been no counseling; but rather, a chat.

Achieving closure may take several forms. The other person may specify people he or she is going to approach and further discuss the problem with. Or he or she may want to indicate what things will be done differently. Perhaps the counselor will indicate action steps the person may take. Regardless of how closure occurs, it is important that both parties feel a certain sense of satisfaction over the discussion even though the issue may not be totally resolved. Sometimes we must simply learn to live with certain conditions even if we don't like them. At least we can learn how to cope effectively with the things that we cannot change. Moreover, sometimes acceptance is the prelude of change.

RE-ORIENTING THINKING

Counseling is problem-oriented. However, the existence of a problem is a very subjective matter. Problems reside in a person's subjective perception and not in objective reality. This does not mean that problems lack supporting evidence. Rather, it suggests that problems require a definition and a problem statement. How someone defines a situation makes all the difference in what solutions they will consider. In fact, most of the time people define situations in solution-oriented rather than problem-oriented ways. That is, we define problems in terms of controlling and predicting outcomes rather than by examining blocked objectives.

Problem-solving involves the selection of one or more courses of action in the pursuit of one or more objectives. Knowing what one's objectives are is clearly important in problem-solving. So, too, is understanding the nature of a situation in which the problem is being defined. This includes both constraints and resources that affect any potential solution. Recognizing these distinct components of problem-solving helps a counselor in assisting someone else. These "intervention points" include:

- defining the nature of the situation,
- specifying desired outcomes,
- recognizing constraints that are both self- and situation-imposed, and
- identifying potential resources in implementing a solution.

SPECIFYING OUTCOMES

Most of our problems stem from a dissatisfaction with things as they are and so our problem statements are aimed at getting rid of something we do not want. This reactive approach to problem-solving may result in anticipated negative consequences if the problem is treated as an isolated event. In fact, the more immediate the source of dissatisfaction we are trying to eliminate, the less likely we are to consider the various implications of solutions that occur to us. We lock in on solutions instead of exploring the scope of the situation.

In proactive problem-solving, on the other hand, a person articulates where he or she wants to go and then attention is focused on how to get there. This approach forces a person to be more systematic. It emphasizes that the first task in problem-solving is clarifying what we really want. By rigorously specifying outcomes, we develop standards by which we can evaluate various course of action. This approach also helps us note the interrelatedness of our world and see dissatisfaction with a situation as a link in a chain of events rather than a single event. [This approach is taken in "Nobody told me to do that" which is found in Unit 6, "Performance Problems."]

In counseling a person who is dissatisfied with things as they are, the counselor needs to help the person clearly articulate where he or she wants to go. Once this desirable future is described, it becomes easier to get there. Of course, in some instances this simple activity may either diminish or eliminate the problem at hand. The other person may conclude that things aren't so bad. Minimally, by specifying desired outcomes, a person not only knows where he or she is going, but also will have the feeling of making progress toward a solution that has been thought out and talked out. These two characteristics, noted the famous Swiss psychologist, Jean Piaget, are the foundation of effective problem-solving.[21]

---

[21] Jean Piaget, *Psychology of Intelligence* (Boston: Routledge and Kegan, 1971).

AVOIDING HAZARDS

Most of the foregoing of this chapter has focused on counseling do's. There are also some specific things that counselors should avoid. These counseling hazards, like the hazards on a golf course, are snares that should be avoided when possible, but dealt with in appropriate ways if encountered. The idea of hazards also suggests there are barriers which are natural and almost inevitable in the counseling relationship. If counselors are aware in advance of some of the hazards which so often confront them, hopefully they will be in a better position to avoid or avert them. Five specific hazards and how to avoid them will be outlined in this particular section. These five hazards include intellectualizing, adopting a parental role, giving superficial responses, making social or emotional entanglements, and subtly manipulating the course of discussion.

Avoiding Intellectualizing

Intellectualizing on the part of a counselor is a particularly subtle hazard. Basically, it is an avoidance technique. By selecting certain safe aspects of what the other person is saying, the counselor actually is attempting to dictate the content of the interview. Intellectualizing forces the discussion into artificial boundaries. When it occurs, the counselor is responding only to the surface message of the words that are spoken. The result is the counselor is attempting to talk a person out of the emotional content of the message he or she is trying to convey. For instance, the counselor implies something like, "Well, you don't really mean that, do you? After all, if you were to carefully examine the situation you would find there is no reason for you to feel the way that you do." Although few people might use words as stark as these, the message they convey is just as explicit. Intellectualizing can occur when a counselor is not allowing the other person to fully express his or her emotions or when a counselor suppresses or dampens the emotional content and avoids the feelings conveyed by the other person.

Preconceived notions of what another person or a situation is like also initiate the hazard of counselor intellectualization. When a counselor has a preconceived idea of what a solution should be, he or she may jump too hastily to a conclusion. Intellectualizing is sometimes resorted to in order to save face if the counselor feels temporarily inadequate or embarrassed as he or she listens to a troubled person. If the counselor feels at a loss as to how to respond, yet feels called upon to demonstrate his or her competence, he or she may start a line of questions that keep the conversation going but miss the mark. Questioning is for productive information, not to satisfy a counselor's interests. Questions ought to force the other person to reflect upon and examine a problem.

The likely consequences of intellectualization are to lose the trust and confidence of the person seeking help. By intellectualizing, the counselor may seem to be someone who just doesn't understand. The consequences of intellectualizing, then, are to lose credibility. Perhaps the most important skill a person involved in the counseling process can learn is that of looking for the nonarticulated message of someone who is concerned or troubled. This does not mean the counselor should practice amateur psychology by looking into what someone "really" means by the words they say or the apparent feelings they are trying to express. Rather, what a counselor should do is help someone explore the nature of their feelings and the content of their experiences. Counseling is useful because it helps people examine a variety of implications surrounding their problems. Counseling is much like reading a map of a largely unexplored territory. It is not a well devised blueprint. Instead, it is a joint venture. Intellectualizing can be avoided simply by remaining silent whenever a counselor is unsure about how to respond, with feelings, with words, or even direct questions. A response such as "I don't know" or "I'm not sure" can often times be more helpful than an intellectual expression which may only serve to put the other person in a "one down" position. The key to avoiding the hazard of intellectualizing is to be genuine.

Avoiding The Parental Role

Another common hazard of counseling is that of adopting the parental role. It can be easy for a would-be counselor to slip into moralizing when he or she feels strongly about a particular subject. Adopting a parental role, or otherwise moralizing, can be such a dangerous hazard because it develops resentment in the other person rather than respect. Moralizing can be overwhelming, because at best it helps the other person see how he or she is being judged, how society looks upon his or her actions or feelings. At worst, it blocks examination of self-motivated actions and stifles further expression; it can result in either submission to the moral directives or stubborn defiance. Typically, what it does not develop is self-reliance or self-discovery. Perhaps Thomas Gordon, the developer of Parent Effectiveness Training, has pointed out the dangers of moralizing and adopting a parental role in counseling more than anyone else.[22] Gordon indicates that such actions, although well intentioned, serve to alienate someone with a problem because such people begin to feel that others are more interested in judging them than understanding them. The parental role in counseling is characterized by demanding that behavior conform to a particular standard or telling the other person what he or she should and should not do. This does not mean that there are not both appropriate and inappropriate courses of action at the workplace. In fact, almost every office and factory has rules which employees must abide by in order to remain with the organization. However, simply reiterating those rules is often not very helpful. A more effective approach is helping someone else see the underlying reasons why rules exist and the importance of abiding by them.

The hazard of adopting a parental role can best be avoided by helping someone either (1) see the negative consequences of not abiding by the various rules or procedures inherent in a particular situation; or (2) helping another person clearly identify his or her own values and evaluate the various courses of action relative to the values of that other person, not the values of the counselor. Stress, ulcers, tension, and interpersonal conflict are often the result of people violating their own values.

Avoiding Superficiality

A third hazard in counseling is that of superficiality. Superficiality, like intellectualizing, involves listening and responding only to the surface message that is spoken. Its difference is that no attempt is made to get below the surface or understand the concern the person may have. Superficiality is often the result of a hasty assessment regarding the nature of the other person's concern. The counselor may recognize that a particular situation is similar to others he or she has been involved in, but it is also very unique to that individual who is exploring it with the counselor at the time. A significant hazard involves stereotyping a situation or person without fully seeking to understand the unique aspects of

---

[22] Thomas Gordon, *Parent Effectiveness Training*, (Chicago: Wyden, 1971).

this particular problem to this particular person. The likely consequences of superficiality may be a feeling on the other person's part that the counselor is out of touch with the world. Or worse, that the counselor is only interested in himself or herself.

The antithesis of superficiality is attempting to understand the nature of a situation and the other person's perceptions of why it exists and why it persists. Understanding is not always easily gained. Paraphrasing or asking open-ended questions often convey that the counselor is sincerely interested in what someone else has to say. Perhaps as important as anything in the counseling process, however, is attempting to clearly define the nature of a problem or concern that another person has. Counseling is not simply accepting the problems or concern as given. Rather, it includes getting to the root of a problem—beyond symptoms commonly expressed.

Finally, in counseling it is always important never to begin what cannot be finished. If the counselor lacks the necessary time or energy at a particular moment, it is more important to put the other person off to another day than it is to attempt to resolve the problem under conditions of fatigue or time pressure.

Avoiding Emotional Or Social Entanglements

Perhaps the most common hazard in counseling is that of becoming socially or emotionally entangled in the problems that another person brings to the counselor. Such entanglements can take one of several forms. One form is that a counselor gives back anger for anger. That is, the counselor may be involved in a situation that another person is describing and feels anger over the way the other person is representing the facts of the case. In such situations, it may be easy for the counselor to fall into the trap of defending the actions of others. Another aspect of social and emotional entanglement involves the so-called burnt-out syndrome. The nature of the burnt-out syndrome is that the would-be counselor gets tired of listening to the problems of others and is no longer interested or able to effectively counsel them.

This is not an easy hazard to avoid since its occurrence is so subtle. One course of action which may be effective in dealing with social or emotional reactions could be to express forthrightly the type of feelings the counselor possesses. Although it may seem paradoxical, the person being counseled may actually be benefited.

Not only is the counselor being authentic about his or her own feelings, but the other person will likely see the attempt of the counselor to be genuine in the relationship. In fact, the other person may actually acquire a realistic understanding of the reactions he or she produces in others through such openness.

Avoiding Subtle Value Manipulations

Values are an essential part of counseling. They are part of the process and they are surely reflected in the goals. It is not possible or desirable for the counselor to leave his or her values outside of the door when counseling. The philosophy the counselor holds about life, about work, about the counseling process itself, are all part of being effective. The hazard lies in an imposition of values by the counselor. The experience of counseling is a learning process.

People must have the latitude and opportunity to be active participants in this process. This means exploring, discovering, problem-finding, problem-solving, choosing, and deciding. A common reason people seek counsel is because they are confused about their own values. They may feel that work has no purpose or goal; striving has no meaning; development is a sham; promotions are unlikely. When someone has such feelings or concerns, he or she needs objectivity and the opportunity to sort out purposes and values regarding work and work life. When we are confused, disappointed or anxious, we appreciate the opportunity to be with some other person to talk about these concerns. We do not, however, need or appreciate someone who overshadows us or attempts to manipulate us.

Impatience is probably the reason why we attempt to impose our values on others in counseling. We are afraid that they will not come to the same conclusion we have about a particular problem. We may interrupt the exploratory process in order to have someone arrive at the right solution. But, here is the hazard. What is right for us may not be right for someone else. We cannot give people right answers; we can only help them discover their own answers. Sometimes that takes time. It always takes individual effort. It is like pulling open the petals of a rosebud. The bud has to develop itself from within if it is to be beautiful and alive. If the petals are stripped away rather than allowed to develop on their own, then the rose will die. So it is with people. By attempting to force-feed them—to impose our values to give them right answers—we shortchange them.

SUMMARY

Counseling is not an easy process. It is one that takes time, patience, and skill. Effective counseling is not done simply because someone wants to do it well. Good intentions are no substitute for efficiency and skill. Counseling is an important workplace tool that can help people be more competent in handling problems at work or elsewhere. Counseling works well when a counselor works at it. Counseling is both a perspective and a set of skills that can be developed and applied at the workplace to achieve results that can be gained in no other way.

Chapter 4

Face-To-Face Interview

A newspaper account records the following incident:

The middle manager and the personnel executive were upset. They had lost a tool which they had come to admire and respect. No longer could age 65 be used as a termination point in the employment career of people in the organization. With one single act, the President and the Congress had eliminated the finality of a person's career. Now each person's merits had to stand on their own. Now, it's not age 65 and "Sorry, old boy, company policy, you know, you have to retire." In its place, managers are expected to review each individual's performance and determine which 65 year old needs to gently be urged into retirement and which 65 year old needs the continued support of those around him in order to perform at the same high level.[1]

The Age Discrimination Act emphasized again the importance of human interaction as a basic part of a person's employment contract. Like its predecessors in the Equal Employment Opportunity area, age discrimination regulations have placed a tremendous responsibility upon line managers and personnel executives alike to speak frankly and forthrightly and determine the proper age for retirement to those who approach traditional retirement age.

Too often managers find themselves in an uncomfortable position where they are required to counsel, coach, or problem-solve with

[1] "No More 65 and Out," *The Houston Post* (October 16, 1977).

employees who report to them. Personnel specialists, likewise, are looked to as a source of information and a general resource in aiding in this process. Often, however, neither managers nor personnel executives are skilled enough themselves in the art and science of counseling with people. Those who manage the nation's largest institutions are aware of the deficiency that exists. One recent survey cited the need for counseling skills as the *greatest* need in management development today. Although the need is widely recognized, like many other problems, it is one that is easier to be concerned with than to actually resolve. Counseling is so difficult not simply because fundamental principles are unknown (although counseling techniques are unknown to many), but rather because counselors, be they managers or personnel specialists, must deal with emotional reactions with which they feel uncomfortable. Counseling is not simply a science, a mechanical lockstep of procedures that one can memorize and apply, but rather an art. There are, of course, procedures and principles that are important in effective counseling, but counseling also represents a point of view, a philosophy, an orientation. A necessary foundation of effective counseling is sincerity and genuineness. Too often those who read about managerial techniques tend to impose them in a manipulative way. They want the benefits of the procedures without accepting the underlying premises of genuine human interaction. Although this reality is not always easy, it is certainly necessary. It is the key to an effective face-to-face counseling interview.

Counseling is a general term that is often used to describe a variety of approaches or techniques. Often it is used interchangeably with a non-directive interviewing approach. The focus of this chapter is a wider view of counseling. It recognizes the generic nature of the counseling term, but likewise describes three specific aspects of counseling in the workplace: correcting, coaching, and consulting.

Correcting people who have specific performance problems is a necessary function of counseling. In any organization, there are formal work rules and informal group norms that keep the group or the organization functioning at a productive level. Both work rules and group norms can be dysfunctional and counterproductive. But likewise, any organization needs both these formal and informal ways of doing things in order to function on a daily basis. Those who violate the more formal work rules must be confronted and dealt with appropriately if group efficiency is to be maintained.

Perhaps no one has illustrated the negative effects that result when a manager allows violation of work group rules to continue as much as David McClelland of Harvard. Professor McClelland has written an intriguing article entitled "Good Guys Make Bum Bosses."[2] The basis of the article revolves around those who try simply to please subordinates and not enforce work rules and who are inevitably going to be accused of favoritism. In their efforts to please everyone, they will please no one. Rules and standards provide a sense of security for people in the workforce. They demonstrate a concern of supervisors for the welfare of everyone. When they are followed, cooperation results. When any employees are allowed to indiscriminately violate work rules, chaos results.

Coaching is another counseling process. This aspect keys on performance discrepancies. If people know what to do but are not performing adequately, a coaching interview may be needed. The basic notion of coaching is that someone else observing our actions is usually more aware of things we do than we are. Like an athletic coach, a person doing coaching in an organization is skilled in observing, describing, and assisting someone else to improve performance.

The third aspect of counseling is that of *consulting* or one-to-one problem-solving. When people have concerns which derive from their work group environment or their home environment, consulting may be needed. Unless they are adequately dealt with, concerns developed either at work or at home can spill over into other aspects of the person's life. Most of us from time to time enjoy and appreciate simply discussing our worries, anxieties, disappointments, and fears with others. If we know that we can get an empathetic ear and perhaps some good information, we are much more eager to share those often-hidden concerns we carry with us. The intent of consulting is to enable a person to more accurately define a problem he or she has encountered, identify a course of action, anticipate possible unintended negative consequences from this course of action, and plan a specific personal strategy to improve the situation.

Throughout the remainder of this chapter, each of these three specific aspects of counseling (correcting, coaching and consulting) will be discussed more thoroughly. In each section, a basic overview will be presented and specific procedures will be identified and summarized. It is important to recognize that one cannot simply mechanically apply the procedures and expect the desired results. Instead, the effectiveness of each counseling approach is based on genuine concern and a realistic desire to improve competence; this ingredient cannot be feigned or neglected.

2 David C. McClelland and David H. Burnham, "Good Guys Make Bum Bosses," *Psychology Today* (December 1975) pp. 69-70.

CORRECTING

The prime function of this type of counseling is not to determine an appropriate punishment for poor performance, but to administer correction principles in such a way that it will prevent the particular person from breaking the work rule or failing to perform as expected in the future. The effectiveness of discipline really has nothing to do with the severity of the punishment. If anything, the ratio is inverse. The intent of correction as helping someone improve, then, must be paramount as a guiding principle in reviewing effective correction techniques. How can a supervisor or a personnel specialist correct the performance or behavior of others in a way that motivates rather than demotivates and is positive rather than negative?

Most people in an organization tend to obey most of the rules most of the time. Supervisors' and personnel specialists' roles would be impossible if employees didn't. They would have to spend most of their time and energy identifying, processing and evaluating infractions if people did not obey most of the work rules. On the other hand, there is something very real in the fact that many people like to flirt with taboos. D. H. Lawrence, in fact, quipped that "Mankind invented sin in order to enjoy the feeling of being naughty." Rulebreaking perhaps affords analogous attractions. People are titilated by the thought of breaking a rule and getting away with it. All rule-breaking behavior may not fall into this category, but it is certainly true that many people break rules in order to establish the limit. They want to know just how far a manager or personnel specialist will go before defining a firm standard.

One possible way of dealing with the problem of how to achieve positive discipline is to determine the conditions under which an employee feels the least resentful towards correction. Douglas McGregor formulated what he called the "hot stove rule" as a basis for identifying conditions that promote positive discipline.[3] McGregor said effective discipline was analogous to touching a hot stove. When you touch the stove, you know that you have done something wrong; a reaction is immediate, impersonal, predictable, and consistent. Each of these characteristics constitute the hot stove rule. To extend the analogy, when a person touches a hot stove, he or she knows immediately that the stove is hot. The outcome every time a person touches the stove is predictable. A hot stove will not burn a person some of the time and leave that person unburned at other times. It will be impersonal; that is, the stove will

3 Douglas MacGregor, *The Human Side of Enterprise,* (New York: McGraw-Hill, 1961).

not burn one person and not another. It will be consistent. Every time any person touches a hot stove, he or she will be burned.

Effective discipline incorporates the same principles. Correction needs to be immediate. Many problems can be nipped in the bud if they are dealt with at an early point. Talking about a problem as soon as a supervisor or personnel representative becomes aware of it can be the key to fairness and the sense of security that people desire at work. Adherence to work rules should be seen as similar to natural laws; that is, there are predictable consequences of following the rules and of not following the rules. People will feel better about following them and be more likely to obey them if consequences are certain. The third aspect of the hot stove rule is to be impersonal. By being impersonal and focusing on the act, not the person, initial resentment is more likely to be minimized. In fact, a person who does get upset during an impersonal correction interview may be likely to feel the sheepishness of the cook who kicked the stove when she burned her hand. The final aspect of correction is consistency. The greater the inconsistency in administering work rules, the fiercer the resentment for the discipline. Individuals resent being singled out.

Correction that is immediate, predictable, impersonal, and consistent is more likely to achieve its intended aims than correction that lacks these characteristics. Other important aspects of this type of counseling are the recognition that unless a person knows where he or she wants to go, has a clear picture of the ideal target, and has a clear idea of the first step, as well as some particular incentive for changing, correction is not likely to produce the desired result. Simply, one needs a direction, a starting point, and a destination. A clear picture of the ideal target is necessary in order for a person to know that the future outcome is going to be worth the journey. A clear view of the ideal target impels a person to desire the change. Likewise, a clear perception of the first step enables a person to go from the abstract to the specific with knowledge of what and when. An incentive to change is the third key element. Without an incentive to perform differently, a desired destination and a road map won't get a person off dead center. A discrepancy between where a person is and where that person wants to be is a very effective technique in providing an incentive to change. Hope or optimism is an alternative to the discrepancy idea for enabling a person to change; conveying an optimistic sense of "you can do it" can be a tremendous fuel for a person whose energy seems to be limited. [Situations included in Unit 7, "Work Rules", all show how to apply these methods and the following procedures.]

CORRECTING PROCEDURES AND TECHNIQUES

Procedures	Assessment Questions	Techniques
State problem	What work rules have been violated? What standards of performance are not being met?	State position briefly boldly clearly unemotionally
Listen to other's point of view	Are there extenuating circumstances? Is the person denying a problem exists? Are there reasons or excuses behind the explanation?	Clarifying questions Active listening
Summarize both perspectives	Is there agreement that a problem exists? regardless of who may be responsible? How far apart is my perspective and the employee's perspective?	Paraphrase
Explain: Here's what I want from you.	Does the employee know I'm serious about this? Can I articulate what specific changes need to be made?	Contracting
Ask: What would you like from me?	Is the employee willing to take some responsibility for improving matters? What resources does the employee need to improve matters?	Problem focusing
Agree on action steps	Who is going to do what? When will we discuss this again? Are the action steps realistic and attainable?	

State Problem

The first step in correcting is for the supervisor to unequivocally state the problem as he or she sees it. This lets the employee know the purpose of the discussion. Sometimes supervisors utilize questioning techniques at the beginning of a correction discussion which may be appropriate for another type of counseling interview but achieve negative results in this type of situation. If a supervisor is aware of poor performance on the part of an employee, it should be plainly stated. Asking leading questions will only signal to the employee that there are hidden agendas being worked and so all his or her statements must be cautious and guarded.

In stating the problem as the supervisor sees it, more will be accomplished when he or she adopts the role of a detached observer. When a supervisor becomes emotional in correcting an employee, the employee's reflex may also be an emotional one. Sarcasm begets sarcasm, anger produces anger, and to accusation is added counter accusation. When people get caught up in an emotional whirlwind, everyone loses.

Listen to Other's Point of View

Once the supervisor has described a performance problem, the subordinate should be given equal time. If the employee is resentful, the supervisor should take extra steps to help the employee describe the situation from his or her point of view. It is possible that new information may be brought up that was previously unknown to the supervisor. Minimally, the employee will feel that he or she had a fair hearing and consequently will be more motivated to improve.

If the supervisor's documentation is not substantial, it is likely to be challenged by the employee. Good documentation consists of a running record of poor performance and specific dates and details written in a factual manner. In discussing such documentation, if the supervisor has recorded actual events (rather than inferences or opinions), the employee is more likely to accept the fact that performance has been substandard. Even under such circumstances, however, the employee is likely to offer an excuse or alibi. The most common excuse is that "other people do things that are a lot worse than this." Such denial can almost be predicted. When it occurs, a supervisor should give the employee a full hearing. Then, without agreeing or disagreeing and in an unemotional tone of voice, remind the employee of the documented performance problem that the employee has and indicate that the employee's observations on the actions of others are not pertinent to this discussion. Of course, if others are in actuality being treated differently, the resentment of an employee would be justified and the entire correction discussion will be ineffective.

It is essential in correcting not to react negatively to the emotions or the point of view the employee expresses. It is important not to disagree, not to argue, and not to attempt to paint the other person into a corner. In the long run, methods which impart such objectives will prove fruitless. Instead, attempting to listen empathetically to the other person will convey a sense of justice and fairness. Just as a judge listens to both sides of a case, it is important that a counselor listen to the opposite point of view being expressed.

Summarize

The third step in these procedures is for the counselor to summarize the perspective that he or she has heard. Again, this conveys that the message the person has spoken has actually been heard by the counselor. Furthermore, it lets the employee know that a counselor has not particularly been swayed by the opinions expressed. It is natural for most of us to feel that we are overworked and underpaid, that others do not appreciate our full worth, that we are actually better performers than our performance is recognized as being. When a counselor summarizes both perspectives that have been conveyed, it establishes a sense of equality if the perspectives are presented in an unemotional but empathetic way.

Summarizing does something else. It puts the supervisor back in control of the tone and direction of the discussion. It allows the supervisor to let the employee know that the substance of the employee's remarks has been heard, but a problem still exists that needs to be corrected.

Explain: Here's What I Want From You.

After the supervisor has summarized both perspectives, it is important once again to explain precisely what change in performance is needed. Such an explanation should simultaneously reinforce the rule or performance standard that is not being met plus motivate the employee to improve. Timing, the supervisor's tone of voice, and the manner in which the supervisor conducts the correction interview all play an important part in determining whether this objective will be met.

The effective supervisor will explain why a standard exists and how it can be met by the employee. If the supervisor can do this in a detached manner and view the employee's initial reactions as "blowing off steam," the supervisor will remain in control of the entire discussion. However, in explaining a mistake or a performance problem to an employee, it can be done well or done poorly. As one observer noted, "There is all the difference in the world between falling down on the job and being accused of being a loafer, of committing an unwise act and being told you're a fool. The employee will remember and instinctively resent any downgrading aimed at him personally."[4]

Ask: What Would You Like From Me?

At this point the role of the counselor changes dramatically from impersonal judge to helpful resource. The discussion focus becomes one of how the situation can be improved. The focus becomes one of resolving a problem and steers clear of blaming or justifying. The counselor, after explaining what he or she would like to see done differently and how he or she would like to see the situation changed, improved, or altered, then asks the employee, "What would you like from me to improve the situation? How can I be a resource to you in changing conditions so that the outcome I've have outlined can be realized?" This shifts responsibility back to the employee and emphasizes the employee's role in improving the situation. It involves the employee in dealing with a substantive question pertaining to the problem at hand, rather than being dictated to, moralized with, or preached to.

A common trap that counselors often fall into after mutual agreement on an existing problem has been reached is making certain the employee does not forget it. Both the counselor and the employee lose when such situations occur. The negative self-esteem and resentment which result are lasting and are always counterproductive. Inviting the employee to express his or her views on how the situation can be improved and how the supervisor or personnel representative can be a resource puts responsibility back where it should be. The supervisor does not assume responsibility for changing conditions but agrees to be a resource to support, aid, and help; but he or she still recognizes that the primary responsibility for improving the situation belongs to the employee.

Action Steps

Action steps should be agreed upon next. In developing such follow-through, the supervisor should make it clear that improvement, not penitence, is desired. Moreover, it is important that the person feel a sense of commitment to actions that have been decided upon.

This step should not be taken lightly. In fact, some employees may be looking to agree to action steps simply to remove themselves from the uncomfortable situation that is often times created in correction interviews.

Knowing that they have not been as diligent as they should or that they have violated specific work rules, they are all too happy to agree in order to avoid further questions and commitments. A quick and easy commitment, one that will not last or long be remembered, is one that this employee is only too eager to make.

The supervisor should not simply press and apply pressure, forcing an employee to commit to specific action steps, but rather ensure a recognition that a problem exists and that the employee must do things differently for the problem to be resolved. It may be useful as a concluding step in the procedure for correction to have the employee summarize the essence of the discussion. This enables the counselor to know what the employee has actually heard, what message has actually been received, and the likelihood that it will be acted upon.

If an employee summarizes the essence of a discussion, it enables the counselor to see if important critical points have been accurately conveyed. Such follow-through is important not simply for the counselor, but also for the employee, for it lets the employee see the situation more clearly and more objectively for himself or herself.

COACHING

Perhaps there is no more traditional aspect of the management function than that of coaching. Managers are expected to help their subordinates improve in specific ways. Trainers and other personnel specialists are likewise oriented towards performance and productivity improvement. Increasingly, personnel specialists are expected to aid the organization and encourage it to improve the overall output and competence of its employees. This coaching emphasis is one that operates on a somewhat different scale and in a different manner than correcting.

The intent of coaching is not necessarily to alleviate a problem or to eliminate behavior that is not appropriate. Rather, its focus is to improve the performance or competence of a person who is not performing at a desired level. Obviously, coaching assumes that there are standards of performance that are currently delineated in a job. Not unless people know a desired performance level will they be able to strive to achieve it.

Describe Performance Gap

Almost every manager or personnel specialist finds it useful to employ quantitative performance measures. They are seductively simple. Regrettably, they may not be as effective or simple as they appear. In theory these provide the critical feedback that will encourage subordinates to strive more vigorously. The dilemma faced is this: Obviously, followers are motivated by clear, unambiguous feedback on performance. However, no incentive works as simply as its advocates would allow.

The questions of equity, reward, intergroup comparisons and pressures against rate rustlers for self-protection all serve to work against the effectiveness of simply identifying clear standards of performance and encouraging people to achieve them. Nevertheless, the existence of targets and feedback on performance in relation to these targets do motivated people. Energy and enthusiasm are released by having reasonable goals and learning how one performs in relation to those goals.

But it is likewise important in coaching aspects to be wary of these potent tools and notice the possible unintended negative consequences that they include. Here are some examples[5]:

1. The telephone company began measuring the performance of wiremen who handle changes in telephone numbers. They did this by counting the number of new connections wiremen made each day. The wiremen, aware of this increased emphasis on this particular standard of performance, began neglecting to remove excess wires associated with disconnected numbers and the panels grew overweight with excessive waste wire. Some even collapsed. Because removing unnecessary wire was not specifically measured and went unnoticed, the procedure became neglected.

2. A computer company began measuring the performance of customer repairmen by the speed with which they accomplished specific repairs in a customer's home. To look good on more difficult repairs, the repairmen ignored early reports from customers on diagnostically difficult problems and waited until the problem worsened or was repeated. The customers were incensed by this increase in down time. The repairmen, on the other hand, were rewarded for the speed with which they were able to diagnose these difficult problems.

3. School teachers in a local school district, measured on students' examination results, began to teach the tests and ignore other classroom activities. Priming sessions were conducted in advance on national tests and, rather than reinforcing the basics, students for several months of the year simply learned how to pass this particular test.

The total organization may be the loser when motivation targets are overly stressed or misused. Unmeasured aspects of the job may

[5] Examples are from Russell Ackoff, *The Art of Problem Solving* (New York: John Wiley and Sons, 1978) and a seminar conducted by Synectics, *Managing for Innovative Teamwork* (Cambridge, Massachusetts, 1976).

then be ignored, and larger organizational interests may be disregarded. Often, cooperation between groups becomes a thing of the past. Subordinates, singlemindedly pursuing a goal of increased performance, are in no mood to consider the needs of adjacent work groups for better quality, change in schedule, or any other accommodation for that matter when only performance is emphasized. There must be a balance between overall standards of performance and other aspects of the work that are important, necessary, and contribute to the overall performance of a work group or an organization.

A specific approach to employee motivation that has been recently identified and regularly used is called the Path-Goal Theory.[6] This theory reverses the long-standing assumption of most managers that satisfied employees will be more productive. Instead, the notion maintains that employees must perceive productivity and performance as necessary steps along their paths to satisfying their own goals. That is, improved performance is something that is related to the employee's own self-interest. There are many links in the chain for the Path-Goal theory to work—for employees to be motivated.

The leaders, managers, and personnel specialists must do much more than offer a reward for a job well done. The link of the extended chain must be satisfied. The following basic elements seem to be necessary for Path-Goal conditions to be met:

1. Employees must have the capacity, based on past experiences and their self-confidence, to improve their own performance.
2. This improved performance will not be excessively costly in terms of devoting individual energy, disrupting friendships, or making other personal sacrifices.
3. This improved performance will result in demonstratively good results; that is, something that others can measure, assess or perceive, some significant difference from the situation before. Again, the results may be in the areas of energy, friendship, or other personal satisfaction.
4. The result will be rewarded and the reward will be perceived as equitable by the subordinate in this particular matter.

[6] Robert House, "A Path-Goal Theory of Leadership Effectiveness," *Administrative Science Quarterly,* (1971) pp. 321-338.

COACHING PROCEDURES AND TECHNIQUES

Procedures	Assessment Questions	Techniques
Describe Performance Gap	What is the difference between actual and desired behavior outcomes? What are the standards of performance?	Discrepancy methods
Assess Nature of Deviation	Does the person possess the information and skills to perform better? Are there good reasons not to improve? What incentive is there to improve?	Probing questions Hypothetical situations
Show and Tell	Can helpful skills be demonstrated? Are there other people who could serve as role models (examples)?	Modeling
Relate Why	Does the person know why this is important?	Cognitive restructuring
Reinforce Results	Are successive approximations recognized? Is clear, specific and valid feedback utilized?	Reinforcement methods

Subordinates obviously have their own interests, often different from the manager's and their own views of situations. Either or both may cause them to sidestep their responsibilities or to participate in gold bricking on the job. Such nonperformance can embarrass and handicap managers seeking credibility and support. How do they confront the reluctant subordinate? The "no" may be a subtle refusal to accept a change in methods, a new procedure or activity; or refusal to finish an assignment in the face of an obstacle; or a reluctance to redo an unacceptable assignment. There may be a hundred other possibilities in which the manager's perceptions of what is needed differs from the subordinate's view of what is equitable or desirable or necessary. And in most organizations there will always be good and sufficient reasons why something can't be done: lack of time, resources, another department having failed to fulfill a commitment, contrary policy, conflicting rules and the like. Whatever the source, and whether it's due to simple recalcitrance, misunderstanding or a desire to challenge the boss, it can become a crucial test of the manager's coaching skills. Managers who aren't followed soon lose whatever status they had originally.

Experienced managers know they cannot afford such losses and take pride in their persuasive skills. Good coaching is helping a subordinate see that it is in the subordinate's self-interest to complete an assignment or to do it in a proper manner. Such persuasion does *not* include using threats. Threats can take subtle as well as overt forms, such as, "Remember how much I've done for you. Is this how you pay me back?"; "How much do you feel I will be willing to go to bat for you to get another raise if this is the way you are going to treat me?" Sure threats can be more overt and direct such as: "If you don't do this you may be fired or put back," or "I'll make your life miserable." It may not be communicated as directly as this, but the message still comes through loud and clear. Threats have unintended negative consequences, however. A person may do the job in a slipshod manner just to finish it, or may feel that he or she is being treated unfairly and take appropriate action to reduce the imbalance, either directly, by trying to get back at the supervisor, or indirectly, by reducing work output over a longer time frame.

Describe Performance Gap

It is important to realize that people do things for which they will be rewarded. These rewards may not always be direct or monetary. Likewise, we all seek satisfaction; and when we feel we are able to satisfy our own needs and meet our own expectations in performing work objectives, we are much more likely to do so. Thus, a key to improving work performance is to help an employee see that it is in his or her own self-interest to complete a job in a timely and appropriate manner. There are several types of performance problems that coaching can be effective in relieving. These include the following:

1. Tasks are not being done to the desired standard.
2. Desired performance gradually deteriorates over time.

3. Employees don't believe that it's necessary to work as desired.
4. Work is seldom completed on time.
5. Work is done but seldom done well.
6. Some tasks are not being done at all.
7. Employees do the job correctly only when a supervisor or an authoritative person is present.
8. An employee appears not be be motivated.

These are typically symptoms of problems and only point to circumstances where a problem exists. These problems are generally either in work group relations, in supervisor/subordinate relations, or in other situational aspects of the job. [See vignettes in Unit 5, "Boss/Subordinate Relations", and Unit 6, "Performance Problems", to see how to apply these methods in assessing and resolving coaching-related problems.] The coaching interview can be the basis not only for determining the real root of the problem but also for developing solutions to resolving it. The first step in coaching is to seek to establish through mutual give-and-take a common understanding of the nature of the problem and the surrounding constraints. This does not mean that both people involved in the coaching dialogue will have the same values about how the problem arose or what should actually be done, but agreement that a problem exists is an absolute prerequisite to searching for a specific solution.

Assess Nature of Deviation

A useful way of agreeing that a problem exists is to describe a discrepancy between what a supervisor sees as necessary and important in the completion of work requirements and the actual performance or behavior of people on the job. Pointing out this discrepancy without pointing fingers is a useful beginning point. It establishes the basis for a discussion and confirms that, rather than affixing responsibility and having someone take the heat, it is more important to the supervisor that gaps be closed and improvement made.

The importance of the problem definition is well illustrated in a remarkable book by Russell L. Ackoff entitled *The Art of Problem Solving*[7]. In this book, Ackoff cites specific examples of the impor-

[7] Russell L. Ackoff, *The Art of Problem Solving* (New York: John Wiley and Sons, 1978).

tance of the old adage that half of solving the problem is defining it well. One of the examples used by Ackoff is instructive in the importance of asking the right questions in accurately defining a problem. A Mexican government agency responsible for the development of water resources decided to build a dam and use it to irrigate a large farming area. When the plans were completed, the agency sent representatives to the rural area that would be affected to explain the project to the local citizens to determine whether they wanted it. Their answers were uniformly affirmative. The dam and irrigation system were built at great expense, but they never produced the expected increase in productivity from the land. The puzzled experts went out to determine why. They found that the farmers had reduced the amount of land under cultivation, thereby obtaining more time to work in nearby towns or relax. They felt that the amount of work required to use all their land was not justified by the small increase that would come about in their income. People will often accept gifts, just as they will accept definitions of a problem, even though they may not accept the solutions which follow from them. This example illustrates the importance of *mutual* problem solving.

It is very important, critical, in coaching procedures to define a problem well. Thus, a second procedure in coaching is to obtain a subordinate's views of why the problem exists. This means that the counselor must seek to understand the employee's values, interests, anxieties and desires. Through appropriate questioning and letting the employee both explain and listen, the counselor can usually get an understanding of how an employee sees a particular problem. Thereby, a better problem definition and a solution can be developed. In assessing the nature of a deviation in performance between what is necessary and what an employee is actually doing, a counselor should be prepared to handle excuses as to why improvement can't be made. Recognizing the reasons why people give excuses and how to deal with them is discussed by Sisselia Bok in an intriguing book entitled *Lying: Moral Choice in Private and Public Life.*[8] In one particular chapter, Bok describes excuses and reasons why people justify giving excuses. An excuse seeks to extenuate, sometimes to remove the blame entirely, from something that would otherwise be a fault. It can extenuate in three ways. First, it can suggest that what is seen as a fault is not really one. Second, it can suggest that though there has been a fault, the person is not really

---

[8] Sisselia Bok, *Lying: Moral Choice in Private and Public Life* (New York: Random House, 1978).

blame-worthy because he or she is not responsible. Finally, it can suggest that though there has been a fault, and though the person is responsible, he or she is not really to blame because they had good reasons for doing something.

Excuses are given in self-defense and in order to protect one's interest, position, or simply to save face. In listening to an employee's point of view about why a problem exists, it is important for the counselor to sort through the information being given and be perceptive of whether or not excuses are being offered to:

1. provide some benefit to the person,
2. avoid some harm that may come to the person, or
3. be a distortion of what the person feels is a fair and justifiable course of action.

In listening to an employee's point of view, it is not necessary to agree. In fact, avoiding taking sides may be as useful a strategy as any the manager or personnel specialist may adopt. Defining the problem and listening to the employee's point of view is essential in getting acceptance that a problem exists. Once a problem has been appropriately defined and commitment given, the coaching process becomes much easier.

Show and Tell

The coaching process assumes that an employee needs some help in making an initial definition of the problem. If it were apparent to the employee that a problem existed, the employee would take some type of action to eliminate the problem. But because there were good reasons for the problem's existence, no such action has been taken.

A function of coaching, then, is to help the employee see, understand and act on circumstances which keep a problem from being solved. It is important in this regard for the counselor to spend time observing, inquiring, and attempting to understand the skills and values of the employee.

The old admonition to "show and tell" is a useful operating principle in effective coaching. It is important to encourage the employee to practice new behaviors, new techniques, or new skills. This practice may be something that is done in a simulated way through a role playing situation during the coaching interview; it may be something that is implemented later on; or it may take the form of actual practice on the job with the employee reporting back to the counselor on successes, problems, and frustrations in implementing the agreed-upon solution.

Relate Why

It is important during these practice sessions for the counselor to be certain that the employee understands the basis for why new skills or a new orientation is needed. By relating why, an employee will better understand what to do in the long run to implement the solution. R.D. Laing, in writing about the influence parents have over their children, maintained that parents are so persuasive because they can give their children a basis for knowing who they are. An understanding of this perspective means that children do not need to be taught "how to" in every instance; rather, because they know who they are, they will be better able to act in an appropriate way. This is the basis for moral judgment as well as the basis for transmitting parental values through the generations. Likewise, in coaching, it is not sufficient for the counselor to teach "how-to" skills without additionally imparting a perspective as to why these skills are necessary. This perspective can become the basis for behavior change in many instances.

Reinforce Results

The last important step in the coaching process is for the manager or supervisor to reinforce results that are obtained. Reinforcing results can take several forms. It is important to recognize that praise can be overused and misused. Praise that is insincere and not genuine obviously has no motivational impact. But, likewise, praise can fall flat if a person feels it is not warranted or justified. Additionally, praise can often reinforce the person giving the praise rather than the person receiving it. For instance, if a supervisor

[9] R.D. Laing, *Politics of the Family* (Pantheon, 1971).

says, "Gee, you really did a good job. I'm really proud of the way that you were able to improve your performance," who is being reinforced? Well, who is proud? The supervisor. The supervisor has only created a sense of dependency, a sense of allocating praise, rather than developing independence by helping the person recognize progress when it has been made. There is a subtle, but important, difference when a supervisor says, "Gee, you really did a good job. I'll bet it makes you feel good." Or, "I noticed that you are able to make progress in this area."

How does it feel when you have been able to achieve something that you have consciously established goals to achieve? Praise given in this way helps the person recognize the source of achievement, the fact that it is the employee that is able to do things differently. Likewise, the employee's internal generator will be switched on and will continue running on this kind of praise because it recognizes and reinforces the employee's capabilities and competence. It enables the employee to recognize that he or she can improve through conscious goal setting, and that improvement has been realized and noticed by others.

In giving recognition in this regard, it may be useful for the counselor to recognize even the smallest incremental improvement. By recognizing progress, the employee can be prevented from becoming discouraged, and he or she will realize that performance improvement is noticed and appreciated.

CONSULTING

The process of giving advice and imparting information is much more complex than we initially realize. On the surface, it seems rather easy and straightforward to tell someone who asks for advice exactly what we think. However, someone's request for information may be anything *but* a request for information. This is well illustrated by an example developed by S. I. Hayakawa:[10] Suppose you have a flat tire along the roadside and a passer-by notices your predicament and stops. The first thing that the motorist is likely to say to you is, "Got a flat?" Certainly this is not a request for infor-

[10] S. I. Hayakawa, *Language in Thought and Action* (New York: Harcourt, Brace and Jovanovich, 1964).

mation. The person knew you had a flat tire before stopping. The question is rather one of testing for receptivity to the motorist's need for help. It is a method of introduction and not a question that is intended to be taken literally.

Perhaps the most difficult aspect of consulting is attempting to determine how much advice and information the other person may be seeking and how much reassurance or support for a preconceived idea that is waiting to be expressed is exactly being sought. Many people want to "test the water" before they are willing to openly express a particular concern or reveal their predetermined solution to a particular problem.

Norman R.F. Maier of the University of Michigan has extensively studied the essential role that talking a problem out plays in most of our lives.[11] When we have a chance to discuss a problem, opportunity, or disappointment, we not only feel better ourselves but are more likely to develop a better and more stable solution to the situation we face. There is more than catharsis in the consulting relationship. There are also the seeds of effective problem-solving and decision-making.

The distinguishing feature of consulting is that an employee has a problem or concern and begins seeking the assistance of someone else. The focus of both correcting and coaching is with the manager or personnel specialist who wants some form of changed behavior. The locus of control as well as the nature of the dialogue thus differ significantly, although the general goal of each is problem-solving to develop enough competence and stability to deal with particular problems.

Some Problems in Consulting

The fundamental difficulty in consulting is in overcoming the imbalance that exists. A manager or personnel specialist not only occupies a position of authority and prestige but also is placed in the position of someone who can be a help and resource. The person *asking* for help puts himself or herself "one down" with respect to the helper by admitting that a problem exists and the helper is automatically "one up" by being forced into the position of pre-

---

[11] Norman R.F. Maier, *Problem-Solving Discussions and Conferences* (New York: McGraw-Hill, 1963).

sumed expert. Building an effective relationship requires restoring a sense of compromise and balance between the employee and the counselor.[12]

The reluctance of many employees to put themselves "one down" often prevents them from discussing difficulties they are encountering in their work life and work relationships. They fear being taken advantage of, being used, or losing face. It is especially difficult for employees who are ambitious and eager to demonstrate their abilities to their superiors to admit that they are experiencing difficulties. Yet, it is often these same employees who would benefit most from consulting discussions. These employees, if drawn into a consulting dialogue, may attempt to equalize the inherent imbalance by not listening, denying the counselor's assessment of a situation, belittling the quality of the information offered or the skills of the counselor. Such reactions occur because of the embarrassment felt when a personal weakness has been exposed. Defensiveness, such as the following, may then be expressed:

- "Your idea won't work because of thus and so."
- "You just don't understand. You haven't been through it and so you really can't relate."
- "I've already thought of that and it won't work."

Such defensiveness is a natural reaction to a threat to one's security. The imbalance that is inherent in the consulting relationship makes the potential for being taken advantage of so obvious that most people will feel a desire to reduce dependency in some way. If the counselor recognizes the occurrence of such defensive reactions and is prepared to deal with them, he or she will be more likely to return the consulting dialogue to a more even keel. If the counselor attempts to counter an employee's expressed or implied defensiveness with more pressure or additional argument, the results are likely to be self-defeating. Defensiveness is best handled by allowing the other person to fully express his or her emotions without agreeing or disagreeing.

Responding to defensive reactions with acceptance and understanding can also assist the other person in putting the discussion on a more equal basis. Discounting can also be dealt with by turning the

[12] This idea of imbalance was presented by Edgar Schein in a workshop on "Process Consultation."

problem back to the person and asking, "Given your concerns, what do you think would be useful?"

Another difficult aspect of the consulting relationship is the tendency to use the discussion to seek sympathy or confirmation of a preconceived course of action rather than realistically evaluating possible alternates. Often people conceive of problems only in terms of solutions that are familiar to them. Rather than doing problem-solving by gathering and evaluating information that may be available, they simply work backwards from a solution to a problem definition.

For instance, an obvious solution to overpopulation in under-developed countries is to widely distribute contraceptives and information on family planning. Since the solution is so apparent, over-population is typically conceptualized in terms of these solutions. However, a major study of the reasons for the singular failure of family planning activities over a 10-year period had some surprising developments.

A consulting team decided to assume that Indians knew how to control the size of their families since, though they were typically very large, most couples had fewer children than they were biologically able to have. The team decided that the real problem they faced was in understanding *why* the Indians *wanted* as many children as they did. The *reason* the Indians wanted large families became apparent after some investigation. It seemed that ever since India had gained independence, the government had been able to significantly increase the expected life span of the average adult. But nothing had been done to increase the employable life span. A typical adult could be expected to live years beyond the time he was still able to work.

Since India had few and very limited old age pension plans that were either publicly or privately supported, most couples had to rely on their children to support them in their old age. The facts are that in India the infant mortality rate is high and generally only males work, therefore, a couple needs an average of four sons to ensure they would be adequately cared for in their old age. The consultants found that most low income families had this very characteristic. Therefore, to ask most Indians to have fewer children was to ask them to remove their source of support and security in their advanced years.[13]

---

[13] Cited in Russell L. Ackoff, *The Art of Problem-Solving,* (New York: John Wiley, 1978).

As important as it is to recognize the imbalance that is inherent in the consulting relationship, it is just as important not to over-react to it. Overreacting to an employee who has a concern by being sympathetic, coddling, overly friendly, denying the responsibility the person shares in the problem, and the like, can be just as counter-productive as not even recognizing the inherent imbalance in the consulting relationship. When a counselor overreacts, the situation is unlikely to change. Overreaction is exemplified in the statements which follow:

- "Gee, you've really tried hard to do the right thing."
- "It's really not your fault and the solution would work if other people will only let it work."
- "You really have been dumped on. I don't know if I could take what you have as well as you have."

Ingratiating sentiments such as these, although intended to develop a bond between the counselor and the employee, tend instead to emphasize only the distance between their worlds. A counselor must help others deal with their own worlds and will be ineffective when he or she attempts to do otherwise. We cannot make our individual worlds free from anxiety, disappointment and frustration. We can only learn to cope with them and minimize their effects on us and others.

The counselor's ability to get involved with an employee who has a concern is a necessary part of the consulting relationship. This aspect of the consulting relationship is not to be minimized. However, the price of personal involvement is not dependent upon being obsequious.

William Glasser, a noted counselor himself, indicates that the way two strangers get acquainted is similar to the process of effective consulting.[14] According to Glasser, some of these personal attributes or qualities which promote successful outcomes include the counselor's ability to be demanding, yet sensitive; openly share his or her own struggles, disappointments, etc; be genuine and not maintain an aloof stance; allow his or her own values and perspectives to be challenged by the employee; not accept excuses for eva-sion of responsible action; and demonstrate courage by confronting perceptions and biases the employee possesses.

[14] William Glasser, *Reality Therapy* (New York: Harper & Row, 1965).

CONSULTING PROCEDURES AND TECHNIQUES

Procedures	Assessment Questions	Techniques
Build Rapport	Does the person feel at ease? Does the person feel one down? Does the person perceive the counselor as a resource? Can the person see the problem as one of choice? Has an obvious problem been identified?	Active listening General questions Verbalizing concerns Paraphrasing Role playing
Identify Problem	Are the person's emotions getting in the way? How would someone who has no stake in the outcome define this problem?	
Encourage Self-Analysis	How does the person see his/her part in contributing to the problem? How would the person like to feel? What would the person like to do? What does the person seem to want from you?	Probing questions Inventories and models
Develop Options	What infromation-gathering has the person done? Has some "imprecise" thinking been done? Have the desired outcomes been identified? Has the person ever "broken set" and considered unusual or even undesirable options?	Metaphorical thinking Brainstorming Modeling Problem-solving skills development
Reach a Conclusion	Has there been closure? Did it seem premature? Does this fit with the person's desired outcomes? Has the person "counted the costs?" Does the person have the necessary skills?	Simulation Behavior rehearsal Awareness of rationalization Reality testing
Follow Through	Can progress be recognized if it's made?	Contracting

When applying this list of procedures, it is not necessary to perform them in a rigid manner. The steps represent a synthesis of more than a dozen models of problem-solving and decision-making. The procedures are intended as guideposts that enable a counselor to set his or her bearings, using them as reference points. Likewise, the assessment questions are examples of the types of questions the counselor needs to feel satisfied with before continuing on through the counseling procedures. The actual process of consulting is an interplay between assessment and intervention activities. The counselor determines which skills the employee lacks and what procedures the other person may be inclined to overlook or ignore—then attempts to foster them. This is the essence of the consulting relationship. [Consulting methods are scattered throughout the Applications Section. However, Unit 9, "Personal/Work Problems", highlights the use of consulting techniques particularly well.]

Building Rapport

In order to help an employee increase his or her competency in a particular area, a counselor must be seen as an understanding and respected resource. Active listening (attempts to understand a problem without evaluating it) is useful in accomplishing this objective. If the counselor presents a nonjudgmental, positively-reinforcing demeanor, the other person is likely to pick up these nonverbal cues and approach the problem in a more dispassionate and clear-headed manner. A principle of physics developed by Niels Bohr is applicable to the consulting relationship. Bohr's principle of complementariness maintains that the observer and the subject are an inseparable whole—changes in one are likely to affect the other. If a counselor can bring the aware detachment of a film critic to a consulting discussion, it is likely to be picked up and mirrored by the other person. A counselor can be like a child watching ants—engrossed but not interfering. This disengagement is necessary. It allows the other person to calm down and more accurately assess feelings, beliefs, and events. This does not mean all emotions are banished and a rational approach invoked by the counselor. Instead, emotions themselves become a target of assessment. When people can analyze and assess their subjective reactions to events in their lives, they not only increase their own self-awareness, but also are more in control of their actions and attitudes.

Besides active listening, asking general questions and verbalizing what the counselor considers to be real, although not expressed, concerns also builds rapport. Asking open-ended questions communicates that the counselor is interested but also demonstrates the counselor's desire to gather information before doing or recommending anything else. Reading between the lines and then voicing what the counselor believes to be the other person's concerns often legitimizes a discussion of these unspoken feelings and perceptions. We are often inclined to avoid discussing our disappointments, frustrations, and dilemmas. We are afraid that we will be thought less of or ridiculed. We may feel that by expressing a weakness, we are admitting failure. Our image of ourselves as being self-sufficient or above pettiness would be altered. Tension can be released and credibility established if a counselor can accurately decipher and voice the unspoken concerns another person has. It establishes a foundation, a bond between the counselor and the person being counseled, that is important to maintain throughout the rest of the consulting dialogue.

Identify The Problem

A primary objective of this phase of consulting is to enable the other person to realize that the real problem faced is one of making an effective decision. Few people enter a consulting dialogue with a statement such as this:

> My problem seems to be one of knowing how to make a good decision. I have many different feelings churning inside of me, and I see several ways of taking action, but I'm not sure which option is best.

Paraphrasing is a useful technique to help someone else articulate their concerns and see the root issue as one of effective decision-making. Paraphrasing involves paying attention to the verbal, nonverbal, and unexpressed cues that someone else may be sending. Paraphrasing means reflecting feelings and words and unexpressed beliefs.

Paraphrasing, of course, requires that the counselor understands what the other person is saying. Because we all fail to speak in clear, unambiguous ways, especially when we are concerned about a matter, paraphrasing can be particularly useful. Role-playing can also be useful in identifying problems, particularly conflict situations where the counselor adopts the role of another person the employee sees as a source of conflict. When utilizing this technique, the counselor and employee attempt to act out various situations and then critique their own dynamics to better understand the nature of a disagreement.

Reframing can also be a useful technique for more accurately identifying and defining a problem. It is especially useful if a counselor believes that the other person has defined a problem in a way that benefits him or her and places responsibility for the problem on everyone else. Useful reframing questions include:

- How would your boss see that situation? Why?
- What other ways are there to define this situation? That is, could there be completely different ways of looking at it?
- Can we identify together some of the assumptions you've made? If you had a different set of assumptions, how would that affect your point of view?

It is important to appreciate that it is unnecessary for the counselor to understand the *whole problem* to offer ideas or even begin to develop options. If the counselor is sensitive and listening carefully to the feelings, words, and beliefs of the other person, he or she will probably understand the other person's *wishes* very quickly. The counselor will see what the employee wants to have happen and can thereby begin to plot a course for directing the person there.

Encourage Self-Analysis

Self-analysis provides its own rewards. When we better understand our strengths and weaknesses, we can improve ourselves. When we better understand our parental and cultural heritage, we can accept ourselves. When we better understand what is important to us individually, we can fulfill ourselves. Self-analysis is the key not only to self-improvement, but also to self-acceptance and self-fulfillment.

Probing questions can be used by the counselor to encourage self-analysis and to help the other person see how he or she typically reacts to certain events. For instance, did the other person react negatively to missing a promotion by *denying* what happened ("I wasn't really passed over.") *blaming* others ("I didn't get it because my boss was unfair.") *projecting* personal feelings onto others ("He is really being snooty about this.") or *blaming himself/herself* ("I guess I'm just no good.") Probing questions are helpful when they enable the other person to see how he or she reacted to a specific situation and face the realization of other choices and options .

In addition to probing questions, there are a number of exercises and instruments available which encourage self-analysis. Firo-B by Will Schutz is probably the best of these. Encounter groups, with a skilled facilitator, can also be useful in developing self-insight. An important reason for encouraging self-analysis in consulting is to recognize that many problems are within us. Our anger, resentment, disappointment, etc., are as much problems as the external events that promoted these reactions. Until we come to grips with these problems, we will not be able to see clearly to solve other problems caused by external events.

Develop Options

A realistic search for options is another key to effective consulting. Sometimes poor decisions are made by people because they have not considered available options. Of course, it is rarely possible to consider all options, but some time spent searching for alternatives can provide a big pay out. In fact, an objective of the entire consulting process is to slow a concerned employee down, prevent him or her from acting impulsively, and make a good choice regarding available courses of action.

One technique for increasing the search for options is metaphorical thinking. This involves comparing the current situation to an analagous one, determining what useful courses of action exist in that situation, and then relating these to the problem situation at hand to assess their utility. For instance, the anxiety of the first men to walk on the moon may be conjured up and options that might be useful in preparing for it considered and then compared to the anxiety a newly appointed foreman feels. Options for reducing anxiety in both cases may be similar. Analogies and metaphors keep a person from thinking too narrowly when developing options. In fact, precise thinking blocks creativity and typically surfaces only familiar options. Imprecise thinking, on the other hand, can often develop better outcomes.

Sometimes people doubt the solubility of a problem and express their reluctance to even consider options. A workable alternative, even if it were identified, may be dismissed for various reasons.

Brain-storming, without regard to the workability of solutions, may be useful in such cases. The counselor should encourage the employee to "fantasize" and say anything that comes to mind. The person should be encouraged at this point to say how he or she would like a situation to be resolved. With this end result in mind, the counselor could propose options as well as encourage the employee to do the same. The employee could then be urged to develop pros and cons of each of these options. Those pros and cons can be used to further develop the specifications for a workable option.

Despite the use of such techniques, the employee may not consider options known to the counselor. Thus, the counselor may wish to model or demonstrate these options. It is important that the counselor indicate that such options *might* be considered rather than what *ought* to be done.

Reach A Conclusion

Simulating an outcome may be a particularly useful technique to use to enable an employee to consider the possible consequences of an option. Simulation allows a person to partially experience an event and analyze his or her likely reactions. Behavioral rehearsal is similar to simulation except events are reviewed in one's own mind rather than acted out. Three-time Olympic gold medal winner Jean-Claude Killy reported once that he did not have time to ski down a particular course before he was required to do it for a competitive event. His only preparation was to mentally ski it several times. He won and said later that it was one of his best races. Mentally practicing how one wants to act in a particular situation is the essence of behavioral rehearsal. A counselor can use this technique to help someone reach a conclusion and prepare for implementing it.

When the other person reaches a conclusion, an effective counselor is careful to do reality testing and to confront the employee regarding any rationalizations given for the particular option chosen. The assessment questions included at the beginning of this section on consulting are especially appropriate in this regard.

Follow Through

Any good decision can go awry if it is not well executed. Implementation is not only the final phase of decision-making, it is also the most important. Without following through, without acting on one's intentions, nothing has changed. Depending on the nature of the problem an employee has, follow through may be implied or explicit. In some cases, procedures for following through may be important details to discuss and agree upon. An explicit contract may even be drawn up where the other person records his or her intentions in writing and leaves them with the counselor. In other cases, follow through actions are made less explicit. The nature of the problem and the people involved will determine which course of action is best. Importantly, however, some decision should be reached during the consulting dialogue with the next steps clearly identified on paper or in the minds of the counselor and the employee.

SUMMARY

Correcting, coaching, and consulting objectives and methods have been described in this chapter. These three terms have been used to describe different counseling orientations when working with people on improvement of their competence in dealing with typical problems they face. We all encounter day-to-day problems and appreciate those who are willing to listen, able to understand, and capable of helping us with them. Counseling is a cathartic function—we feel better when we've experienced it. When talking about our problems out loud, we understand them better ourselves. But counseling also has a remedial and a developmental function: we can change and improve through counseling. We can appreciate the importance of work rules, learn to do our jobs better, and get more satisfaction from our jobs through the counseling process. It is well worth the time for managers and personnel specialists to become skilled in counseling.

Section II

Counseling:
Applications

Applications

Perhaps one of the most important skills that anyone can develop to be both successful and effective in organizational life is the ability to learn. Learning is not easy. It is not easy because learning opportunities can slip by unnoticed so easily. Learning is so often thought of as gaining more information, which it is, but it also results from being more aware. In fact, using information to increase awareness is the basis of learning.

The vignettes contained in this section will be the most helpful if the reader will likewise use this information to more earnestly examine what works for him or her. We learn by gaining new information, deciding how to use it, trying it out and then reflecting on its utility. Through this process, we can better generalize principles that will work in most situations and personalize those that are effective under certain given conditions. One thing that we can all be certain of is that because people are so different, we must continually test what we "know" so we don't use the right tool in the wrong situation. The late Abraham Maslow encouraged his students to avoid this by gaining as many interpersonal tools as possible and assessing each situation in order to determine the appropriate one to use. "When the only tool you have is a hammer," he said, "you tend to treat everything as if it were a nail." The key to "knowing" ahead of time what will work lies in our individual ability to correctly define key elements in a situation. The structure of the vignettes in this section is designed to aid in that process.

Each vignette is written so that it contains three basic parts: a situation description, a dialogue, and a critique. The situation description sets the stage and provides key background information.

The dialogue shows the interplay between counselor and employee and illustrates methods presented in the various chapters in Section I. The critique is a brief commentary depicting what happened and what can be learned from the approach taken by the counselor.

There are several objectives that the applications attempt to realize:

1. To be specific and pragmatic so that the reader will see principles and concepts applied to a realistic situation;
2. To show the give-and-take that goes with counseling;
3. To demonstrate some likely consequences from counseling methods; and,
4. To emphasize that counseling is partially an art and partially a science.

Since this book is intended as a practical reference work for managers, trainers, and others, the vignettes are intended to be representative of the type of counseling situations typically encountered at the workplace. They are not intended necessarily to be read through at one sitting. Instead, by reading a vignette, deciding how to use the approach described, experimenting with it, and then thinking about its application to similar situations, the reader will be more effective when counseling others. This is the essence of self-directed learning. It is vital to the understanding and application of counseling effectiveness.

Pay, Promotions and Appraisals

Why Was I Passed Over For A Promotion?

The Situation

The promotion committee had met and made their selections for the vacancies that existed in the plant. Several technical foremen positions were available and were filled during the course of the meeting. After the various offers were extended and accepted, the results of the committee's actions were posted on bulletin boards throughout the plant. Frank had not been asked.

Frank felt before the meeting that this time he was sure to get a promotion. After all, he reasoned, he had more experience than any other senior operator in the section. He had always received good performance reviews and was noted for his loyalty to the company. He got along well with most of his co-workers and tried to help new operators learn the various functions of the equipment in the section.

Why, then, with all of this going for him was he passed over for a supervisory position? He decided to ask his boss, Jim Jamison, about the matter this time, rather than just keeping quiet about it as he had always done before. Their discussion began.

Frank: Can I see you for a minute, Jim?

Jim: Sure thing. Come in and sit down, What's on your mind?

Frank: Well, I was wondering why I didn't get a promotion to technical foreman again this time.

Jim: You're disappointed that you weren't selected?

Frank: Yeah. I think I'm better qualified than some of those younger folks who got promoted. Why, I was doing my job when some of them were still taking time out for recess everyday. Why was I passed over?

Jim: I can see that this is really bothering you, Frank. I can sense your disappointment. Do you feel that people were promoted who shouldn't have been?

Frank: Well, not exactly. The ones that I know are all good employees. But what about me? I work hard, too. Are you saying that my performance isn't good enough? That I'm really not as good as they are?

Jim: You're a solid performer, Frank. You know that from our performance appraisal discussions. Your knowledge of the equipment in this section is invaluable and your willingness to work with some of the new employees has helped a great deal lately.

Frank: If I'm so good, why then was I passed over? Why don't you give me a promotion? You don't know what it's like to see people 10, 12, 15 years younger than you are advanced while you stay in the same job. I'd like to do something different myself is all.

Jim: Is that it? Is that what you would like to do the most? To do something different than what you've been doing?

Frank: Now don't get me wrong. I like my work. I like it a lot. I like knowing that I can make those machines out there jump through hoops. In fact, the one thing I wouldn't like about a supervisory job is not being able to spend as much time doing mechanical work. But I like to do different things too. I like a good challenge as much as anybody else and would like to try a new challenge.

Jim: I think you are good at working mechanical problems, Frank. You're good with your hands and you seem to really do problem-solving in those areas. But what about administrative problem-solving? I've heard you say before *that supervising was just a lot of paperwork. Although I think supervising is other things too, it certainly does involve a lot of planning. scheduling, checking, and reporting. Is that the kind of work you want?*

Frank: *Well, I guess I do enjoy the mechanical work more. Is that the only reason I didn't get a promotion?*

Jim: *It's the basic reason. Your strengths are really in the mechanical area. You're good at trouble-shooting problems. That's where your strengths lie. In fact, rather than thinking of yourself as being passed over for a promotion, it may be more realistic to think of yourself as being saved from the hassle of administrative tasks—letting others have it who like that kind of work. Do you agree?*

Frank: *Well, sort of. I guess I see others going to jobs that earn more money and having "supervisor" as their title and all that.*

Jim: *Sure, there are some rewards. No denying that. But I guess the question we all have to ask ourselves is: "Are the costs worth it?" Only you can determine whether or not it's worth it to you.*

Frank: *I really don't like doing paperwork.*

Jim: *You said something earlier that I've been thinking about, though. You said you thought your job was losing some of its challenge for you.*

Frank: *That's right. I know the equipment pretty well. It makes my work easier, but it's not as exciting to me as it once was.*

Jim: *As I see it, there are two angles to approach a situation like that. One angle is to examine ways to make your current job more challenging. The other way is to prepare yourself for more challenging and sophisticated mechanical work.*

Frank: *I think I've milked all the challenge and innovation I can out of my current job. What can I do to prepare for something else?*

Jim: *Oh, I can think of a couple of ways. You could talk to people in the plant who do other work and see what you think about their jobs. You can take a vocational class at a local college or trade school. Can you think of others?*

Frank: *No, not off hand. Maybe I should take a vocational class on something related to my work, and maybe I can take it on something that will help me out in doing odd jobs around the house, too.*

Jim: *You may want to think about it for a few days. Why don't we get together on it again next week? You may have some other ideas then, or if you decide to take a night class, we can discuss what the various schools in town may have to offer.*

Frank: *Sounds good to me.*

Critique

Perhaps there is nothing so basic to our self-worth as our feelings and beliefs about how we are doing in our job. Most people want to do well and want to be recognized for their contributions. A survey conducted at General Electric some years ago verified this when more than 80% of the employees asked about their performance indicated they were certainly above average. In fact, most of us, when we are introduced to someone else, will ask, "What do you do?" One's job is more than a source of livelihood; it is a primary source of self-identity. Thus to feel passed over for promotional opportunities is to feel a sense of loss—the "identity crisis" that was the catch word of the late 1960s.

The significant contribution Jamison made in this counseling discussion was to convincingly assure Frank that he was respected and valued. He reminded Frank of the things he did well and reframed the nature of a supervisory promotion. Jamison helped Frank see that a promotion was not simply more money and a certain status. It also involved doing a different type and kind of work—detailed, administrative work. Work that Frank neither enjoyed nor did well. In addition, Jamison listened to Frank's concerns and avoided giving Frank reasons for not receiving a promotion. The words and the context of the discussion show that Frank was not really seeking information on why he was not offered a promotion. Rather, Frank believed that he had been treated unfairly and came to the conclusion, only upon reflection, that such was not the case.

Jamison did more than reassure and reorient Frank. He also gave him some direction. As it turned out, Frank was looking for something new to do. He was a skilled craftsman and no longer found the work he was doing very challenging. Jamison offered a suggestion, as did Frank, which they discussed. Importantly, no attempt was made to bring closure to the *new* problem: how Frank could feel a greater sense of challenge in his work. This new problem deserves some additional time and thought. By avoiding a hasty conclusion, a better solution will likely be developed. It is enough to have dealt with Frank's feelings of injustice and self-worth.

In dealing with problems of "felt injustice," it is important not to take sides. Determining whether or not the employee is right or wrong in his or her perceptions is less important than helping the person cope with disappointment. Usually this can be accomplished by focusing on what the person does well and reinforcing this success identity. Then, appraising *interests* (not performance or skills) can aid the person in identifying what he or she really wants to do. If action planning ensues, the realistic and everyday costs of realizing a goal should be counted so that the forward thinking will not create erroneous expectations. Moreover, no favors or special preferences should be extended to the employee at this time. If offered, they will only serve to convince the employee that he or she has, in fact, been "done in," and this is the counselor's attempt to make up for it.

Why Doesn't The Company Pay Me What I'm Worth?

Dale: You got a minute? Can I talk to you?

Clint: Sure, c'mon in. What's up?

Dale: Well, I'm concerned about something, and I thought you might be able to help me.

Clint: I'll do what I can. What's your concern?

Dale: I feel like the company's not paying me what I'm worth. I've worked here for five years now, and I'm not making that much more than a recent graduate. My bosses have all told me that I'm doing a good job, but I don't think my salary reflects that. Why they were stringing me along, I don't know. But I do know what we are offering new *hirees fresh off the campus. It doesn't seem like the company is very interested in keeping the people it has, since they're paying those of us who have some experience the same as the new recruits.*

Clint: *Mmm. Sounds like you are concerned. But how can you be so certain you are only making a little more than recent college graduates?*

Dale: *I've hosted three prospective job candidates in the last two weeks. We've talked about the offers they are getting, and they're pretty good.*

Clint: *They may also be inflated. I'm not saying anything about any one of them, but such recruits do have a tendency to relate what they are asking for and ignore what they are being offered. It's a form of one-upmanship. Maybe their offers are better than you think they should be, but maybe they are not as good as you've been led to believe.*

Dale: *Sure, they probably are inflated a little, but I doubt the difference is that much.*

Clint: *I agree. I just think that you may not be getting correct information on what our starting salaries are like. But it is true that salaries are based primarily on market conditions, supply and demand, while salary increases are based on several factors: competition, performance, internal equity. It's different administering a salary system than it is determining initial salary offers. The two are obviously related but they are different processes and require different considerations.*

Dale: *I can understand that they are different processes, but I could walk out this door and probably have two offers at better pay than I'm making now.*

Clint: *You probably could—and if that is what is most important to you—you should consider it. I firmly believe that almost anyone with four or five years of experience could go to work for someone else at higher pay.*

Dale: *Why don't they, then?*

Clint: *Lots of reasons. Some stay for security. Some out of loyalty. Some see more long term opportunity where they are. Some don't want to sever friendships that have been developed. The reasons vary, but the bottom line is that gross pay is only one way most people measure their compensation. It is quantitative so we talk about it a lot, but it is only one of several factors as to why people stay or leave.*

Dale: *Sure. Okay. I'll accept that. But don't you think employees should also be paid fairly?*

Clint: *Yes, but I don't know what that means. What is a fair day's pay for a fair day's work? It is an issue that is debated continuously by union leaders and company officials. Fairness is a difficult criterion. Basically, it is undefinible. It is what people agree to and is not some universal standard. Now just for the sake of discussion, tell me, why shouldn't the company pay you less?*

Dale: *Because I might quit or be more dissatisfied than I am.*

Clint: *Okay. Now you are using some economic criteria, something that can be measured or quantified. Turnover and morale. The company is concerned about minimizing turnover and keeping morale high, but although these are measurable criteria, they are shifting ones. At least it helps you see that the same economic criteria used in every other decision made by the company are also applied to pay. The company pays what it must to keep employees, to reward them, and to motivate them. Criteria used to meet those multiple objectives are based on performance increase categories, competitive salary surveys, and internal opinion surveys. The company doesn't want to underpay you because you might quit or not work as hard.*

Dale: *Are you saying the company pays me as little as it has to keep me?*

Clint: *I'm saying that's one way to think of it, and that's also the only good way to think about fairness and paying employees what they are worth. If we are generally competitive in pay practices—and we are—then it is difficult to deal with the issue of paying fairly. Instead, it seems to me that how pay practices can reward and motivate become important matters of consideration.*

Dale: *So what if I say I'm not feeling rewarded or motivated?*

Clint: *Part of motivation is being dissatisfied enough to want more or to try harder. If you are totally satisfied or completely dissatisfied, the system isn't working. If you feel like you're not where you want to be, that's not all bad. I don't want to be rhetorical about all this. I just want to represent things as they are. You are a good employee, and you are well regarded. You are being paid at the right salary level considering your service and performance.*

Dale: *I can see what you're saying about pay practices. I guess I am like everyone else, I want all I can get. You've helped me see how things work. Even if I don't feel any better about my salary, what you've said makes sense.*

Critique

It is not uncommon for someone to feel underpaid and to believe that a supervisor or manager does not really understand all the work that an employee does. It is a means for us to protect our self-image to attribute the success of others to undeserved factors ("He's just a brown-noser," "Her promotion was based on a pretty face," etc.) rather than to look inward and realistically evaluate our individual contribution and our overall capabilities. It is difficult for many to evaluate all the benefits they derive from a particular job and compare them to the prospective benefits of another job. It is unfortunate to see the dissatisfaction some experience when they take a job simply because of the higher rate of pay that job offers. Statistics from several sources suggest that people who leave one employer primarily because of a more attractive salary offer are inclined to move on again when another higher bidder comes along.

Data collected in recent years shows that almost half of those who graduate from major universities with business degrees will not remain with the organization that hired them from the campus more than five years. These new employees get anxious about their compensation and feel underpaid when they hear about salaries of former classmates. Such information, however, can be misleading. Besides concerns for accuracy, such information conveys a "snapshot" perspective and says little about future salary growth for either employee. Timing, promotability, and salary grade data are all unaccounted for in such one-to-one comparisons. This factor should be pointed out to an employee who feels underpaid. Total compensation including nonmonetary items may also be discussed and thereby help an employee feel better about his or her salary.

There are cases, however, where an employee is being paid competitively (based on available data) but believes he or she is not being paid competitively. In such cases, discussions such as the one which took place in this example may be useful. This discussion attempted to redefine the issue as one of determining fairness and equity. By realizing such terms are vague and abstract, the employee can see why salary matters are best thought of in economic terms. Competitive pay practices can then be described, and the employee can come to realize that paying fairly means paying competitively. Of course, the effectiveness of this discussion rests on the assumption that the organization does salary surveys and maintains competitive pay practices.

I Don't Think My Boss
Gave Me A Fair Appraisal

Situation

Fred is an engineer for a major company. He has been working about 5 years, and has recently been transferred to a new location. He was transferred about a year ago to his present assignment, which is a startup facility for a new plant. He is in his early thirties, pleasant to be with, and considered easy to get along with. He received mediocre marks when he recently attended technical seminars sponsored by the company. His supervisor has talked to him about his performance and indicated to him that he wasn't a very hard worker and his lack of ambition might prevent him from obtaining future advancement opportunities. Eric, an employee relations coodinator for engineering, is acquainted with Fred and has talked to him on several occasions.

Eric: *Hey Fred, I was in the area and thought I would stop by.*
Fred: *Glad you did. I'm always interested in talking to you and today I have something particular on my mind.*
Eric: *Oh? What is it, Fred?*
Fred: *Well, I just had my annual performance appraisal with my boss, and he didn't see me as doing very well. Eric, what do you do if you feel like your boss didn't give you a fair appraisal, that he just has it in for you?*

Eric: *Oh I guess it depends on how strongly you feel about it. Fred, I guess there is always an opportunity for an appraisal to be reviewed by you personally with your supervisor's boss. But that kind of bypassing could have negative results. Why don't you tell me a little bit more about your feelings before you consider taking such drastic action as that.*

Fred: *I can't put my finger exactly on why I think he's unfair. I guess it's because we really don't have a very good relationship.*

Eric: *Is there something in particular that you may have said or done that your boss indicated that would cause you to feel this way?*

Fred: *Well, nothing in particular, I guess. He did say that he didn't see me as working hard enough, which is something I don't agree with. I work hard while I'm here; in fact, I usually eat my lunch at my desk.*

Eric: *Oh, What do you suppose he meant by that statement, then?*

Fred: *Well, the only thing I can figure out is that I don't stay late or work as long as some of the other engineers. Usually when it is five o'clock and time to go home, I go home. I know some of the others work later at night, but I guess I am getting paid for what I do and if I do as much in eight hours as others do in nine or ten, why should that be held against me?*

Eric: *Well it shouldn't if your work output and quality is as high as others. But I guess I'm still interested in why you feel like your boss was unfair in the appraisal.*

Fred: *Well, he did talk to me a little about my technical skills and how he thought I could improve in that area. But I work on so many things that seem to have a pressure deadline. It's hard for me to really improve my skills.*

Eric: *Oh, I see.*

Fred: *My boss did say he also thought that I wasn't very good at judging priorities, but I think that is partially his fault as well. If priorities have changed, he should be giving me more directions and better instructions so that I'll know what is really expected and what is important.*

Eric: *Hmmm.*

Fred: *I guess I feel like I've worked hard the last five years, and I hate to see all that work go down the drain through one appraisal.*

Eric: *Oh, I don't think one appraisal makes or breaks your career. But it sounds to me like your boss has given you some specific reasons why he evaluated you the way he did.*

Fred: *Yes, he has been pretty specific.*

Eric: *I guess the question, then, is whether or not you feel like your boss's appraisal has been unfair. You can either talk to him specifically about it again, talk to his boss, or decide how you're going to meet future work requirements better. Do you see any other options?*

Fred: *No, I don't. I guess now that I think about it and talk about it, I know how my boss feels. I wouldn't want to approach him again. I also know that he talked to his boss before he gave me the appraisal, and I don't see that as a viable option.*

Eric: *It is always a risky course of action to bypass your current supervisor. It may be necessary in some instances, but it sounds to me like you feel there is some basis for the evaluation you were given.*

Fred: *Yes. But I feel like it's not all my fault, that my boss has some responsibility as well. Although I can also see his point. Other people do work hard and longer than I do, and I didn't do very well in the technical seminar. I just don't feel like it's all my fault.*

Eric: *Yes. I also think that oftentimes problems at work are a function of the interaction between several people, not simply one person or one event. Blaming, however, usually prevents problem solving. It focuses the attention on who is responsible, rather than what to do about it. What, Fred, do you think you could do about the current situation to improve it?*

Fred: *I know that if I spent more time at work I could get more things done, that I could improve technical skills, as well as have more time to work on projects when the phone is not ringing as much.*

Eric: *It sounds as though you're not positive you want to do that.*

Fred: *I'm not real sure that I want to do it. I'm not sure that I want to spend the extra time that it takes to get ahead away from my family. I really enjoy my children. I also have a wood shop and enjoy working in it. I don't know if I want to give up all my free time in order to do better on my job.*

Eric: *It's always difficult to determine where to put your time. I guess that's part of the same choice your boss talked to you about in determining priorities. Priorities extend not just in determining what work assignments to pursue, but also where to split your time, between work time and nonwork time.*

Fred: *That's right. I don't want my life to be consumed by my work. I have other interests. But I also don't want to be left behind in advancement opportunities. I guess I want the best of both worlds.*

Eric: *Trying to get the best you can of what you have is something that we all want. I guess it's important as well to realize that each of us has to choose. And likewise, when you make those choices, to live with the consequences. One thing that I think would help, regardless of your choices, is for you to talk to your boss about some of your priorities and preferences, about things you want for yourself. I think you also need to look at things from your boss's point of view, and see if he has some expectations as well of you. The essence of a boss's job is to provide predictability in an organization. If things take longer than they're scheduled to, that makes him look bad to his boss. The essence of an organization is to be able to plan and to be predictable.*

Fred: *I guess I know that, and I probably ought to communicate to him about some of my interests on and off the job so he'll be able to plan his work better.*

Eric: *I think that would help. It sounds like it's important for you as well to decide what you really want, if you prefer time away from the job. Other people who are willing to spend more time on the job can not only do their own work but can also improve their technical skills and will tend to advance faster. Coming to terms with that, who you are and what you want, is important.*

Fred: *I think you're right.*

Eric: *One thing that you might do, as well, is to solicit from your boss his priorities in your work. That's not always easy, but it's a starting place to know exactly how to improve.*

Fred: *I guess my most conflicting thought is: if I spend all of this extra time, am I sure that I'll really get ahead?*

Eric: *That's a promise nobody can make. I think it's possible for all of us to improve and do better on our jobs, but that doesn't mean we can become the best, or that we are going to advance the fastest. The problem is sometimes we think we've improved until we see other people who are just as ambitious as we are, have been just as diligent in striving to improve, but who have a little more natural ability. So, it's not possible simply to invest time and expect the outcomes we want. That's part of what happens in organizations, though. But I think we can at least determine for ourselves what kinds of things we like to do, determine our own goals and priorities and balance off our work interests and our non-work interests, so that even if we don't run the company, we are satisfied with the compromise that we have struck.*

Fred: *I'm sure that's true. I guess what I really need to do is consider myself, what I think is important, and then take a look at my job in the same way. Then I should talk to my boss about those priorities, both what I consider important in my job and what I consider important in my life. That way he'll be able to better plan my workday and my career.*

Eric: *I think we all need to be in control of our own careers and lives, to plan them and to decide what is important to us. Once we've made those decisions, we will realize that we're not really giving up other things but just doing what we really want to do.*

Fred: *That's right.*

Critique

Fred exhibits a common conflict: How to get ahead and do the best he can in his job while not letting his career control his entire life. Constant outside interests are so varied and important to him that he will probably never be regarded as a high performer. Consequently, appraisals that are only, at best, mediocre, can be expected. There is nothing wrong in being an average performer to people who consider their job as just another part of their life.

In this counseling section, Eric did several things that were particularly helpful. First, he let Fred talk about his feelings and reactions to the appraisal that was given. He did not take sides, but stayed neutral. He listened. He was empathetic. He sought to understand Fred's feelings from his own point of view, without agreeing or disagreeing. Then he pointed out to Fred some of the things that Fred had noted about differences, about performance deficiencies that his boss had identified. Fred agreed that there was a problem in meeting work objectives, although he blamed his supervisor for the fact that the situation existed. However, once an acknowledgement had been given that there was some basis for the appraisal, the issue of fairness could be set aside and other issues explored more extensively. For instance, Eric helped Fred see that other things were really more important to him than his work. He also helped him see that his lack of setting priorities between his work and his nonwork was probably a reflection of his own lack of priority setting on the job. This was a major criticism of Fred by his supervisor and established again some basis for fairness in the appraisal that was given of him. Fred was also able to see that his supervisor had given him feedback on several other topics, although Fred did not always carefully listen or consider the impact of this feedback from his boss. Finally, Fred was encouraged to talk to his boss about his own priorities, so that his boss would be able to plan work better and more consistently. Through this means, Fred's performance in the coming months would likely improve even though his work output might not. This is because his supervisor would be able to plan with more certainty and greater predictability and not be encumbered with missed deadlines or unfulfilled expectations.

Performance appraisals are intended to serve a number of important functions in most organizations. They are supposed to provide feedback to employees about their performance, identify employee development needs for the basis of getting awards and aid in planning and control. The debates about which approach to performance appraisals is the best have been many and long. At present, there is no one approach that is unanimously claimed as the best. However, it seems that the mutual give-and-take appraisals which rely on clearly based work behaviors are generally better than approaches which rely solely on raises. For example: How friendly is the person? High, Medium, or Low? It is difficult to simultaneously appraise performance for the purpose of giving awards and discussing the development needs of an employee, although they are commonly combined. The evaluation and appraisals of our performance in an organization strikes basically at our self-esteem. Most of us consider ourselves good performers. In fact, research at General Electric found that 80% of all employees considered themselves above average. By definition, it is simply not possible for 80% of all employees to be considered above average. It is unfortunate that there is such a stigma surrounding being average, but it is surprising as well. Although we all want to be considered normal, none of us want to be considered average. Yet, for someone who has sorted out what is important in his or her own life, being average at work provides another opportunity to be above average in some other aspect, e.g., his or her hobby.

In this discussion, Eric encouraged Fred to do two things:

1. To determine what was important to him, and then to pursue those priorities and not be deterred when he did not do as well in areas that were not important.
2. To improve priority setting with his boss so that they would each understand how much the other was willing to accomplish at work. By setting better priorities at work, Fred would be able to improve his performance by making his boss's planning more certain and predictable.

Why Doesn't The Cost-Of-Living Factor Match The Inflation Rate?

Ray: *Say, Betty, I want to say something to you. I think the company's gone chintzy on us. It made all those big profits last year and gave us a lousy 5% inflation increase.*

Betty: *Oh, you don't think 5% is enough?*

Ray: *Yeah, that's what I think. I think the company is making profits because all the little people work hard. But it's the big shots who get big salaries.*

Betty: *Do you think they make too much or that you don't make enough?*

Ray: *Both. But what I'm upset about is this measly 5% cost-of-living increase you announced yesterday would be in the next paycheck. I don't think 5% is near enough. It's not even close to an inflation rate that may be twice that amount this coming year. Don't tell me the company can't afford it, either. I read the papers and know the company made a lot of money last year. All I want to know is why doesn't the cost-of-living factor you use in figuring up merit increases match the inflation rate for our city?*

Betty: *That's a good question, Ray, and I'm glad you asked it. Short and sweet, part of what causes inflation is salary and wage increases that are out of line with productivity increases. No company that I know of attempts to match the inflation rate with its cost-of-living increases. If it did, without comparable productivity increases, it would eventually "spend" itself out of business. But I'm wondering if your concern doesn't reflect some deeper anxiety.*

Ray: *Like what?*

Betty: *Like a concern over whether your standard of living will be drastically affected by inflation.*

Ray: *Sure, that's a concern to me. Isn't it to everyone?*

Betty: *Sure, but do you realize that your personal inflation rate is much lower than anything reported in the newspapers?*

Ray: *What do you mean?*

Betty: *The Consumer Price Index or CPI is the way the inflation rate, if we can use that term, is officially measured. The CPI is a comparison of what 100 specific items cost at one time compared to some other time. It is a weighted average of these 100 items.*

Ray: *So?*

Betty: *So, did you buy a house last year?*

Ray: *No.*

Betty: Then your personal inflation is much less than anything reported in the papers. This is because about 30% of the CPI is weighted according to the increased cost for financing a house. Since you bought a house when interest rates were lower your personal inflation rate in that category didn't increase at all.

Ray: That's interesting. I didn't know that.

Betty: Increases in the company's benefit plans also mean that your personal inflation rate is offset in this area, too. 5% of the CPI is reflected in the costs of healthcare which didn't increase at all for you because of the company subsidy of hospital/medical plans for all employees.

Ray: We do have a good benefit plan here.

Betty: If you drove your car less because of higher gasoline prices, grew food in your garden, or did bargain hunting while shopping for either food or clothing, your personal inflation rate would be lowered even further. Your own inflation rate may be less than half of that reported in the papers.

Ray: Gee, that's interesting. I didn't know all of that. It's just that I work so hard for what I get, it doesn't seem fair that I'll never be able to get ahead and provide something more for my family.

Betty: I sense, Ray, that part of your concern is not inflation itself but the uncertainty that accompanies inflation.

Ray: I am concerned about that. Where will it all end? What can we do about it?

Betty: Well, I'm not sure that I know, Ray. Lots of people have their own ideas. So far, what's been tried doesn't seem to be working. I think a couple of things would help but it would require sacrifice on everyone's part. Besides productivity increases, if the government would print less money and not try to spend its way out of debt, things would get better.

Ray: If it's that simple, why doesn't the government do it?

Betty: We won't let it. Each of us wants someone else to pay the price. We subsidize buses, roads, schools and the like instead of paying the full price for services. The government likes some inflation, too, since it puts people in *higher tax brackets and generates more revenue for its own programs without voting a tax increase. The government, like business, has its own way of passing on cost increases to consumers. However, it usually doesn't compete with anyone for customers so there's no direct incentive to economize. As a company, we do what we must to remain competitive, both through pay practices and pricing practices. When we make more, we have more to invest in new technology or plants. Being competitive is the key to job security as well.*

Ray: *That's certainly important. Tell me, Betty, do you think inflation will ever slow down?*

Betty: *I don't know, Ray. I just don't know. Some countries have higher rates than we do and seem to have accepted it as a way of life. We may have to do the same. Surprisingly, lots of people in those countries have learned to cope, even thrive, during inflationary times. They've done it through good personal money management.*

Ray: *Oh? How?*

Betty: *You may want to look into a course that's being taught at the Junior College on personal investing. I've heard it's excellent. Or you may want to read something like Sylvia Porter's <u>Money Book</u>; it has some good ideas.*

Ray: *I will. Thanks. I've got to run. I really enjoyed talking with you.*

Critique

This discussion represents a common concern, although it may not always be expressed in these same terms. Many people are concerned about the cost of living and the impact inflation has on their life style. Inflation also brings with it uncertainty. Inflation makes it difficult to plan for the future because of erosion of purchasing power of dollars saved over time. It tends to make people cynical about the future.

There is only so much that any one company, or agency or individual can do about inflation. It is important, however, for employees to realize the things their employer does for them to fight inflation in addition to pay increases. When people believe they are not being adequately compensated, they are more likely to steal office supplies, make strictly personal long distance phone calls, pad their expense accounts, and the like. It is very much in an organization's interest to let its employees know how much it is doing to help them cope with the rising cost of living.

In this dialogue, Betty did several things that were effective in reorienting Ray's thinking so that he recognized the company's efforts in somewhat defraying the impact of a rising cost of living. Specifically, she *confronted* him with the fact that no company she knew of attempted to match the rise in cost of living dollar for dollar. She also told him *why* this was not possible. With this basic premise established, she was then able to explore his *anxieties* concerning inflation and *reorient* his thinking by showing how Ray's personal inflation rate compared to increases in the Consumer Price Index. She listened to his generalized concerns and offered her *personal views* on ways Ray could further cope with inflation. The *timing* of this sequence of counseling events left Ray feeling that the company was doing more than he realized.

Unit **2**

Career Counseling

What Do I Do If I Don't Want To Be A Secretary Anymore?

Situation

Anne hesitated momentarily in the doorway, shuffling and sorting papers erratically in her hands. She had worked for the Chamber of Commerce for 12 years as a secretary. As an executive secretary to the Associate Director, she appeared to her co-workers as competent, thorough and very satisfied with the position she occupied. Phil Reynolds, the Associate Director, was certainly pleased to have Anne on his staff and had developed a good relationship with her since assuming his current position 18 months ago. Seeing Anne pause in the doorway, he called to her.

Phil: Got something for me, Anne?

Anne: Yes, Mr. Reynolds. I do have some papers for you to sign. Routine letters mainly. But I also have something I'd like to talk to you about when you have a few minutes.

Phil: Now is a good time. Why don't we talk first, and then I'll take care of the letters. What can I help you with?

Anne: I don't know how to begin exactly. What I want to talk about is my future here. When we had my performance appraisal review last month you said to feel free to come in anytime and talk about my job and my career. I feel that I have a good job here, but not a good career. I'm an

121

executive secretary now and moving on to be the director's secretary doesn't have much appeal for me. What can I do in the Chamber if I don't want to be a secretary anymore?

Phil: *You seem quite definite that you want a career change. Is there something that has prompted these feelings?*

Anne: *This is not a quickly-made decision by any means, but something has caused me to think more about it. A neighbor of mine who held a similar position in a local manufacturing company was recently promoted and given a job in the company's personnel department. Her job change has caused me to think about my own career.*

Phil: *Events such as that can often stimulate us to think about what we personally want out of our jobs. I would like to talk to you about some of the jobs outside of secretarial work that become available from time to time. But before we do that, I would like to better understand your feelings about your current job and what you are looking for in the way of a change. Anne, can you tell me more about your reasons for wanting a change and your feelings about broadening yourself outside of secretarial work?*

Anne: *There are several reasons actually, none of which have anything to do with you or my work. I like my job, I like the constant variety and excitement, and I feel that we have a good working relationship. That's why it's difficult for me to say what other types of work I would enjoy. Basically, the reasons that I would like to try something else are because of the additional money and advancement opportunity that would be available outside of secretarial work.*

Phil: *As you know, the only higher level secretarial position in the Chamber is the one Patsi occupies as secretary to the director, and you're saying that job doesn't hold a lot of appeal for you. Is that right?*

Anne: *It isn't that I'm not interested. I think I'd like that job. But Patsi is in her mid-forties and will probably be there a long time. I don't want to simply wait around until she retires.*

Phil: *I think I understand what you've been saying, but let me summarize and see if I've gotten your intended meaning.*

You're saying that you like your job but feel capable of handling assignments that would be outside of the secretarial area. You feel that there is limited opportunity for advancement beyond your current position and would like to get into a line of work that holds more promise of advancement with commensurate increases in salary level. Is that right?

Anne: *Yes. Is that realistic?*

Phil: *I think so, depending on what you want to do and how soon you want to do it.*

Anne: *I'm willing to try almost anything, and I certainly don't expect it to happen tomorrow. I know these moves take time. Does that help?*

Phil: *Well, a little. What type of work would you like to get into, Anne, and what have you done so far to prepare for such a position?*

Anne: *That's part of my trouble. I don't know exactly what is possible for someone like me, nor what I'd have to do in order to be in contention for some of the jobs I think I would like.*

Phil: *You have identified some of the things you would like in a job, and that's probably a good place to begin in determining what kind of job you might like. This isn't an easy task, Anne, nor is this whole process one for which I can provide a lot of answers. But I do think there is a general strategy you can adopt if you want to spend time working at it that will help you determine what alternatives are worth pursuing.*

Anne: *That sounds great to me. I would certainly welcome your advice.*

Phil: *As I see it, there are three activities that can help you determine what you really want to do. These are to take an inventory of yourself, talk to some people who are in jobs that you might like, and do some reality testing to determine if you want that type of work and are willing to prepare for it.*

Anne: *Gee, that sounds good to me. Where do I begin?*

Phil: *With the self-inventory. There are lots of ways you could do this. Let me suggest one I've found useful and see what you think about it. Think back on some specific work experiences that you've had in the last several years. Select a project that you worked on or a series of related events. Select something where you felt challenged and where you felt you really did a good job even if no one else noticed. Select four or five events or experiences. Then, write down all of the activities you were engaged in. In other words, what kinds of things you did in order to complete the assignment or fulfill the task. You can then use this same list to evaluate whether or not you would like the work of other people who are in jobs that you think you'd enjoy.*

Anne: *Is that the second basic activity you see me engaging in— sorting out what I'd really like to do?*

Phil: *Yes. When you've identified some of the activities you like the most, we can talk about entry level jobs that utilize those activities. I'll see if I can arrange for you to talk to some people who are already in those positions so you can find out what they actually do. We can also talk about some of the questions you may want to ask so that you'll find out what the job incumbents really do.*

Anne: *I'd really appreciate that.*

Phil: *However, I wouldn't see the process as complete without an essential third step. Reality testing. I think you've got to rigorously sit down and say, "How do I compare with others who may also be candidates for this type of job?" Being somewhat objective when doing this reality testing is not any easier than when you do the self-evaluation. But to minimize your chances of disappointment in not getting what you want after you've clearly identified your interests, it is absolutely necessary to objectively look at what you have going for yourself and what gaps in experience, training, and the like you may need to fill. I'll give you a list of questions you can ask yourself to help you do some reality testing, and then we can talk about it. As you can see, I've got lots of lists.*

Anne: *You certainly do. And I appreciate your willingness to share your ideas and time with me. I value your opinion and respect your point of view. It has really been helpful to me.*

Phil: *Good, I enjoy working with you and hope that I can be helpful to you in ways like this. As I think you realize, there are some good opportunitites here with the Chamber. There are also some very qualified people like yourself who are concerned about their careers and how to advance in them. Consequently, competition is keen for most of the openings we have. If you are willing to pay the price in terms of experience, training, and high work performance in your current job as well as prospective ones, I think that doors will open for you, Anne. There are many things you could do if you're willing to pay the necessary price. Your continued high work performance and positive work habits are the necessary minimum. They get you to the door. Appropriate training and demonstration of relevant skills will get you through the door.*

Anne: *Well, I'm certainly willing to try my best.*

Phil: *Fine. Why don't we plan on talking about the results of your self-appraisal next Monday morning. Say about 11:00 A.M.?*

Anne: *Great, I'll look forward to it.*

Critique

The concern Anne expressed in this situation is becoming an increasingly common one. In the headquarters facility of a major manufacturing company, 65% of the more than 250 secretaries recently indicated a desire to have a career outside of the secretarial field. Many of them had college degrees and had accepted secretarial positions because there were no openings in their preferred field or they had seen a secretarial job as a stepping stone to something else. Large organizations or those which do not require specialized or technical skills can often promote people who have good analytical and interpersonal skills from secretarial positions. Of course, these same organizations need capable secretaries and need to reward them as secretaries when they perform well.

In this situation, Phil had time to talk when Anne first brought her concern to him. If he would have been pressed for time, he should make a specific appointment at a later date to talk to Anne. It is a myth that bosses must always be available when an employee has a problem. Setting aside time later demonstrates a boss's concern for his or her employees.

Anne began by very specifically describing what was troubling her. But Phil did not immediately accept this as a prelude to develop options and solutions. Instead, he noted that she seemed quite definite about wanting something else, and he asked her what prompted this decision. Basically, Phil was trying to get Anne to identify why she wanted a change. Were her reasons due to current job dissatisfaction or perhaps a specific incident where Anne felt slighted? Or did she feel unrecognized in what she did or dissatisfied with her pay? By searching for the primary *motive*, Phil could avoid solving the *wrong problem*.

By listening and asking clarifying questions of Anne about how she felt about her current job, both Phil and Anne are in a better position to set objectives regarding future courses of action. Once Phil saw that Anne wanted to do some other kind of work and was confused about what possibilities were available to her, Phil became very directive. His career counseling is instructive as well. Since Anne was somewhat confused about what she wanted to do, Phil's approach was to get her to clarify what she enjoyed *doing* rather than what she wanted to *be*. This process approach to counseling is useful because it focuses on skills and interests instead of aspirations. There are too many people already who enter medicine or business or law because of the extrinsic rewards and yet are frustrated with those activities they engage in on an everyday basis. There is nothing wrong with pursuing interests that provide lots of rewards, but one should consider both the extrinsic and intrinsic rewards available in any occupation. This was the approach taken by Phil.

If You Haven't Worked Here For Five Years, They Think You Don't Know Anything

Situation

Dale is a comparatively new employee. She graduated with an MBA from a prestigious business school about 18 months ago. On graduation, she came to work in the audit section of the company, where she spent about six months. Because of her accounting ability, she was transferred to the controller's unit where she has worked the last twelve months. She is in her early thirties, bright and aggressive. She met Pete Molan at an orientation seminar, where Pete represented the personnel department.

Dale and Pete have just bumped into each other at the cafeteria and decided to eat lunch together. They are in the course of discussing their mutual careers.

Dale: I don't know, Pete, I guess I get really frustrated sometimes. The company has a program of planned frustration, of keeping you one step behind all the time.

Pete: What do you mean by that, Dale?

Dale: Well, I thought I could sell people with logic and was amazed at the hidden agendas people have, irrational objections-really bright people come up with dumb excuses. They have their own little empires to worry about.

Pete: Oh, what do you mean by that?

Dale: Well, it just seems that because you're young, nobody respects you around here. If you haven't worked here at least five years, they think you don't know what's going on. It's so hard to break in.

Pete: Something in particular caused you to have this evaluation, or are you just talking about things generally?

Dale: Well, I could name lots of specifics, but it's a general attitude. It's not explaining things until you absolutely need to. It's not treating employees who are young as if they know what is going on. It's not my boss, but people in my work group—older, more experienced accountants.

Pete: I think it can be difficult to break into any new organization. People are suspicious, and they do not want to be put in an uncomfortable position because of something a new person might say or do.

Dale: Isn't that odd that we feel threatened by each other? That we're trying to protect our little domain as if that's all that mattered?

Pete: I guess we do it to protect not just our self-interest, but to protect our identity as well. Without change, we all know *how things work, how things fit together, and who's who. But change, especially with a new person who's young and eager and bright, threatens the balance, throws things out of kilter.*

Dale: Well, what do I do about it? You're supposed to be the personnel expert?

Pete: I don't know about expert, and I don't know all of what to do. But I do know that everybody needs to sort out the informal procedures that go on in an office and work with them as well as with the formal procedures.

Dale: Yeah, you mean through the politics?

Pete: You could say politics, but politics is kind of a dirty word. Nobody likes to think of politics as being positive, they think of them as being negative. People get something they're not entitled to. I think of the informal organization as what people do to get information that they know is reliable.

Dale: You see it as an inevitable process, then. Regardless of the situation there will always be this informal organization?

Pete: Yes, I do. I don't see it as something unnatural or bad. In any organization, information is a scarce resource, and you can't rely on a formal organization to make sure that people are always informed or that information is appropriately passed on.

Dale: So you see the informal organization as something to work with rather than against.

Pete: Yes I do, and I see the importance of gaining a mentor as critical.

Dale: You mean somebody who can look out for you?

Pete: Yes. I think there are several kinds of mentors—informational mentors, sponsors who help you get ahead, others who can show you around. But mentors are very important.

Dale: How do I get a mentor?

Pete: Well, I see it as a process of mutual exchange. When you have something that somebody else wants and likewise. Like any process of buying and selling, people feel like they're both giving something and getting something of value. I think mentors can be gained by identifying people who seem to know what's going on and then developing a *positive relationship with them. A relationship that's built on more than just liking. A relationship that is built on exchange, where you provide information. In your case, probably technical information. Information about computers—something I know you are very good with. The mentor can provide information about the informal system.*

Dale: *I know somebody like that. Somebody with whom I think I could work well and establish a mutual bond.*

Pete: *I guess in some ways, everybody needs to know that an information source is reliable before they are going to rely on the information. What may seem to be bureaucratic blocks to your getting ideas accepted or programs implemented, may be just the function of people not knowing you and not knowing whether or not your information is reliable. A mentor can help in that way too. The mentor can identify opinion leaders and how those opinion leaders need to be approached.*

Dale: *You see the mentor's role as pretty important, I take it.*

Pete: *I really do. What advantages do you see of having a mentor?*

Dale: *Well, I guess a mentor could help me see the pressures and goals that my boss and colleagues have. A mentor could also help me test my own assumptions about problems and approaches to solving them.*

Pete: *I agree.*

Dale: *Well, thanks for talking with me. I've got to run.*

Critique

Young, ambitious employees are often impatient. It is a natural consequence of being highly motivated. They want to achieve, and they are eager to make changes and see the results of their efforts. Sometimes, more experienced managers want to help such employees and will counsel them not to expect too much, to take things easy, to roll with the punches, to be patient. Such advice, though well intended, is misdirected. Highly motivated people deserve to be encouraged, to be shown how to make the system work for them so their personal energy can be spent achieving work objectives.

It is important for young professionals to learn to work with the informal organization that is a part of their work life. This means knowing how to work with different kinds of bosses and their preferred ways of doing things. Every organization wants people who are industrious and take the initiative. But while a subordinate may see his or her actions in such a light, a boss may see the subordinate as overworking problems and pursuing unnecessary ideas. The point is, "being industrious" and "taking initiative" are abstractions that only have meaning in the context of a mutually agreed upon working method between boss and subordinate. Moreover, it is not the boss's responsibility to clarify this relationship, but the subordinate's.

Subordinates have many opportunities to influence their bosses and establish a working relationship that is beneficial to both. Pete, in this counseling situation, offers several ideas to Dale that are useful in effectively managing work relationships. Initially, Pete listened to Dale's definition of why a problem existed, but he did not agree with her definition. Pete encouraged Dale to see the situation as the result of natural consequences that warranted understanding and not blame the suggested ways for gaining understanding. Then, by asking Dale's views on the advantages of a mentor, Pete was able to see what influence he had had on Dale.

I Don't Want To Be A Manager — How Do I Grow As A Professional Engineer?

Situation

Harry is 30 years old and has six years of service with a large corporation. He has a good relationship with his boss, Owen Barrett, who is only 35 years old. They have talked openly about company personnel policies and practices from time to time, so Owen looked forward to the appraisal and development discussion he had scheduled with Harry. During the development discussion, Owen asked Harry about his career aspirations.

Owen: *Harry, you know that I think your technical skills are excellent and you seem to really enjoy them. How about the administrative aspects of your work? Do you enjoy them as much and are you interested in supervisory assignments?*

Harry: *I do really enjoy the technical challenge of my work, much more than the administrative part. I know it is necessary, but, frankly, it's a burden to me. I wonder if I'd really like being a manager.*

Owen: *What aspects of being a supervisor most concern you?*

Harry: *What concerns me the most is the loss of technical skills that goes with being a supervisor. I see lots of young supervisors whose technical skills are just not that good. And to be honest, I don't like the politics that seem a necessary part of supervision. I'm not saying it's bad altogether, it's just not for me. I also don't like the long hours that seem to be expected of supervisors. I enjoy my private life too much to spend as many extra hours as you do on the job. Don't get me wrong—I'm ambitious, I'm just not that ambitious.*

Owen: *Do you feel pretty strongly about this?*

Harry: *Yes, I do. I've thought it over a lot. The only trouble is, I wonder if I'll feel as strongly 10 years from now.*

Owen: *Oh?*

Harry: *You know, I see people like Dennis Wilson who is about 40 years old and only a Senior Project Engineer. It seems that he has lost a lot in both money and prestige because of his decision not to pursue a management career. Is there something in the company for senior technical people?*

Owen: *Dennis Wilson may not be a good example for several reasons, all of which I think are confidential matters between Dennis and myself. Your concern, as I understand it, Harry, is whether or not the company recognizes the contribution senior technical people make.*

Harry: *Right. Are they on par with the managerial personnel?*

Owen: *We try and recognize the contribution every employee makes through both advancement on the technical ladder and merit increases. It's important to appreciate the fact that supervisors have some responsibility for the work turned out by everyone in their group and that this responsibility is recognized monetarily as well as in other ways. We do try to compare the total contribution of each employee, supervisory and nonsupervisory, and reward it appropriately. A lot depends on your own growth and development as a professional.*

Harry: *That sounds good to me, Owen, and I believe you about advancement opportunities. But if I don't want to be a manager, how do I grow as a professional engineer? What do I do to get recognized?*

Owen: *I don't think there's a formula that you just plug yourself into, Harry, and I'm not inferring that you thought there was. The process of selecting people for advancement is partially subjective. That really isn't all bad because if you think about it, no one wants to be treated as an object, an inanimate thing, which is what complete objectivity implies. This doesn't mean advancement is capricious or arbitrary. I do think that advancement for a professional engineer does hinge on passage through several specific stages.*

Harry: *Yeah? What are they?*

Owen: *Stage I is entry level. An engineer needs to learn the system, learn the informal ways of doing things, and establish himself or herself as completely dependable in working problems through to completion. Stage II is when the engineer seeks and is given more independence. In this stage, a person is expected to finely tune his or her technical skills and develop an acknowledged specialty. Without this base, an engineer will likely lack the confidence and the capability to make a full contribution throughout his or her career. Many engineers move into Stage II but never leave it. Stage III involves assuming some responsibility for others and is often equated with the mentor function. It involves acting like a project leader who shares what he or she knows with project members although his or her formal authority may be limited. Stage III people spend a lot of time in technical counseling and are not unlike a college professor working with graduate students, although the context is certainly different. Stage IV people are involved in defining the direction of some major unit of the company. Such people occupy a position of influence because of their expertise and their contacts inside and outside the company. These people are the innovators whose ideas are now integrally incorporated into our product line.*

Harry: *You seem to have it all worked out in your mind, but does it all work like that? I know people who work on innovative things but don't seem to get recognition or encouragement for them. They're told to stick to the basics of their job and avoid the frills.*

Owen: *Maybe they are seen as being in Stage II but are trying to do Stage IV type work. My experience is that you can't skip a stage. What you seem to be asking is how you attain recognition if you go through each of these stages. Is that right?*

Harry: *Yeah, how to avoid getting lost in the shuffle.*

Owen: *I think you must both be a mentor and have a mentor. The Stage I requirement for sponsorship never really stops.*

Harry: *So it all goes back to politics, huh?*

Owen: *That's one way to look at it. Another way is to know you have good ideas and convince others that they are good. Knowing who needs convincing is a part of the process, don't you think?*

Harry: *Yes, but good ideas should speak for themselves.*

Owen: *Mmmm. Can you think of reasons why they might not?*

Harry: *Oh, uh, I don't know, unless because they are so new that they might not seem workable. If you haven't tried something you tend to be skeptical.*

Owen: *The concept of these stages may be like that to you. I'd suggest you think about them. Look at technical people you respect, maybe even interview some. I could arrange that for you. See if they haven't gone through these stages and test their reactions to the recognition they've received. You might also consider other options to professional growth that are takeoffs from this one.*

Harry: *Like what?*

Owen: *Like involvement in professional societies, as an example.*
Importantly, though, you need to decide what you want in
your career. There are different rewards and costs for
every type of assignment. Adding them to what you want
is important.

Harry: *That's good. This stage notion has given me something to*
think about. I would like to talk to some folks if you can
arrange it.

Owen: *I sure can. Also, I don't think you ever need to make*
final decisions on your career. In fact, as long as you
know what you like to do and don't like to do, you'll
have what you need to help you make good career choices.

Harry: *Thanks.*

Critique

A typical career path in an American corporation is to move up a
technical ladder, then to functional management, and lastly to
general management. Many people who have good technical skills
experience quite a bit of conflict because they have no real desire to
perform general management assignments. They may enjoy their
day-to-day technical work, but see management per se as "playing
politics." Research conducted by Ed Schein at MIT has shown that
such people who are strongly technically oriented rather than
managerially oriented will tend to leave companies rather than be
promoted out of their functional area.

Even though someone who is technically oriented may not prefer
management, he or she may experience internal conflict over lost
opportunities in the way of perceived promotions and salary
increases. Coming to terms with who we are and what we really
want out of our professional life is not easy. In fact, someone who
doesn't want managerial assignments may be all the more interested
in professional advancement.

The description of career stages presented in this dialogue is based
on a model developed by Gene Dalton and Paul Thompson and
validated by literally hundreds of interviews. In this counseling
session, Owen did several things that were particularly useful. After
beginning with several open-ended questions, he followed with

probing questions that revealed more of Harry's true feelings. Importantly, Owen did not attempt to either change Harry's mind or pacify him when Harry related his beliefs regarding the negative aspects of supervision. Instead, Owen attempted to determine *how strongly* Harry felt about it. In such cases, it is often better not to try to dissuade any employee who is strongly oriented toward technical work. Such efforts would likely be perceived as putting down technical assignments relative to managerial assignments.

Owen presented a "practice theory" or some personal rules of thumb for developing one's self as a professional and thereby qualifying for additional recognition. This was offered in response to a request for information with encouragement for the employee to validate it by interviewing longer serviced engineers. Owen did *not* tell the employee what he *should* do; rather, he provided a model based on his own experience. This method of giving advice is usually very effective because it points the employee in a certain direction but excludes any pressure to follow a particular path.

I'm 50 Years Old And
I Want To Change My Career

Situation

Tom Brandon has worked as an accountant for a major corporation for 25 years, and though he is not a supervisor, he has been able to relieve in a supervisory position quite often. He works in the division office of this corporation in a small town in the midwest. He has a good relationship with his boss, Irene Jensen. Irene and Tom have known each other for the last four years. Irene has moved around from time to time and has reached this position after about 15 years of service. Irene is 42 years old.

Tom: Irene, I'd like to see you if you have a few minutes.
Irene: Sure, Tom. Come on in. What is it?

Tom: Oh, I've been thinking about something and I'd like to talk it over with you.

Irene: Sure, I am always glad to talk to you, Tom. What's on your mind?

Tom: Well, I've been thinking, Irene, about quitting my job and doing something else.

Irene: Oh?

Tom: Yes. You know I'm not getting any younger. In fact, most of my life is over, and I decided I wanted to spend the rest of it doing something I really wanted to do.

Irene: Tom, is there something that has prompted this feeling? Something happen on the job or at home?

Tom: No, no, nothing in particular. Nothing on the job certainly. I don't want you to be thinking there is anything wrong with my job, there's not. It's just that I've done a lot of things that other people wanted me to do and nothing that I wanted to do. Now I finally want to do some things that matter to me.

Irene: Well, Tom, I can see you have thought about this. It is something that seems to have been on your mind for a while.

Tom: Oh, it hasn't been on my mind for too long, Irene. It's just that so many things really just don't seem to matter much. My son and daughter are married and live elsewhere. My career, well, it's at a dead-end. I'm not complaining about it. I've had a good career, but it's not going anywhere. The mortgage is almost paid off. I remember when I was young, full of dreams. I followed the program in the now generation—get a job, get married, raise a family. All that's done and what now? What is there left for me to do? I don't see any advantage to just continuing with this job—to earn some more money. I want to do something else. I want to do something that really makes a difference in other peoples' lives and my own.

Irene: That certainly is a noble objective. Have you thought about ways to fulfill it, to reach that objective?

Tom: No. I haven't thought of anything specific, anything that I could devote my energies to. I guess that's one reason *why I wanted to talk with you. Can you give me some advice, recommend some activities, things I might do?*

Irene: *Well, I don't know specific kinds of occupations or jobs. I guess, to a certain extent, I feel it would be useful for you to decide what kinds of things you like to do now. Maybe look at some of your pet projects and see whether you can just continue them full time, if that's something you want.*

Tom: *Well, I have been working with the boy scouts in my community, and I find that at times they are fun and exciting, but at other times, I find it a real drag. The boys don't seem to obey me; they aren't very interested in learning; there isn't a whole lot of parental support. I'm not sure I'd like doing that for very long.*

Irene: *Well, I think that is kind of a necessary search process that you might need to be involved in, Tom. It seems to me that the most important objective you have is to identify the reasons why you want a job change. If you can really write down on a piece of paper why you want a change, then I think you can determine whether or not this is just a reaction to specific events, or a generalized concern, or if there are real reasons—reasons strong enough to compel you to get out and get retraining and the skills necessary to do the job you want to do.*

Tom: *Well, I think that's good advice. I know it does seem that I am just kind of troubled and that I just don't seem to know what I want to do, which is partially the case.*

Irene: *I think people go through periods where they question and examine themselves and their life's work. They ask themselves, "Is this something that is worth the time that I've been spending on it?" I guess I have to admit, Tom, I've asked myself this question and asked myself, "Is this something that I really want to do?" There have been times when I've just felt like I couldn't give myself to my career. I personally enjoy working with antiques, and I've often sold antiques during my spare time. It would seem to me that a useful process would be for you to, first of all, as I said, identify your reasons for change. If you feel like life is just passing you by, that you've missed out on things that you've really wanted to do, then that's different. Decide if you have reached a plateau and done some things that you've felt were unsatisfying. I guess that's what I heard you say earlier, that your son and daughter are married and live elsewhere. You've gotten married and raised a family and followed that earlier program and now you question whether or not this is all for the program, or whether that programming was right in the first place.*

Tom: *Yes, that's true. I guess, Irene, I don't feel badly about the things that I've done in my life. I feel like I have done some good things, some worthwhile things; and I don't feel bad about what I have done today. It's just that I am asking myself, is this all there is—is there something more?*

Irene: *Tom, here's what I would encourage you to do. Before you make a decision about changing your career, do this first: make a list of people who are important to you. People whose friendship or love and respect you value and want to keep. Decide on ways to strengthen these relationships. Decide on ways to let these people know of your care and concern and desire to be involved in their lives. Make a similar list of pet projects. Decide what kinds of things you really like to do and decide on ways to improve your abilities and outcomes in them. I think if you can do this, it will help you in two ways. First, it will help you see that it is possible, perhaps, to just keep the job you have. You have done a good job. You have had a good career here. Possibly keep your job, but spend your spare time doing other things—things that you really enjoy and focus your time and energy on those things. Additionally, by investing more time and energy in these relationships or those pet projects or activities, it will help you to see how you might turn one of those projects or relationships into another career, into doing something else.*

Tom: *You mean like the old idea of turning a part-time job into a full-time job?*

Irene: *Yes, that's exactly right. Before you make any decisions, get as many facts as you can about opportunities that are available. If you like what you're doing, continue with it,*

and use your free time to pursue other interests. I know a
school teacher who likes teaching school. I guess he felt
like you when he was in his mid fifties he'd almost been
teaching school all his life. He wanted to do something
else, but he didn't want to give up school teaching. He did
like to work with his hands, so he started building houses
in the summer part-time. He got his own contractor's
license, and now he's got a small but prosperous business,
something that he likes doing. He doesn't want the
business to grow too much because he wants to be
involved himself in making the houses. He is not after the
money anymore, but his own satisfaction.

Tom: Hmmm. I guess there are several things that I do like to
do, and if I had another full-time job, I probably wouldn't
be able to do them. This job does allow me a certain
amount of flexibility.

Irene: Tom, regardless of what you do, whether or not you
change jobs, do go out looking for another career. Try and
develop a big picture of what you want to do with your
life. Assume that you have 30 years left in your life. What
do you want to do in those 30 years? Think about not just
what you want to be, but what kinds of activities and
accomplishments you would like to have. After you develop
that big picture, write down some necessary first steps in
its direction—specific routine day-to-day things. You would
have to begin right now in order to get that big picture.
When you have done that, try, as well, to identify some of
the costs, some of the sacrifices. There is some sacrifice
involved in realizing any goal and any objective and you
should see whether or not these costs will be more than
the expected benefits.

Tom: Big picture—first step, cost and expected benefits—well,
that sounds like good strategy, Irene. Tell me what do you
think, am I just going off on some wild kind of idea?

Irene: No, I don't think so, Tom. I think that you have spent
some time looking at yourself, looking at your life and
that you want to make sure that what you're doing is
worth it. Self-examination is useful. It is something I do
from time to time. I don't always come up with definitive

answers, but when I think it is important to ask the questions, I do that. Such reflection allows me to reinvest my energy in job requirements or with my family. You may find, as a result of your own introspection, some new directions or some emphasis in some old directions. Either way, you'll find you will be able to pursue work interests and other interests with a lot more enthusiasm.

Tom: *Well, at least you have given me some food for thought. Something I am going to think about and consider.*

Critique

An oft-quoted remark attributed to a marriage counselor regarding mid-career orientations is that "...between the mid-forties and the mid-fifties, a man either changes jobs or changes wives." People who are at this point in their lives may experience a considerable amount of anxiety. If they have not experienced the career success they once hoped for, they may feel disappointed and resentful. If they have realized their aspirations, they may wonder, "Is this all there is?" During their late forties and early fifties many people re-examine their lives and their values. An important counseling function may be to point out the many experiences the person has had and indicate ways the person may find fulfillment through a reaffirmation of his or her current life goals.

Douglas T. Hall of Northwestern University has catalogued some concerns which an employee may experience during this period:

- awareness of physical aging;
- recognition of the number of career goals that are likely to be attained;
- sense of dispensibility, even obsolescence; and
- apprehension regarding job security.[1]

These concerns arise out of a person's sense of place, of his or her feelings of fitting in. Personal identity, in this regard, hinges upon a person's recognition of individual values, goals, interests, and

---

[1] Douglas T. Hall, *Careers in Organizations* (Santa Monica, California: Goodyear Publishing Co., 1976)

opportunities. Defining or reaffirming personal identity is not simply answering the question "Who am I?" As the noted psychologist Erik Erikson has said:

> I can now register a certain impatience with the faddish equation of the term identity with the question, "Who am I?" . . . on occasion I find myself asking (someone) who claims that he is in an "identity crisis" whether he is complaining or boasting. For most, the pertinent question really is, "What do I want to make of myself and what do I have to work with?"[2]

In this counseling situation, Irene was able to help Tom see how to determine what was really important to him. Irene did not ask leading questions or attempt to force Tom to admit that he really did like his job. Rather, through appropriately worded questions, Irene helped Tom realize that there were many things Tom liked in his job and alternate ways, beside pursuing a new occupation, for developing his outside interests. This reframing caused Tom to reflect not only on what he *liked* doing, but also on what he was capable of doing, considering his age, commitment, and resources.

How Do Most People Handle Retirement?

Situation

Ray Johnson has worked for a government agency for 35 years. He's had several responsible positions in the accounting department and has learned to do his job well. For the last 15 years, he's been a department head in the Accounts Payable section. Two months ago, Ray announced his retirement. Since then, several people have noticed changes in his mood, especially his supervisor, Stan Williams. Stan has known Ray for a number of years; their friendship has been long and enduring. Consequently, Stan felt a desire to be a resource to Ray and appeared at his office one afternoon just to talk.

[2] Erik H. Erikson, *Childhood and Society* (New York: W. W. Norton and Co., Inc., 1963)

Stan: Ray, got a few minutes so we can talk?

Ray: Sure, come on in. I've got lots of time now.

Stan: OK, good. What I thought I'd do is just drop by and see what kinds of things you have planned in regard to your retirement. We have some plans of our own for you, too.

Ray: Well, I've got a few things I'd like to do.

Stan: Yeah, you've got some specific things in mind?

Ray: I guess I just want to work around the house for a while. I don't know exactly on what projects, though.

Stan: Well, I know retirement will be a big change; it's a change in anybody's lifestyle. Is your wife looking forward to it?

Ray: I'm sure she isn't. I'll probably just be in the way around the house.

Stan: That certainly will be an adjustment. Is there any way in particular I might be of help as you look forward to retirement?

Ray: Oh, I don't know, I don't know exactly what I want to do. There are a lot of things I've thought about for years that I'd like to do. Now I feel like I'm getting old so I won't be able to do some of them.

Stan: With some things, it can seem you're too old to start at retirement.

Ray: Yeah. I've done this job for so long it seems like all I know how to do is supervise these people. There aren't too many people at home to supervise.

Stan: It's going to be a change of focus in your activity.

Ray: Yeah, I guess it is. Once you retire, you wonder what else there is to do.

Stan: Is that a concern to you, that you won't find enough things to do?

Ray: Well, I've got a lot of things that I'd like to do, places I'd like to go, but that can only last for so long. I wonder if I should try to find another job. During these inflationary times, I may need to work. I don't know whether I want to go back to school; I might get bored just sitting around the house. A lot of things are worrying me. All of a sudden I'm not needed here, and I've been needed here for a long time. I'm beginning to wonder, will I be needed anywhere anymore?

Stan: I think retirement can be unsettling. As you think about your own change of focus as you retire, what do you think is your biggest concern? What do you worry about the most?

Ray: I have always hoped that I'd be useful and do things that needed doing. When I think about retirement, I wonder whether or not I'll be doing things that are worth doing. I thought I was fairly useful around here. Suddenly not to be needed by anyone, to be dispensable, is a little disconcerting.

Stan: Such feelings can result from a change in your life; once you've been doing something all of your life, suddenly to be without that constant factor is an adjustment. It's not only something to do but also the orientation about who you are to a certain extent. Most importantly, by admitting your fears and exploring them, instead of pretending that they don't exist, you are better able to analyze them. At least you can identify them for what they are and that makes it easier to take appropriate action. Are there other things that concern you about retirement?

Ray: Oh, I guess the retirement money is pretty good. I can't complain. Worked all these years, and it's really good except I wonder how long it's going to be good with inflation so high and the cost of living continually going up. I wonder if I'll have to go to work again in a few years just to support my wife.

Stan: So one thing you're really concerned about is whether or not your retirement income, your annuity, is going to be enough to cover your expenses.

Ray: Yeah.

Stan: Do any other things concern you?

Ray: I guess I also feel frustrated in my work to some extent. There's no one really here to train to take my place, and I feel like the employees aren't really working for me as hard as they did before. It's kind of like, well, "We know that you're leaving pretty soon and you don't really have any power over us." A lot of the work that I know needs to be done before I leave isn't getting done.

Stan: So you feel like a lame duck?

Ray: I guess to some extent I do, but there are things that I want to accomplish as well, and I can't do them by myself. I don't want to leave everything in an uproar when I walk out the door so that it's left for someone to try and pick up the pieces and figure out what has been going on. I want my shop to be in as good a shape when I retire as it's been while I've been in charge of it.

Stan: Sure. What kinds of things do you think could happen to help that take place?

Ray: Well, maybe if we get my replacement in here so that people in the shop here will not be left in suspense, that would help. Even if they're only trying to impress the new person, they'll at least get the work done that needs to be done.

Stan: You'd like to train a replacement, then?

Ray: Sure.

Stan: I think that would be good. I'll really try and push as much as I can from my end to get a replacement in. I think that would be good from a work point of view and also as a transition. You really seem to enjoy that one-to-one contact, being able to teach somebody else a new job, new techniques, or new ideas. Would you say that's an accurate assessment of the satisfactions you've gotten out of your work?

Ray: Yes, I really like to work with new people. I won't miss the deadlines and pressures of the job, but I really will miss the interaction. I'll miss feeling that someone can come to me when they have a problem and knowing the job well enough that I can be an expert. I feel I'm successful in this area. Sometimes I ask myself, "Why am I leaving this all behind for something I don't know anything about?"

Stan: Knowing what you like to do is important. If you derive satisfaction out of teaching/counseling, you may want to consider some way to do what you like outside of the accounting profession per se. What do you think about teaching or counseling jobs after you retire?

Ray: Oh, I've thought about putting up my own shingle or something, maybe as a tax consultant. But I'm not so sure

I want to tie myself down to any one thing right now, though I feel like I want some direction. I guess part of what I feel right now is not knowing if I want to be tied down. I do know that I don't want to change one eight-hour day for another. I want something that will give me flexibility.

Stan: *Well, maybe working with a volunteer agency or with some kind of part-time agency that's funded by the government would be appealing.*

Ray: *That might work out well.*

Stan: *I think that is a good direction. Again, it's something that you enjoy doing—or maybe something that may require some additional schooling or courses. Likewise, if there's anything I can do to help or give references, I want you to know that I'm available. As you look at your own retirement, Ray, think about those dissatisfactions you've had with your job that you'd like to avoid. The kinds of things you could identify and see as things you really didn't like. Things that have been a particular source of frustration for you.*

Ray: *Oh, I guess as much as anything it's the pressure of doing things that please other people whether the job's done right or wrong—like pleasing the top brass, or in our case, the military, or whoever else. It just has to meet their approval whether I do it right or wrong. I feel like I want to have some control over quality, not just approval.*

Stan: *As much as anything, it sounds like you prefer an unstructured environment where there aren't too many layers of supervision, or at least not a formal structure, necessary to the work being done. Right?*

Ray: *Right.*

Stan: *That's good. That's good. Well, I think these ideas are useful and important. The more realistic you can be in taking inventory of yourself, of your values, then the easier the transition from work to retirement is going to be. I don't think retirement necessarily has to follow the old cliché of closing one door and opening another. I think it can be a continuation of doing things you like to do, if you can identify those things you like and then be realistic about what you may need to do, to support yourself financially and emotionally in order to do them. Any particular obstacles you see in your path of doing this well?*

Ray: *Nope, I guess I'm pretty well free to do whatever I want. I've got no debts, got a home, and can do just about anything I want. So, I don't see too many obstacles. The only obstacle I can see is that I'm not ready to settle down to anything for a while until I decide what I really want to do about these things.*

Stan: *Sometimes an incubation period can help ideas grow. Putting them in cold storage for a while and then coming back and looking at them is a good idea. I would encourage you sometime to take out a piece of paper and write down some of the things you'd like to do—some of the kinds of things you'd like to accomplish with the rest of your life. As much as anything, having goals and having hopes are incentives for us to try to make our lives full and rich. And putting them in writing really brings more clarity to our ideas. In addition to writing down those goals, you should ask yourself, "What do I need to do, what plans of action do I need to take?" Again, be realistic in your inventory and do the kinds of planning you need to. I think you can make retirement something that's very satisfying. Well, Ray, I've enjoyed talking to you. I look forward to some of the other meetings and associations in the next couple of weeks prior to your retirement. I hope you'll feel free to call on me.*

Ray: *I will.*

Stan: *Good.*

Critique

A cartoon in a news magazine depicted two men dressed casually at a social event. The caption had one fellow saying to the other: "Who were you before you retired?" Although humorous, the cartoon represents the concerns many have about retirement. Cyril Sofer has identified the various functions served by work and, thus, the losses which may accompany retirement:

1. Work roles provide economic returns that are a means to other ends.
2. Work provides the individual with opportunities to view himself or herself as contributing to society.
3. Having a work role enables a person to maintain status and self-respect.
4. Work roles structure the passing of time.
5. Work roles provide scope for personal achievement.
6. Work provides assurance for oneself of being able to deal effectively with their environment.[3]

It is natural for a person to be anxious concerning retirement and the changes it inevitably brings. Planning for retirement can reduce such anxiety, but not eliminate it. Helping someone effectively make the transition can produce several benefits, including aiding the individual, the work group, and others who are thinking about retiring.

In this situation, Stan did several things to keep Ray in a problem-focused mode rather than feeling sorry for himself. He did this by not directly responding to Stan's "unanswerable questions" such as, "Will I be needed anywhere anymore?" There is no appropriate answer to such a question.

Instead of reassuring or discounting it, Stan acknowledged the *intent* underlying the question (" . . . retirement can be unsettling") and then asked *probing* questions to find out what was bothering Ray the most. Stan remained in this problem-focused mode until it appeared that all of Ray's concerns had been expressed, and then they jointly began problem-solving. They could realistically plan together using as *criteria* for possible action steps acknowledged areas of concern and types of activities from which Ray derived satisfaction. By following these steps, Stan performed the counseling function well.

---

[3] Cyril Sofer, *Men in Mid-Career: A Study of British Managers and Technical Specialists* (Cambridge: Cambridge University Press, 1970).

Male/Female Issues

I Am Tired Of Being Treated
Like A Second Class Citizen

Situation

Nan had worked 3 years as an internal accounting auditor for a
large multinational company in a major metropolitan area. Only
recently she had relocated in a small college town, accepting employment with the county hospital while planning to attend night classes
and obtain her MBA degree. She enjoyed her work and seemed to be
adjusting well to the local pace and ways of doing things. Thus,
when Steve Fisher, a training specialist with the hospital, interrupted
Nan late one afternoon to discuss her interest in attending a writing
course, he was surprised to find her visibly upset.

Steve: *Something wrong?*
Nan: *Oh, no. It's nothing really.*
Steve: *You seem disturbed about something. I noticed when I
      walked through the door that you were preoccupied, but
      you're not working on anything on your desk.*
Nan: *It's nothing I can't handle.*
Steve: *I'm sure of that. You seem to be able to handle most
      things pretty well. Is there something, though, that you
      just want to talk about?*

Nan: I don't think you'd understand.

Steve: Maybe not. But just talking outloud can sometimes help a situation.

Nan: Oh, I don't know. I've tried to talk to the administrative section heads, but they just don't seem interested in my advice. They don't seem to appreciate my telling them about cost savings or ways to cut some of their expenses that I've discovered. I think that all the males in the hospital are so used to having women who are nurses do their bidding that they don't know how to handle it when a woman tells them how to improve something. I'm tired of being treated differently from the men on the accounting staff. I'm just as good an accountant as anybody else, and I'm simply tired of being treated as a second class citizen.

Steve: It sounds like you have some pretty strong feelings churning around inside of you.

Nan: I do. And I don't know how much longer I can take the condescending attitudes I face every day.

Steve: I'm trying to get a handle on the nature of your feelings. Do you feel like there is hostility directed toward you, or is it that you feel your advice is not taken seriously because you're a woman, or do you feel that you are being stereotyped into a role that doesn't fit you very well?

Nan: Some of each.

Steve: Can you tie it to a specific example?

Nan: Sure can. The staff meeting I attended with the maintenance services group is a good example. Skelly, the manager of the group, was talking with his section supervisors when I walked in. No sooner had he introduced me, then one of them popped off with: "You're not one of those women libbers, are you?" I was so mad.

Steve: What did you say to that?

Nan: Nothing. I just glared. Somebody else came in and the meeting started. But my composure was gone. I really didn't make a very good presentation on the changes I was recommending even though they were well-researched.

Steve: The comment about being a women's libber was so disconcerting that you lost control of the situation. Is that right?

Nan: More or less, although I don't like to think of it in those terms.

Steve: But putting it in those terms helps to put into perspective what you want to do; that is, to be in control of situations such as this so you can demonstrate your competence.

Nan: I've been trying to demonstrate my competence ever since I got here.

Steve: Good. But let's not approach the situation from such a broad perspective. Instead, let's look at what you really want to accomplish when you feel put down by something someone says in staff meetings such as the one you just described.

Nan: What I feel like saying is, "Screw you."

Steve: Okay, let's put that down as an option. What other ways do you see of responding?

Nan: I could say, "What do you want to know for?" or "What's a women's libber?" or something clever like, "Are you a men's libber?" or just something simple like, "Gee, I don't know, what do you think about it all?"

Steve: So if we say these are the options, what responses are they likely to produce?

Nan: Saying something like, "Screw you," is likely to produce a negative response—but I'd sure feel good, even if no one else did. Whether or not the other statements started a meaningful discussion would depend on the tone of voice I used. That's what I'd really like—a discussion. This would give me a chance to say what I'm _for_ and _against_ and avoid being stereotyped. So asking someone else what they think about women who work would probably be the best approach.

Steve: I agree. It would help you keep your feelings more under control while giving you an opportunity to say what you really believe. You'd feel more in charge of yourself and the situation and less like you were reacting to the remarks of others.

Nan: Yes. This has been a good discussion. I'll feel more confidence in handling such situations, now that I have a place to begin.

Critique

Steve's sensitivity to people and their concerns is revealed by the fact that he noticed Nan was upset and initiated a discussion to find out why. Without being demanding, he started with an open-ended question. When Nan reported nothing was wrong, Steve provided a description of her actions that suggested otherwise. By doing so, he was, in essence, saying that he was not asking the equivalent of, "How are you?" with his first question. He was doing more than exchanging pleasantries. Nan's retort was a defense mechanism to try to conceal her hurt. Once the discussion continues, it becomes apparent why Nan was so defensive at this point. She was smarting from experiences where she felt others had not accepted her as competent and capable. Steve responded to her defensive reaction with a compliment and a final invitation to talk when Nan accepted. Persistence paid off.

Being persistent carries its own implicit message when a would-be counselor is not overbearing or demanding. It is not possible or desirable to make people talk. However, by staying in a relationship and not reacting to initial rebuffs, a message of real concern is conveyed. People want to know how serious someone else is in their willingness to discuss problems. The type of ritual displayed earlier in this discussion is natural and characteristic of people who feel independent. Many opportunities for counseling and problem-solving will be missed if managers, trainers, etc. always wait for others to see them. Some people would not feel comfortable inititating a discussion with people they perceive as authority figures. Others might hold back because they would feel in a one down position—in effect, admitting they had a problem they could not handle on their own. Moreover, when a counselor initiates, it immediately establishes a feeling of equality between the two people. Steve's actions provide a role model in how to initiate.

Steve used a question-asking technique called "laundry listing" in getting Nan to identify what was really bothering her. This technique of asking someone if their concern is this or that or something else can reduce generally abstract thoughts or feelings to something specific and manageable. It focuses attention. Such convergence is necessary and useful if it is not premature. Occurring as it did in this discussion, after Nan had an opportunity to unload her feelings of hurt and anger, it focused attention on the cause of her concerns. The nature of the question also suggested the scope of the problem-solving. Instead of dealing with generalized problems of women in organizations, Steve's question showed his interest in helping Nan develop a functional solution to her pragmatic problem.

Steve gave some nondirective responses to Nan's strongly worded statements. He let her talk and avoided being prescriptive when she talked about what was bothering her. He asked her to be specific and asked probing questions, not only so that he would better understand all that Nan felt and believed, but also so that Nan herself would identify her reactions. Steve did, however, become directive when it came to defining the crux of the situation. He offered his observations that what Nan really wanted was to feel in control and not embarrassed or angry when others were sarcastic or failed to accept her as a professional. Steve's observation and insight caused Nan to examine what *she* might do when she felt put down. This definition of the situation avoided simply blaming others and sought instead to deal with *Nan's* problem: her feelings and beliefs.

This reframing is important. A counselor must deal with the person that he or she is with. There is no need to judge who is right and who is wrong. Taking sides is dysfunctional. Instead, a counselor needs to help the person he or she is with develop competence in dealing with situations he or she faces. In this discussion, Steve was able to assist Nan in seeing for herself that angry reactions to put downs may make her feel better in the short run, but are likely to produce negative results in the long run. Nan saw for herself that by being nondefensive she would feel more in control of circumstances and more likely to have others accept her advice as a knowledgeable accountant.

I Don't Want To Work For A Woman!

Situation

Susan Brown is an engineer working in a medium-sized company. She has about five years of experience and is considered a good performer. She has worked on several projects and has always been viewed as a particularly knowledgeable engineer technically. Recently, her supervisor was promoted and a new supervisor, a woman, appointed. Several years ago, Susan met Frank Benson, a personnel representative with the company, at a social. She and Frank have talked from time to time and, consequently, she felt comfortable in going to Frank's office to talk to him about a problem that she had.

Susan: *Mr. Benson, Frank, may I talk to you for a few minutes?*

Frank: *Sure, come on in. What's on your mind?*

Susan: *Well, I don't know quite how to approach this, but it is something I feel strongly about.*

Frank: *Oh? What is it?*

Susan: *Well, you know that recently Mary was made supervisor in our office . . . and, well, I have problems working with her.*

Frank: *Oh?*

Susan: *I don't feel comfortable around her. I just don't feel good about working with her. I don't want to work with her.*

Frank: *I can see you're upset. You seem to be a little anxious in expressing how you feel as well.*

Susan: *Well, I guess, sometimes I feel like as a woman, we ought to stand up for each other, but since she's been in this position there have been more problems than I've experienced in all the time I've been in that job. And I really feel like I need to go somewhere else or do something different. The whole atmosphere of the office is terrible.*

Frank: *Bad, huh? I'd like to understand this better, Susan. Is there something specific that Mary has done or said that makes you feel this way?*

Susan: *I don't know. I think I have a pretty open mind about women's roles; I'm an engineer myself, not exactly something that all women go into, but I feel like she's so concerned about herself. It's the way she comes across, she's on the fast track, she's looking for promotions, she does everything to look good and everything that looks bad she blames on someone else. She wants everything to be done perfectly and has put more pressure on us than any male supervisor I've had.*

Frank: *Hmmm, I see. You feel that this is a function of Mary's being a woman, or of her own personality, or of pressures of the job? I'm not exactly sure.*

Susan: *Well, it seems like she's always trying to please others. She doesn't seem to really care about her work group. Like the other day, she called me and asked if I could come in on the weekend to work and I said sure. I'm willing to work; I've worked hard; I'm willing to work weekends if something needs to be done. I came in and worked all weekend. She came in Monday morning and said she was disappointed because I wasn't finished with what she wanted. And I told her I was waiting for some data that I needed from one of the plants. She said that was no excuse. She said she didn't care, I was to get it done. She doesn't seem to be willing to listen to our side. It's not just me that feels this way. Other people in the office have the same kind of feeling. She jumps all over me or any of the others for not doing what she expects, and then the next day she wants to be our friend, our buddy and confidante. And there's a tension that makes it uncomfortable to even work.*

Frank: *How long has Mary been in the supervisory position? Just a couple of months, isn't it?*

Susan: *Yeah, two months I guess.*

Frank: *Have you ever had a supervisor before who was in his or her first supervisory assignment?*

Susan: *I don't know. I don't think so.*

Frank: *That may have something to do with the relationship. I don't know. I'm not there; she's not my boss. But it's something that maybe is a consideration. Do you feel that, technically, Mary knows her job?*

Susan: *Oh, I think that she's a good engineer. She's done well. I'm not saying that she hasn't. Personally, I think she shouldn't have been put in as supervisor. I don't think she's ready to be a supervisor, but because she's a woman, I think she's gotten preferential treatment. I know there are quotas to fill, but those of us below her are losing out because the company has to have a woman supervisor. Someday I'd like to be a supervisor, but I don't want to be selected because I'm a woman but because I'm skilled and ready to be one. Other women may lose their chance if Mary doesn't do well.*

Frank: You don't think she deserves the job?

Susan: I don't think she's ready for the job. She may deserve the job down the road a little way, but I don't think she's really ready for the kinds of things that a supervisor needs to be ready for. Obviously, a supervisor is going to take some blame for things that happen, but not her. A supervisor has to make some decisions; I feel like a supervisor needs to be concerned about the people she works with, and she doesn't watch out for us. If there is trouble with something, she doesn't go to bat for us. As engineers we are coming up with new ideas. It's not like we just sit and write down answers to problems. We're coming up with new ideas, and she won't support us in our promotions or initiations. We come up with an idea and take it to her. If there's any kind of negative feedback against that idea she throws it out. As a supervisor she should give us a little more support in the jobs we're doing. Also, if something goes wrong, it's all of us as a group that has the problem, not us against her. She wants everything to be rosy red, and if it's not, we're the bad guys.

Frank: Sounds like you have two concerns. One is that she's really not ready and capable to be supervisor, and, in fact, she may not deserve the supervisory position. And the other is a concern about recognizing the effort people put forward and looking at the contribution that people make, especially by working long hours or working overtime.

Susan: But we do work hard, and we do a good job. That's what we get paid for and we want to do a good job.

Frank: Have you talked with her about any of your concerns?

Susan: No.

Frank: How do you think she would react?

Susan: Well, I don't feel real good about talking to her about them.

Frank: Do you think that she would react negatively? Or don't you have a good enough relationship to talk about it?

Susan: Both—Negative reaction and poor relationship. She's not willing to break down the barriers. She comes on as wanting to be our friend, but she puts up a barrier there.

I can understand that to some extent, but she isn't willing to let her hair down a bit.

Frank: *I guess I understand the nature of some of your concerns, Susan. I think the concerns are legitimate, that they are valid. I see some of the same concerns expressed by employees whenever a brand new supervisor is put into a supervisory position. I think the transition is a little bit difficult, it's something that's not always easy to make, and as much as anything it's important to identify now how to make the situation better. What kinds of things may be possible to improve on the situation. As you look at it with that kind of focus, what options do you think you have for dealing with the current situation?*

Susan: *Well, I could always work on being transferred.*

Frank: *That's certainly an option. What other kinds of options do you think are possible for dealing with the situation?*

Susan: *I don't know. I guess we could all go talk to her. I don't know whether anybody else would agree to do that, though.*

Frank: *What else?*

Susan: *I guess we could go above her head.*

Frank: *Okay, you could bypass her, talk to her supervisor. Anything else?*

Susan: *Well, I don't know, is there anything else?*

Frank: *I guess as you think about those options for dealing with the situation, what do you feel good about?*

Susan: *I think the easiest thing would be a transfer.*

Frank: *I think a transfer would be easy, and, if you think the situation is really unworkable, that may be the best thing to do. But a transfer is essentially withdrawing from the situation. It seems to me that without speaking to Mary about what bothers you, you aren't really giving it a chance to work.*

Susan: *OK. So, what do you think I ought to do?*

Frank: *I think you owe it to yourself to try to understand why things are the way they are and see if they can be worked out. You may have the roles reversed someday. If you decide to try to work it out, express your concerns, identify some goals and go through some kind of planning process to work on those goals. Assuming you stay in the relationship, what kinds of things in terms of goals would you want to work on?*

Susan: *I guess the first thing is that I don't want my performance to be hampered by her. I want to do the best job that I can.*

Frank: *Okay. What about in terms of your working relationship with Mary?*

Susan: *Truthfully, what I'd like to do is let her sink or swim on her own merits; and let me do my job and ignore her. I don't want to bend over backwards just to please her. If I don't do what I think is right, I'll feel a little dishonest. I'll feel like I'm doing the same kind of thing that I see her doing—pleasing the boss just to be an apple polisher.*

Frank: *If you did that, would you see yourself as just giving in?*

Susan: *I don't know. I was hired to do a job, not to worry about a relationship with her. I guess I wouldn't really be giving in. I'm still concerned about the conflict between us that exists. I guess what I need to do is sit down and think about things that seem to stimulate the conflicts, that, is, things that make it worse and then try to eliminate those kinds of things. For instance, if I let her know ahead of time that an unmeetable deadline is coming up, maybe she won't think I haven't done my part. This may cause a conflict, but at least it keeps her informed of what we're doing.*

Frank: *That's a good method, a good technique. In a sense it sets up some mutual expectations, some guidelines which you can work within and identifies potential conflict areas before they arise. Every manager, every supervisor has his or her own style, his or her own preference for doing things, and it doesn't necessarily mean giving in to accommodate those ways of doing things. It's like the difference between principles and preferences in terms of giving in or giving up, versus working cooperatively. As you look at your own motives behind your concerns, (concerns which we discussed earlier about Mary getting preferential treatment and really not being prepared to be*

*a supervisor, maybe not having enough experience or
being the most worthy, and about looking good for the
boss and other people in management), what bothers you
the most about working with Mary?*

Susan: *Well, I feel like I'm a good performer. I do my job well.
In the past I've had bosses who have liked my work, and
all of a sudden I have a boss whose only feedback is
negative. It makes me feel inadequate and I'm sure that's
part of my motives. I don't feel as good about the job
I'm doing because she doesn't seem to appreciate my
work. And yet I don't think I'm doing any worse than I
ever have.*

Frank: *Do you feel resentful?*

Susan: *Sure, because I'm working as hard or harder to try and
please her, and I never get any positive feedback. When
things go right, then she's the heroine.*

Frank: *What problems do you anticipate if you were to mention
something like this to Mary, "Gee, I feel like I don't get
enough feedback when I do things right (recognition) nor
do I always know in advance how to do something that
would fit your personal style."*

Susan: *I don't know. I feel like she's not quite sure of herself in
her job either, so she's on the defensive probably as much
as I am.*

Frank: *So her lack of confidence may be part of the reason she's
putting on the pressure and trying to look good.
Confidence is a function of competence. People who feel
capable, who feel secure in their job and in work relationships, tend to be more confident. Again, one of the things
that may help her is for you (or somebody) to take the
risk and say, "Here's how I feel as a subordinate. Here
are some of the things I'd like to do." That way it
doesn't come across as complaining. Tell her the things
you expect from her and your job, such as more feedback,
more recognition when you do something well, more
direction if she sees you going into an area on a crooked
path.*

Susan: *It would probably help a lot to talk to her about those things,
so that she would better understand me and vice versa.*

Frank: Do you foresee any problems in doing that?

Susan: Sure. I don't want to confront her.

Frank: What kind of things do you think you could do so it wouldn't come across as adversarial?

Susan: I guess if I went in and said, "Gee I really like my job, I want to do a good job. I'd like to know the kinds of things you expect of me that would help me do my job better."

Frank: If you were in her position and somebody came to you and expressed those concerns, how do you think you'd react?

Susan: Somebody asking me what they need to do? I'd feel good about that.

Frank: Would Mary react in the same way? Will she see your desire to do well and see your job concerns not as criticism but as useful information?

Susan: She probably will. I would.

Frank: One thing it's important to recognize is that you have noticed things she does well. You recognize some of the pressures on her. The fact that she is in a new supervisory position, she is somewhat insecure, wants to look good, wants to justify the fact that she received a promotion as early as she did. By going to her and letting her know that you are very interested in doing a good job and that you'd like to establish a good working relationship is likely to be very positive.

Susan: I think it will work.

Critique

The two most frequently cited generalizations about women managers are their demanding nature at times and their unwillingness to reach out and help other females. If women do tend to be less flexible and demand more from their subordinates, it is probably the result of organizational pressures they may only faintly recognize and not have skills to deal with. How women respond to these pressures may vary, but there is likely to be a common pattern that can be observed. If they are ambitious and capable enough to be selected as supervisors, they are likely to be aware that they are being carefully observed and closely monitored. They may overcompensate by trying too hard, expecting perfection, and making sure no man will accuse them of being soft with the women in a work group.

These dynamics can be expected when there is a relatively small number of women in an organization. They will be visible and others may gloss over their own weaknessess by accusing women who advance as being undeserving. Making changes under such circumstances requires at least a two-pronged approach.

First, the women supervisors must understand these organizational dynamics and deal with them effectively. Counseling a woman manager regarding these issues is explored in two vignettes in this section entitled "Sometimes I Feel Like Their Token" which deals with peer relationships, and "I Don't Think They Like Working For A Woman" which explores subordinate relationships and women bosses.

Besides equipping women managers with effective organizational skills, peers and subordinates can also help by understanding how these organizational processes combine to put pressure on a female manager. They can better act as a resource to their boss, defuse tense situations, and develop better on-the-job cooperation.

While counseling, Frank listened a long time to the pent-up emotions Susan had. Once Susan had unloaded all of them, they were better able to consider why a problem existed. Frank never accepted Susan's definition of the problem as "Mary is a poor supervisor," nor did he attempt to defend or apologize for Mary. Instead, he reoriented Susan's thinking by encouraging her to consider how *any* new supervisor might feel in his or her first assignment. Several options were discussed and considered with Frank helping Susan see that the situation may someday be reversed. She should see this as a chance to solve a problem she may encounter when she is a supervisor.

Frank effectively helped Susan see that she was somewhat envious of Mary and that her resentment contributed to a poor working relationship. By being instructed on how to present her work-related concerns to Mary, some of Susan's personal feelings diminished, and she acquired the means for effectively dealing with the situation at hand.

Sometimes I Feel Like Their Token

Situation

Cheryl is a competent mid-level manager. She has almost fifteen years of service with the company and is highly respected and regarded. She is, however, one of a kind. There are few if any real women peers in the organization; consequently, she is often asked to participate in external social events and represent the company's point of view. Stan Taylor is a personnel representative whom Cheryl has known for some time. Stan is well aware of Cheryl's potential in the organization and has discussed company policies with her on several occasions. Thus, it came as no surprise when Stan saw Cheryl in his doorway, and she asked if he had a few minutes.

Cheryl: *Stan, I'd like to talk to you if I could.*

Stan: *Sure, be happy to do whatever I can, Cheryl. Come in and close the door.*

Cheryl: *Thanks. I don't know if I can take it anymore. I just don't know if I can take it.*

Stan: *Take what, Cheryl?*

Cheryl: *I don't know, It just has gotten to me today. At times I just feel like their token. I feel like I'm not respected for who I am or for what I can do because I'm a woman.*

Stan: *I can see that you are upset about something, but I'm not sure exactly what has triggered it. Did something specific happen?*

Cheryl: *No, it's nothing in particular. It's just, well, today a newspaper reporter called. The president had given him my name. He wanted to interview somebody about corporate life, and I've been singled out. It just seems that I'm put on a pedestal so many times. It just really gripes me.*

Stan: *I see.*

Cheryl: *It's not just representing the company at outside events. I don't mind that. It's lots of other ways as well that I'm singled out. Generally, singled out and put down. Like at the interdepartmental financial analysis meeting that we had last week. When I came into the room, several of the other men were making a joke about something, and then suddenly became quiet when I entered the room. Then during the meeting, I made several comments, and it didn't seem that anyone was really listening to me. It didn't bother me just that my ideas were not being respected, but other people brought up almost the same thing later on in the meeting and everyone seemed to think their ideas were valid and necessary to implement. They were almost the same things I had said earlier, but no one even noticed that I had said them. All during the meeting the new fellow in the treasury department kept giving me the eye. When we broke for coffee, he came up and looked me over, squeezing my arm, and giving me excessive compliments. I don't like that, and I don't know what to do about it. But that's just another example of peers recognizing me as a token. My boss, too, seems to always be careful about giving me feedback. He doesn't really lay it on the line for me. When I've made a mistake, he tries to cover up to minimize it rather than being straightforward, telling me what I've done wrong and how I can improve. I'm not sure how many times he may have corrected something that I had done, simply because I didn't know any better, and he didn't take the time to tell me what I had done or why. I don't want to be protected, I want to be given experience, and I want to take my own lumps when I deserve them.*

Stan: *I see. I think it is important for you to feel like you are respected for what you do and not who you are. Would you like to talk with me about how you seem to relate to other people, using me as an example?*

Cheryl: *Yes. I would like to do that.*

Stan: *Let me say one thing that I've noticed that has an impact on me, and I expect has an impact on other people as well. I notice that you always dress very stylishly and that you are an attractive woman. I'm sure other people notice that as well.*

Cheryl: *Does that mean if I dress in sackcloth and ashes, that it would help my business rapport?*

Stan: *(Laughingly) No, I'm not saying you need to go to that extreme, but I am aware, because you are attractive, because you dress stylishly, that it's harder for me not to be influenced by your appearance.*

Cheryl: *Oh, I see.*

Stan: *You say that like you're thinking, "He's just like all the rest."*

Cheryl: *Well, if I didn't know you better, I probably would say that. I must confess, the thought did cross my mind.*

Stan: *What I'm trying to point out is the impact that you have on me and, my hunch is, it has a similar impact on other people. They just can't help but notice. Your femininity can be an asset or a liability, just as a Harvard MBA can be an asset or liability, depending on what it is used for and how it is presented. Someone can flaunt educational certificates to try to manipulate people and it will eventually produce resentment. Too much femininity can do the same thing, it's worse than none at all. Being attractive and dressing stylishly may not be helpful. It doesn't have to hurt you, but you do need to positively deal with that aspect of yourself.*

Cheryl: *And how do I do that, Stan?*

Stan: *I'm not exactly sure that I know, Cheryl, but tell me what you did when the fellow at the meeting who was giving you the eye came up and talked to you at the coffee break.*

Cheryl: *Well, I was cordial and had a pleasant conversation with him. I tried not to be too brusque and that was that.*

Stan: *And how do you think other people at the meeting who may have also noticed he was giving you the eye thought about you?*

Cheryl: *Oh, I see what you are saying. If I saw him giving me the eye, others may have noticed the same thing and concluded that I was just another hungry woman looking for a man.*

Stan: *You said that a little more dramatically than I would have, but that's the idea. It's not just that your intentions were good, but other people are bound to have noticed as well and may have seen your friendliness as a come-on. That is not the way to be taken seriously in business meetings.*

Cheryl: *That's for sure. I've seen women who do flirt at a meeting, and it leaves a bad taste in my mouth because I am serious about my job.*

Stan: *I think it's important for you to realize it's not just what you intend, but also what other people may be interpreting that counts. It affects your own credibility.*

Cheryl: *It's just that I try so hard to be professional, to do the kinds of things that will help me be accepted and included and not looked upon as an outsider.*

Stan: *What kind of effect do you think your striving to be included has on others?*

Cheryl: *Oh, I don't know. I do try and be friendly, to show interest, to be one of the boys, if you will.*

Stan: *Your friendliness and desire to be one of the boys may likewise reinforce the feeling among other people that you are not to be taken seriously. One of the things that I've seen is the people who try too hard somehow are seen as not having strength to pursue their own convictions. I've observed that people who are accepted and included are those who are clear about who they are and what they want, rather than simply trying to please others. You might concentrate on being an individual.*

Cheryl: *I think that's a good suggestion. One of the things that I've thought to myself is that I try too hard to please other people and that trying too hard may not be as helpful as I think it is.*

Stan: *Recognizing that some of the things you do may not be interpreted in the same way as you intended is an important realization. How can you improve your ability to be perceived as friendly yet professional at that same business meeting for instance?*

Cheryl: *Well, I could make certain I talked to everyone at the break.*

Stan: *Good. What else?*

Cheryl: *I could talk about general business matters rather than social events.*

Stan: *Uh huh.*

Cheryl: *I could be straightforward with someone if I feel that someone is not fully considering my ideas during a meeting and make them back up disagreement with my ideas with data rather than opinions.*

Stan: *Being straightforward would help people see that you intend to be taken seriously. It is important to disagree at times if for no other reason than to keep others honest.*

Cheryl: *Do you think my situation is unique, Stan, or do other women have the same problem?*

Stan: *Every situation has unique characteristics. There are circumstances that involve you that are unique. I think that some of the concerns you express about acceptance and inclusion face not only women but also new campus hires, minorities, and others. You've described some positive ways of dealing with your situation that may be helpful to others as well.*

Cheryl: *I think that's right. Anyone who is different is tested to see if he or she intends to be a contributing team member or not. I've gotten some good ideas from this conversation. I want to think about it some more, but I think I know now what I need to do.*

Critique

Tokenism is partially a product of the number of women in professional, technical, or production positions in an organization. It is also a product of the myth and stereotypes people carry around with them about other people. Likewise, it is important to realize that stereotypes have some *substance*, otherwise they would not be believed. While it is important to appreciate this fact, it must be realized that stereotypes may fit *some* members of a group, but certainly not *all* members and probably not *most* members. In fact, most stereotypes result from a *single* experience, and the conclusions reached from such an experience may not be generalities at all. Recognizing this is the first step toward changing a stereotype.

Many men and women hold stereotypical views of themselves. There is an old saying, "Ask a woman where she's going, and she'll tell you where she's been." Many women have been conditioned to explain and defend rather than be direct and straightforward. Sharon Kirkham, a management consultant, in a personal interview effectively illustrated this common tendency.

> If you tell a woman, "That's a pretty dress," she will tell you where she bought it, how much she paid for it, and tell you how long she has had it. She will do what she can to defend herself against the compliment. Men in corporations who are successful never speak in this defensive way. There's a big difference between the positive, "Here's what I think . . . " or, "In my opinion . . . " and the negative, "I don't know if you'll agree with me or not, but . . . " and, "You may not look at this the same way, but I think . . . "[1]

Stan effectively counseled Cheryl because he pointed out to her the *impact* her actions had on him. In this way, he *validated* what people in other situations may have thought or felt. He was able to deal *specifically* rather than abstractly with Cheryl because he was *aware* of the feelings she evoked in him. Importantly, as Stan counseled with Cheryl, he let her make her own *decisions* but he tried to help her follow through on those decisions by making some *commitments* to herself and to him.

Just Because I Work In The Plant, They Think I'm Here For Something Else Besides The Job

Situation

Jackie Smyth had been working in the plant as a maintenance mechanic for six months when Ann Franklin, a personnel specialist, decided to visit with her. Ann had conducted an orientation session which Jackie attended when she first began work at the plant. Ann was interested in seeing how she was adjusting to her new work environment and stopped by during Jackie's afternoon break.

[1] Cited in Alice Sargent, *Beyond Sex Roles* (Minnesota: West, 1977).

Ann: Hey, Jackie, I was in the area and thought I'd drop by
          to see how things are going. Ann Franklin from
          personnel.
Jackie: Oh, hello. We met at the orientation session, right?
Ann: Right, so how's the new job?
Jackie: Fine. Just fine. No real problems.
Ann: How are the folks in your work group?
Jackie: Oh, they're okay.
Ann: Do they seem to have any concerns about working with a
          woman?
Jackie: Uh, no, not really. At least not anything too major, I
          guess.
Ann: Oh?
Jackie: Well, there is something, Ann, but I don't think anyone
          can do anything about it.
Ann: What's that?
Jackie: Well, it seems that a lot of the guys think I'm here for
          something else besides the job.
Ann: Like what?
Jackie: Well, they either pinch my rump and wink at me or else
          they gripe about women's libbers taking over the world.
          What bothers me the most is that no one takes me
          seriously. I'm either ignored or given too much attention.
          I don't want to date 'em or antagonize 'em. I just want
          to do my job. The other day I told off one guy who
          grabbed me. Instead of backing off, I think he's taking
          me as a challenge because he gave me the eye again
          today.
Ann: Feeling upset about it, huh?
Jackie: Yeah, I'm about ready to really let the guy have it!
Ann: I know that when I'm upset I really feel like blowing my
          lid. Usually, though, it doesn't really help things. It just
          makes me feel better for a few minutes.
Jackie: What do you suggest I do, then? Just ignore him? That
          won't help.
Ann: I don't think ignoring the situation is the answer. But I
          do think it is important to consider what you really want
          to accomplish first, and then decide what you're going to
          do.

Jackie: *I want the guy to leave me alone.*

Ann: *You also said you want others to take you seriously.*

Jackie: *That's right. So how do I do it?*

Ann: *Well, let's see. Your purpose is to be respected, to let the guys know that you are not on some kind of campaign, and that you're not available to every Tom, Dick and Harry. Is that accurate?*

Jackie: *Yes.*

Ann: *So what are your options besides reading this guy, who is an immediate problem, the riot act? Mmmm.*

Jackie: *I guess I could take him aside and tell him about it one-on-one. Or I could tell my boss and let him handle it, although that would be like being a tattletale.*

Ann: *You think talking to him one-to-one would help?*

Jackie: *Maybe.*

Ann: *I think it's a low risk, possible high payoff option. He doesn't get embarrassed and you show him and others that you can handle yourself. When you talk to him, tell him how you feel about the situation, why it bothers you, and offer him a way out so that he doesn't feel like he's losing face with his friends. Maybe see if you can join his gang at work for lunch and get their advice on how they handle some work-related problem. That'll give you a chance to show him and others that you are interested in your job.*

Jackie: *That sounds like a great idea.*

Ann: *Oh, and why don't you wait until tomorrow in case anyone's seen us talk. They might be thinking the worse—that you're complaining—and if they see nothing directly come of this conversation today, it will help you be accepted even more tomorrow.*

Jackie: *Good. Thanks.*

Critique

Handling sexual advances in either a plant or an office situation is difficult at best. If it is the boss who is making advances, it can be even more difficult. By responding, a woman may develop a reputation that can never be lived down. A rebuff, on the other hand, can put a strain on a working relationship that can seldom be effectively overcome. Although such a dilemma may not be as intense when a woman must deal with the come-ons of a peer, the situations differ more by degree than kind.

Margaret Mead, the celebrated anthropologist, maintains that taboos against sexual relations between people whose jobs require them to work closely with others should be developed to match the taboos in most societies against incest. She maintains that the social fabric of the workplace, like the home, depends on a deep abiding trust in one another.[2] Workplace sex, like incest, is based on exploitation rather than a desire for real intimacy. Trust, consequently, is destroyed.

A simple outline, which was used in this case, can be a useful guide in dealing with sex at the workplace. Firstly, a counselor should discover how the other person feels about the situation and let her (or him) "blow off steam." By asking questions which require *factual* answers (what happened, when it occurred, etc.) the person can be calmed down and will come to consider available options more easily. Then, the counselor should get the person to identify to a purpose or objective for improving things. "If the situation were really better, what would it be like?" "How would you like things to be different than they are now?" Thirdly, the counselor can discuss the likely reactions from others which various options would produce. "If you did that would it promote resentment? More kidding? Game playing? Cooperation?" Lastly, evaluating the risks of a particular course of action may provide some hints on how to effectively implement it. This basic outline was followed by Ann in this discussion with Jackie.

I Don't Think They Like Working For A Woman

Situation

Kevin and Vickie are good friends who have worked together on past projects although they have not done so recently. Vickie was

[2] Margaret Mead, "What We Can Do Now for Our Children's Future," *Redbook*, (May, 1979), p. 54.

promoted to her first supervisory position about four months ago.
Kevin, a personnel specialist, has decided to look her up.

Kevin: I was in the area, Vickie, and I thought I would stop by.
How are things going?

Vickie: Oh, hello, Kevin. Fine. Things are just fine.

Kevin: Good. Say, I really enjoyed your participation in the
supervisory training program we had two weeks ago. You
really seem to take your supervisory role seriously.

Vickie: I think a lot about how I can improve. I am interested in
being a good supervisor. Sometimes I wonder if the fact
that I'm a woman makes my supervisory style different
than it otherwise would be.

Kevin: Are there any particular problems you are facing as a
woman supervisor?

Vickie: Yes. I really don't think people around here like working
for a woman.

Kevin: Oh?

Vickie: Yes, it's true. I know you probably think I'm being
overly sensitive, and maybe I am, but I just don't think
either the men or the women in this group have gotten
used to the idea of a woman supervisor.

Kevin: Ummm.

Vickie: It's nothing I can't handle, of course. It is just different.
It's just an additional challenge. It's like . . . uh . . .
Kevin, I've got a problem. I really need someone to talk to.

Kevin: About what?

Vickie: I think several people in my group resent me. I felt that
it was important to establish myself early when I came
into this job. My old boss told me to assert myself, don't
let people push me around, let them know that I was the
boss and that I was going to run the show. I wanted to
have people share their ideas and participate in some
management decisions, but I didn't want to be a puppet
for somebody else.

Kevin: I see.

Vickie: So, I made some changes that I believed would improve
the effectiveness of the group. I changed some
assignments and set up review procedures to streamline

things. So far it hasn't helped. Now, I don't know exactly what to do about it.

Kevin: *You came on tough and assertive, but it isn't working out as well you had planned?*

Vickie: *That's right. Is this to be expected? Should I just hang in there a little longer and hope things work out?*

Kevin: *Waiting can help sometimes. Sometimes it does take a little while for changes to be fully accepted. There may be a period of anxiety before they fully take hold.*

Vickie: *So you're saying that I just need to be patient?*

Kevin: *Yes and no.*

Vickie: *(Laughing) You sound like a politician.*

Kevin: *I don't mean to. I think you do need to be patient and not expect too much too soon. But I also think you need to decide for yourself what kind of supervisory style this situation calls for.*

Vickie: *What do you mean?*

Kevin: *Well, it seems to me that you've encountered a dilemma that characterizes a lot of situations when people assume supervisory positions. They don't want to be meek and mild for fear that others will run over them, but being tough can alienate others too. There are negative consequences that result from being too tough or too meek.*

Vickie: *Do you think that's what happened? I've alienated my subordinates?*

Kevin: *I don't know. You are in a better position to evaluate that than I am. But it does seem that you've made some decisions that affect everyone in the work group and consulted no one before announcing your changes.*

Vickie: *I can see how they could be interpreted as arbitrary and inflexible even though that was not my intent.*

Kevin: *So what should you do? How do you think you should manage this work group?*

Vickie: *I want to be in charge, but I also want people to feel that they have some input regarding how things are done. Several of the people in this work group have some good experience, while others are very inexperienced. I want to use my subordinates' ideas and get their input in deciding how to implement decisions but avoid putting them in decision-making roles when they lack information or have no stake in the outcome. I want to manage by* <u>*consent.*</u> *This allows others to participate where their ideas can do the most good and be the least frustrating. What do you think of that concept?*

Kevin: *It sounds like something you've thought about before.*

Vickie: *That's right, I have. I know it will work.*

Kevin: *I think the key to your own success is in helping others see that it is in their self-interest to help you. Then give them opportunities to do so. Help others see the benefits of viewing you as competent and capable. You can still be firm and run your own show.*

Vickie: *I know that. Perhaps I've taken the advice of others to be tough too literally. I can be firm and still get the ideas of others. I can make my own decisions but still get my group's input and help in implementing changes so that the results will be beneficial.*

Kevin: *You said something else that I've wondered about.*

Vickie: *What's that?*

Kevin: *You said you think some people in your group resent you.*

Vickie: *I think they do. Not me personally, but they don't like a woman boss. They aren't used to taking directions from a woman.*

Kevin: *How have you taken that into consideration in working with them?*

Vickie: *I haven't taken it into consideration at all. I'm not going to grovel for them! That's what they want me to do.*

Kevin: *Grovel?*

Vickie: *Maybe not grovel, but I want people to meet me on my terms. If they don't like working for me, that's their problem.*

Kevin: *Does it affect the performance of the work group?*

Vickie: *I'm sure it does.*

Kevin: *Then it's your problem, too. You supervise everyone in your work group.*

Vickie: *So what should I do about it?*

Kevin: *I don't know, you're the boss.*

Vickie: Are you playing games with me, Kevin?

Kevin: No, I honestly think you know your people better than I do and know what would improve the overall situation even though it may mean some personal barriers would have to be broken through first.

Vickie: You're right about the barriers . . . on my part, too. I guess I could go talk to a couple of the older men and make an appeal to them to try to get along.

Kevin: Is your objective as a manager to help people get along or meet performance standards?

Vickie: In this business, you can't do the work without getting along.

Kevin: But getting along may be the result of doing the work well rather than vice versa.

Vickie: I see. If I were to help some of my people get their work done easier, that would help overall cooperation and probably have them feel better about me. I could do that especially by running interference between my people and other work groups. That's something that I've seen as needed. Now I realize just how much it is needed. Oh oh, I've got to run to a meeting.

Critique

Some of the dilemmas faced by women managers are illustrated in this dialogue. They include:

- how to be assertive without being domineering;
- how to compete with men without being a threat;
- how to use femininity as an asset rather than a liability;
- how to adapt to a managerial world without being absorbed by it;
- how to be professional without imitating others; and
- how to develop cooperation among subordinates who may feel uncomfortable working for a woman.

The essence of the counseling approach used by Kevin is to show Vickie that her problem is aggravated not because she is a woman but is based on her managerial style. Vickie realized that she would not want to be supervised the way she was currently supervising her work group and related the kinds of reactions she would have if her role was reversed. This *role reversal* caused her to describe how she liked to be supervised and provided a framework for her to describe how she really wanted to lead her group.

With this behind them, Kevin and Vickie were able to explore the concern Vickie had initially expressed regarding how others felt about working for a woman. Initially, she was uncompromising in her expectation that subordinates should adapt to her style. Eventually, she was able to see an alternative to a "confession" in developing a better rapport with her subordinates and quickly saw the merits of such a plan.

Unit 4

EEO Problems

The Company's Gone Overboard
On This EEO Thing

Situation

Walt has 25 years of experience with the company and is considered a loyal employee by management. He works hard as a Field Superintendent to meet company goals and still be responsive to employee concerns. His knowledge of company operations and reputation of interest in those who work for him is widely known.

Thus, it came as something of a surprise to Bill Drews, his boss, when Walt came into his office, visibly upset, and announced:

Walt: *The company's gone overboard on this EEO thing.*
Bill: *Oh, what do you mean, Walt? Come in and tell me about it.*
Walt: *There's nothing to tell. You know as well as I do that we're hiring people who have no business working as Maintenance Specialists. People who've never done this kind of work before and who can't keep up with the pace of our schedule for more than a couple of weeks without being absent for two or three extra days a month. But I guess there's nothing you can do about it either. All I can do is complain.*

Bill: *Complaining isn't all bad. But I'm not sure I understand the nature of your concern. Are you saying absenteeism is a problem that you're having a difficult time dealing with or are you saying that we're having a problem hiring qualified people?*

Walt: *Some of each. But what I'm really upset about is this letter from personnel that says we're supposed to fill some of our vacancies this year with women. Now tell me, what business does a woman have doing a dirty job like this that involves hard physical labor? You wouldn't want your wife or your daughter doing work like this would you?*

Bill: *Being a Maintenance Specialist is dirty and demanding. More importantly than what I'd want for the women in my family is what they want for themselves. A lot of women are seeing jobs like a Maintenance Specialist as well paying with promotional opportunities readily available.*

Walt: *Sure, the pay is good. But can they earn their fair share? Can they do this kind of work day after day? And for how long? A couple of years maybe? And what about all the men who are out of work? They have families to take care of. I personally know a guy who lost his job with another company in a cutback because he didn't fill an EEO quota.*

Bill: *Are you concerned that could happen here?*

Walt: *Oh, not really. But it just doesn't seem fair that we should have to hire a bunch of women who are just not as well suited for this type of work as men. That's what really bothers me.*

Bill: *I can see that it is a concern to you. And I think that it's a valid concern if we say we're out to hire people who can't do the job. But maybe, Bill, we don't know if some women can't do this kind of work. Sure, not all women could, but not all men could either. Some men wouldn't make it a week. Perhaps we've assumed that because no woman has ever been a Maintenance Specialist that no woman could be one.*

Walt: *I'm not saying one or two couldn't do this kind of work. But <u>should</u> they be doing it?*

Bill: Who's in the best position to decide? Is it fair to
          arbitrarily say "women shouldn't do this kind of work?"
          Why not let let them decide if they want to, and we will
          decide if they are qualified?

Walt: Are you saying that we're going to hire women who are
          unqualified just to meet a quota?

Bill: We are not going to hire anyone who's unqualified, male or
          female. But we are probably going to be hiring some
          people who are inexperienced and who will need the time
          and assistance of their bosses. Because few companies have
          had women Maintenance Specialists, the women we're
          likely to hire are going to need a lot of help. Everybody
          has to start somewhere. How do you feel about spending
          some extra time with new hires who are women?

Walt: I've always been one to help someone new learn the ropes.
          It may be difficult to work on a one-to-one basis with a
          woman, though. I've never done it before.

Bill: What problems do you anticipate encountering in effective-
          ly teaching a woman a Maintenance Specialist's job?

Walt: It's difficult to say exactly. I'm sure it would vary
          depending on the woman. But generally, I think I'd find it
          difficult to let her do some of the really heavy work even
          though she would need to do it if she really wanted to
          learn the job.

Bill: I agree. You may feel that you'd like to protect her in
          various ways that in the long run would be detrimental to
          her. What other concerns do you have about working with
          a woman?

Walt: I'd worry that the men would think I was showing
          favoritism to her because she was a woman, especially if I
          was spending a lot of time helping her learn the job.

Bill: Any others?

Walt: If she was good looking, I might worry about keeping my
          mind on my work or if other employees thought that was
          the reason I was being so helpful to her.

Bill: Anything else?

Walt: No, that's mainly it.

Bill: So your primary concerns are (1) that you might protect a
          woman from doing the hard jobs and thereby prevent her

from learning how to do them, (2) be seen as showing favoritism, and (3) be suspected of having intentions other than job training when you spend time with her.

Walt: *That's right. Now what do I do about it?*

Bill: *Good question. What available options do you see that might deal with one or more of these concerns? Let's list any reasonable options that you see without editing. Let's brainstorm what some practical alternates may be and then go back and refine them and examine the outcomes each is likely to produce.*

Walt: *Okay. You got any ideas?*

Bill: *Yeah, I've got some, but I want your ideas too.*

Walt: *Sure, but give me what you've got since you've thought about it.*

Bill: *Okay. Here's one. Why not ask an experienced Maintenance Specialist to work with each new woman employee?*

Walt: *Would that be fair to . . .*

Bill: *Let's get several ideas out before we start evaluating. It'll help us to keep on track, and come up with more ideas.*

Walt: *All right, what else?*

Bill: *Well, I don't have all the answers. What do you think?*

Walt: *(pause) Why can't I just have the employee come to me? I've always had an open door policy.*

Bill: *Okay, that's an option. What else?*

Walt: *That's all I can think of. Let's evaluate.*

Bill: *Okay. What about having some of the other Maintenance Specialists help train the new employee?*

Walt: *I don't like that too much. It won't work for everyone.*

Bill: *Will it work for some?*

Walt: *Yeah, I guess so. I'll try it if I need to. Yeah, I'll look into it and use it if I think it's appropriate. What about the open door policy?*

Bill: *Open door policies are fine except some employees don't feel comfortable in approaching their bosses. They don't want to bother them or confess that they don't know how to do something.*

Walt: *So what if I had them come and see me every once in a while?*

Bill: *I think that would work if there was a regularly scheduled time to do it, say every two months. That way both you and the employee would see it not only as appropriate to discuss how well the employee's learning on the job, but also see it as a kind of requirement. It establishes joint responsibility for learning and discussion on how to perform the work.*

Walt: *Yeah, I can buy that. That makes sense to me.*

Bill: *Good. Anything else?*

Walt: *No, that's it. I really appreciate your time. It's helped a lot.*

Critique

Walt's concern about the company going overboard on Equal Employment Opportunity programs is essentially a concern about fairness. Alleged reverse discrimination cases originated by Bakke and Webber that reached the Supreme Court were initiated because of "felt injustices" which purportedly represent the feelings of many other white males in the country today. As women move into wage jobs previously held by males, complaints about unfair treatment are likely to reach many supervisors and managers.

In this situation, Bill employs a strategy that not only defuses Walt's anger and resentment but also engages Walt in considering how he as a supervisor could provide the necessary help that a woman employee would need to do well on the job. Bill began by listening to and clarifying the nature of Walt's concern. He found out that part of what Walt felt was a mild threat to the job security of current male employees. After reassuring him, Bill tried to establish a basis for hiring women into previously held all-male maintenance specialist positions. Importantly, Bill did not try to *convince* Walt that women should be hired into these jobs, but rather that they should not be automatically dismissed from consideration for such positions. This is a subtle but valuable distinction. Many men, like Bill, have strong convictions about the type of work that should be reserved for males. Attempting to change their beliefs without reference to the performance of specific women in similar work is likely to result in a philosophic argument that produces little results.

After gaining Walt's acceptance of the idea that no one should automatically be excluded from maintenance specialist jobs, Bill involves Walt in problem-solving. He asks Walt what he would do if a woman was working for him. He gets all of Walt's concerns out in the open, summarizes them, and develops some options for dealing with these concerns. Consequently, Walt will leave Bill's office not only with some satisfaction that the company isn't going overboard on EEO, but instead is merely giving women a chance. In addition, Bill has developed support for a company policy and provided a supervisor with some ideas for working with women on the job. Perhaps Walt's basic concern was a feeling that he would not be as competent in supervising women employees as he had been with male maintenance specialists. By expressing his fears, his anxieties could be confronted and dissipated.

You Can't Refuse To Transfer Me Just Because I'm Not White

Situation

Len Thompson is a mechanic who has been working in the plant for almost four years. He is young and ambitious, although it has been noted on his performance appraisal form that he has "a chip on his shoulder" regarding management in general. He has been attending night school at a local college and received an associate degree in accounting at the end of the last semester. He has just entered the office of Steve Robinson, Personnel Advisor.

Len: *Mr. Robinson, I need to talk to you.*
Steve: *Sure, come in. What can I do for you?*
Len: *I've just heard that you hired a fellow, Stan Mason, into the Payroll Accounting section.*
Steve: *That's right. Good candidate. I think he will make a good employee. Is he a friend of yours?*
Len: *Not exactly, although we did have an accounting class together at State College. I can't believe you gave him*

that job. I've had my request for transfer in for weeks and no one has even talked to me about a job like this. I went to school to try and get ahead, but it doesn't seem to matter around here. But I'll tell you this: you can't refuse to transfer me just because I'm not white.

Steve: *Hold it a minute, Len. Being Black doesn't have anything to do with it.*

Len: *Oh, yeah? Well just your saying it doesn't make it so. I'm just as qualified as Stan Mason and now he has a good job while I'm being discriminated against.*

Steve: *Just because you didn't get a certain job doesn't mean you are being discriminated against.*

Len: *The hell you say. I've had a transfer request in for weeks, and nothing has happened. What do you call that?*

Steve: *Do you think we have deliberately ignored your request or just moved slower than you wished we had?*

Len: *I don't know. Why don't you tell me? It has the same effect whatever the reason.*

Steve: *But the reason is important. If my motives are bad, then talking to me now won't help. If I'm devious, I'll just try to cover my tracks. But if I've just been slow or negligent in my duty, or maybe, just maybe, working on your request but have not been able to find the right opportunity yet, then it's a different story, isn't it?*

Len: *What are you trying to say?*

Steve: *That I haven't been trying to do you in or forget about you, I just haven't found the right spot yet.*

Len: *What about the payroll accounting job?*

Steve: *The payroll accounting supervisor wanted someone with experience in computer programming. Stan Mason had several courses and had worked part time while going to school in the computer center at school. You haven't had any programming courses.*

Len: *I see. When's a job for which I'm qualified going to become open?*

Steve: *That's not an easy question to answer, Len. As you know, most of the people we hire into accounting have bachelor's degrees. But I am trying to get you placed in a position that may not be exactly what you want initially but would give you exposure to some aspect of accounting and a chance to prove yourself. A job in an area which also makes it easier to continue on in school and get your B.S. degree. That's important if you are going to really compete with those who we are hiring as entry level accountants.*

Len: *I wonder if I'll ever make it.*

Steve: *It's not an easy row to hoe—to work and go to school—but it can be done. Your work habits help greatly in getting your transfer request seriously considered. Your good marks in both output and attendance make you a desirable candidate. Let me encourage you to continue in that regard.*

Len: *Yeah, sure.*

Steve: *It is important, and it does help.*

Len: *Okay. Well, I hope something comes up soon.*

Steve: *I want you to know, Len, that you are considered for every opening in the Accounting Department. You're not being overlooked. However, since the jobs you qualify for are entry level positions, you must compete with other candidates who meet the requirements of the particular position.*

Len: *Well, thank you, I do appreciate that.*

Critique

Many people are more capable than their position in an organization allows them to demonstrate. A very real problem that faces the modern organization is an overabundance of talent for some position. Len Thompson exemplifies a typical situation of someone who wants to get ahead, but sees roadblocks everywhere he turns. Consequently, he feels discriminated against.

Steve Robinson was able to deal with the anger Len felt because of several specific things he did. First, he was willing to let Len question his own motives. This indicated to Len that neither Steve nor the company had anything to hide. This also caused Len to wonder whether or not he was acting hastily and was thereby more willing to give Robinson a chance to explain. Steve then indicated the basic job requirements of the position in Payroll Accounting and told Len why he was less qualified. Without being able to compare

Len's background to position requirements, Len's charge would have contained at least some substance.

Not everyone who applies for a transfer gets one. How the people who make decisions about who gets transferred describe their criteria for choosing one person over another can make all the difference in whether or not those who are passed over accept the decision. It is not easy for someone to accept that he or she is less qualified for a postion than someone else. Objective job criteria and a discussion of them helps the unaccepted person reconcile his or her disappointment.

Do Minorities Really Get Preferential Treatment?

Situation

Frank Hanson and Roger Davis have been friends for years. They bowl together, their wives are in the same club, and on occasion they have taken days off together and gone fishing. Frank is a plant foreman and Roger, a senior operator. Nearing quitting time, Roger walks into Frank's office.

Roger:　*Hey, Frank, how are things going?*

Frank:　*Pretty good. Going fairly well. How about you?*

Roger:　*Oh just great. Afraid we got a new employee maintenance specialist in the plant today, Bill Spunk. He doesn't seem to know a whole lot about gas plant operations.*

Frank:　*Yeah, I know Bill, I interviewed him when he first came over here. He was kind of new, kind of inexperienced, but I think he has good potential, and will probably work out well.*

Roger:　*Oh, I don't know, Frank. Potential maybe, but he sure doesn't know a lot about gas plant operations. I had to show him how to calibrate a four inch meter. It seems to me that we are not hiring people with the necessary experience to do a gas plant job.*

Frank: Well, Roger, sometimes people we hire don't have the experience that you or I did when we first started, but I guess everybody has to start somewhere, sometime.

Roger: Yeah, I guess everybody has to start somewhere, but tell me, Frank, this new guy Bill, was he hired because he can do the job or because he is a minority?

Frank: What do you mean?

Roger: Well, I mean do the minorities get preferential treatment or not? I've tried for several months to get my son-in-law hired on as a maintenance specialist, and they have just not been willing to look at him. Now if I say he is good, and I know what his work is like, and I know what his work habits and his skills are, why were they willing to hire a minority who doesn't know anything about a gas plant over my son-in-law who has a Class A mechanics certificate from a vocational technical school in town?

Frank: Well, Roger, I don't know exactly why your son-in-law hasn't been hired. I didn't even know he had been interviewed. Employee Relations hasn't talked to me about that. As for Bill Spunk, well, he is going to need some help and need some work. He hasn't had any real work experience and doesn't know a whole lot about gas plant operations, but he is a fellow who did well on his aptitude test, and when I talked to him, he certainly seemed to have a willing attitude.

Roger: Well, he may have a willing attitude, but he doesn't know how to do the work. My son-in-law also has a willing attitude, and I think knows how to do the work well; but tell me, Frank, do minorities get preferential treatment or not?

Frank: Roger, one thing I think we all need to recognize and understand is that everybody is hired because they've passed the test and we think they can do the job. Now, Bill Spunk may or may not work out. I guess what we do and the help we provide is going to make a big difference on whether he works out or not. But I can tell you this, he won't work out unless we help him. Now, as to whether or not some minorities are given preferential treatment, I'd have to say that all things being equal, we

*look at the employee's application form. Yes, we probably
would hire a minority over a nonminority employee. All
other things are usually equal though. That does not
mean that there isn't room for your son-in-law or a lot of
other nonminorities. The company has an affirmative
action plan, a plan that says we are going to hire a
certain number of employees who are minority, if they
meet our qualifications. Now that doesn't mean we have
to hire anybody who doesn't meet our qualifications, but
it does mean that we have to make a special effort to try
a little harder, work a little bit more with some who don't
have all the experience or maybe all the aptitudes, but
still show promise and show a mechanical aptitude
equivalent to what we require for an entry-level person.*

Roger: *Well, I'll be, Frank. You're telling me that if a minority is
not as qualified as I am, he's going to get the job before
I do?*

Frank: *It means, Roger, that we are going to do the best we can
to train, orient, counsel, and coach minority employees,
not just because they are minorities, or are going to be
hired, or going to be promoted. They are going to have to
be able to meet our minimum qualifications, and if they
meet those minimum qualifications, well, then we are
going to give minorities some opportunities even though
they may not have all of the experience that other people
do have.*

Roger: *That just doesn't seem fair to me. It just doesn't seem
right.*

Frank: *Well, on the face of it, it doesn't seem very fair, Roger. It
seems like some people, just because of who they are, are
going to be able to get jobs and promotions. Is that what
you are feeling?*

Roger: *That's exactly right, Frank.*

Frank: *But you know, that's already happened the other way
around for years and years. Just because a man was
black years ago, no matter how qualified he was, he
couldn't get a job. Likewise, a man who was white, just
because he was white, would sometimes get a job even
though he was less experienced.*

Roger: So if we go overboard the other way, is that going to make it right? Are you saying two wrongs are going to make one right, Frank?

Frank: Well, I don't suppose I am, but I am saying some people didn't get experience that they probably would have been entitled to years ago. Now if they have the aptitude, you've got to do something for denying them the experience they would have had if they had been given an equal opportunity years ago. You see, that's the point I'm making, Roger. We've prevented some people from getting experience and now when it's time to compare them, we are saying one has more experience than another. And if we give the job to the experienced person, all we are doing is perpetuating the same condition in this generation that existed over the last generation of people.

Roger: Why can't we just start over again with the next generation? Let this one go on their way, making everything right so that everybody can have the same experience.

Frank: That means you would write off a whole generation, Roger?

Roger: Well, I don't know about that. It's just that it's not fair, Frank, that my son-in-law should be out of work and this young minority who is not half as good as him should have a job. It just doesn't seem right.

Frank: Well, you know, Roger, it may not seem altogether right to us, but they've waited a long time to be able to have good jobs, and I don't know what we owe them altogether. I'm not saying anything one way or another, but I am saying that we've denied them opportunities to get experience and if we go ahead now and deny them experience, we are just perpetuating the same old conditions we've had before.

Roger: Well, I guess that's right too.

Frank: Roger, I guess my strongest feelings are that anybody who is willing to work hard and has some ability, can get a job and can get advancement opportunities. They may not get a job as quickly as they would like and they may not advance as quickly as they would like, but it will *come. There's plenty of opportunity in this old world for everybody who's willing to work and willing to apply themselves. Now you know as well as I do, you've got to pass that test to be a maintenance specialist. You've got to have that ability, too, in addition to working hard, and your son-in-law will be able to get advancement opportunities and so will you and I. It may not come as rapidly as we'd like, but then, again, I guess we have to think that a lot of minorities have waited a long time to get even some of these opportunities. Maybe it's not all fair, but there is some rhyme and reason to it.*

Roger: *I guess that's right. Well, it is quitting time, Frank, and I'm going to take off. I will see you in the morning. I'm not convinced that it is totally fair, but I guess there's some basis for doing things and, at least I feel better about it.*

Frank: *OK, Roger. See you in the morning.*

Critique

Three problems with which the supervisor must cope that involve the work group and the new employee are favoritism, integration, and acceptance. To some longer-service employees, and perhaps to the supervisor, the special treatment that goes with affirmative action will appear to be favoritism, even reverse discrimination. It is very important for a supervisor to communicate to the work group that the minority employee didn't get hired just because he or she is a minority or a female. It's also important that the supervisor recognizes and communicates to employees that it is legitimate for these minority employees to ask for help and assistance, especially when they are just beginning a job. Oftentimes, minorities and females have aptitudes which prove their considerable potential for the jobs for which they are hired. But aptitude isn't the same as experience, and the only way they will get experience is by being given opportunities and the support and assistance of other employees and other members of the work group. Feelings of integration and acceptance are also matters of concern that supervisors must face. If employees feel resentful because a minority or female is hired, it is likely that that minority employee is going to be hassled considerably. It may even be possible that the work group can make a minority's job so intolerable that he or she quits. If such actions occur, it is important for the supervisor to take action, to meet with employees individually or perhaps in a small group with key employees to express concerns, to get the group's commitment to avoid baiting or taunting a minority employee. Normal orientation procedures can greatly facilitate integration. An employee must do a certain amount on his or her own. It is important that the minority employee do things to limit his or her own visibility and uniqueness in the organization, especially if there are only a few minority employees. He or she, no doubt, will feel that to a certain extent, that he or she is on display, that more is expected of him or her than others. The supervisor's assurance and support, and especially the support and assurance of co-workers, can be key matters in this regard. In this dialogue, Frank Hanson did not minimize the importance of meeting affirmative action goals. The company was committed to hiring and advancing minority employees, and Frank made no apologies for this position. He did, on the other hand, feel respect and understanding for Roger Davis' concerns, without acknowledging agreement or disagreement. He stated his own opinion and the opinion of the company. In such matters, it is often important for a supervisor to represent his or her own feelings as well as the company's, and if there is a conflict in his or her mind over the fairness of company policy and company practice, it is important for him or her to clear that up to effectively counsel employees who have concerns such as this. Frank was effective in avoiding stereotypes, either the liberal do-gooder or the hardcore conservative approach. By steering a moderate course, by expressing his own feelings by reframing the situation, he discussed the employment of Bill Spunk, in terms of aptitude and experience rather than simply comparison to Roger's son-in-law. The situation was lifted from an emotional arena to a more rational one, which put the discussion on a positive plane. Frank Hanson did not probe or care about Roger's own personal biases or prejudices. He, rather, emphasized the importance of group morale in total work group effectiveness. He used his friendship as a basis for getting a commitment from Roger Davis to provide support and assistance to Bill Spunk. Instead of dealing on an abstract or emotional level, Hanson dealt on a personal work group effectiveness level, and pointed out the importance of being fair to Bill Spunk by giving him a chance to learn the job well rather than defending or supporting affirmative action generally. He supported Bill Spunk and utilized his lack of experience as a basis for getting commitment from Roger Davis.

They Gave Him The Job Just Because I'm Over 50, Not Because He's Better

Situation

John Mitchell and Sherman Hollis have had a passing acqaint-ance for a number of years. John is a senior engineer in the com-pany. Sherman Hollis is a personnel specialist. Both men are within the same generation: John Mitchell is 53 years old; Sherman Hollis is 48. Both of them have more than 20 years of experience with the company and see themselves as competent and capable contributors. There have been several recent promotions in the last few months in the particular engineering group that John is a part of. John, however, has not received one of those promotions. Sherman was listening to several supervisors in the cafeteria talking about older engineers and their perceptions of the company not being very positive. Since he knew John, he decided to take the opportunity to have a conversation with him and see where it would lead.

Sherman: *Hey, John, how are you doing, how are things going?*

John: *Fine.*

Sherman: *I was in the area and thought I'd stop by. Is now a good time to talk or should I come back later?*

John: *I'm not working on anything too pressing, come on in.*

Sherman: *Thanks, I appreciate that. What are you working on anyway, something important?*

John: *No, nothing I work on is ever very important. Most of what I do is insignificant stuff.*

Sherman: *Gee, I'm not sure I know what you mean.*

John: *Well, it seems like I've been working pretty hard here for a long time, and it doesn't seem to be getting me anywhere.*

Sherman: *I guess I'm still not sure what you are saying; are you saying you're not getting recognition for the work you do, or you're not getting good projects to work on, or something else?*

John: *Oh, I'd say not getting the recognition as much as anything.*

Sherman: *Is that recognition from your supervisor or recognition from the company or what?*

John: *Oh, I think the company probably feels like I've had my useful days and should be put on the shelf.*

Sherman: *Has anybody said anything to you to cause you to feel that way?*

John: *No one has actually said anything; I just feel that unless you're young and aggressive and willing to bow and scrape to the big cheeses at the top, you won't go very far here.*

Sherman: *Are you saying people need to be apple polishers to get ahead?*

John: *I'm saying you've got to be 25 years old, is what I'm saying. Listen, I've been working here for 25 years. I've done a good job, and except for the last few years, I thought I was doing well. Right? Then all of a sudden all these young guys come in and they're doing things that it took me 15 years to get the opportunity to do.*

Sherman: *People with limited service or limited experience are getting opportunities that it took you a lot longer to get?*

John: *Yes, it seems that if you're not young you don't get the opportunities. Those of us who have been around a long time are being passed up by the company instead of being given opportunities for advancement. It seems like they don't value experienced people, they're just watching out to see what the young guys are going to do. It took us a long time to know the business, and we're just being shoved in the background.*

Sherman: *You're talking about yourself and several other people? Have other people talked to you, other engineers, about this same thing or is it more or less your perception of what you think they also believe?*

John: *We haven't really talked about it all that much, but I think others see things the same as I do. Why are we being passed by; why do you have to be young to get anywhere?*

Sherman: *I guess I'm not sure that you need to be young, John. I know that younger people are moved fairly quickly, especially if they seem to have management potential; but in terms of being valued, I can assure you that the company does value its older engineers. I know that it's possible sometimes to look at people and say, "Gee, when I was that age or had that much experience, I didn't get those kind of opportunities." Some of our own demands for engineers have changed as well, since it's a different ball game. I'm still searching to really understand your concerns, John. Are you saying that you're not given recognition from your supervisor in the form of salary treatment or in terms of assignments? Or are you saying that there are things that you'd like to achieve that you don't feel like you're going to be able to achieve?*

John: *It's the achievement part. My salary is fine. I don't think I'm overpaid, but I make enough. But I'd still like to get promotions. I'd still like to have opportunities. I'd still like the growth and the excitement of new challenges. I'm not so old that I don't enjoy challenges and successfully meeting those challenges. I want to get ahead, too, not for money or power or anything but for my own achievement. I feel like I'm being pushed back into a corner because I'm not young and aggressive. I feel discriminated against. I have a mind to file a discrimination charge because I think others are getting the jobs because they're young, not because they're better.*

Sherman: *I see you are really concerned. Are there specific kinds of assignments that you wish you had or are there specific opportunities that you feel you're not being given?*

John: *No, not really. I guess even us old folks like change. If you're stuck in the same job for too many years, it gets boring. It does for anyone; it doesn't matter how old you are. And after a while you get to know it so well that you don't even have to work, you're just doing it. I like the challenge of something different.*

Sherman: *What makes a job challenging? Are there characteristics of any job that make it a challenge?*

John: Oh, trying something new and working with people are challenges.

Sherman: Have you worked with any of the new employees?

John: No.

Sherman: How receptive do you think your supervisor would be to the idea say, on a specific project where you had some expertise, working directly with some less experienced engineer? Do you think you would find that a challenge? Do you think he would find that an acceptable option?

John: Sure, I guess he would.

Sherman: How do you feel about that?

John: Oh, I guess it would be a challenge, it would be something different. I have worked with young engineers in the past. I think it would give some variety to what I am doing because otherwise I know my job pretty well. Besides, they could benefit from what I know.

Sherman: I myself enjoy being around the younger engineers and younger people in Employee Relations because they have a lot of enthusiasm for their jobs. I have found that it can be a very positive reciprocal relationship— spending time counseling and coaching, showing the ropes to somebody who doesn't have a lot of experience, and benefiting from and shaping their ideas. That's something that helps me find challenge and be creative in my own job. It is something that I have even talked to my supervisor about doing. I have found him to be fairly supportive.

John: Okay.

Sherman: Is that something you feel you could talk to your supervisor about?

John: Yes, I think so. I think that will help me enjoy my work more. But I want to get ahead, too. What can I do to get promoted?

Sherman: I don't think there is a formula, John. A question that I think is a better one, moreover, is "How do I improve; how do I gain skills?" Sometimes we look at other people and say, "Gee, they're getting a lot of *rewards, they're getting advancement, they're getting recognition, and they're getting good jobs." Sometimes being at the right place at the right time helps. But if I concentrate on improving, I'll be doing all I can to improve my promotability. That may mean gaining technical skills as well as such intangibles as learning to take initiative, developing good business judgment, and the like.*

John: *I know that what you are saying makes sense, but it's certainly nothing new.*

Sherman: *I know it's not new. I think, though, if you feel that you've done your best, you can certainly be proud of that. I don't see what's wrong with saying, "I'm a good engineer. I do my best. I still keep trying to improve. So what if I'm not the best there is, I'm as good as I can be."*

John: *That's not the same as a promotion.*

Sherman: *No, but if it's true, it's worth a lot.*

John: *I suppose so. Well, I need to go. I did enjoy the discussion.*

Critique

The basis of this discussion, like others included in this book, assumes that personnel decisions are made on objective criteria that are supportable should a charge of discrimination be made. If people are being treated unfairly, no counseling approach will be effective. On the other hand, fairness and objective criteria do not guarantee that employees will perceive decisions as stemming from these factors. Good counseling, however, can bridge the gaps which often exist between fair treatment and an employee's perception of a situation.

People have different ways of dealing with their personal disappointments, Responses range from bitterness to apathy to acceptance. Counseling can help a person deal with his or her own dissappointment in a positive manner, but along this range of responses a counselor should point out options, and the likely consequences of these various options.

One way people attempt to protect their self-image is by ascribing responsibility for an outcome to circumstances beyond their control. Thus, not receiving a promotion is blamed on a supervisor, a performance evaluation made by others, or most easily on the system. But then, some people who think they should be in a higher position than they occupy may indulge in self-deprecation. Such people may experience ulcers, migraine headaches or even attempt suicide if they cannot come to terms with who they are and their niche in life.

There are two responses which are not *simply* in between these two reaction types, but which represent categorically different emotions and enable people to deal more positively with themselves and their world. The technical term for the first of these responses is dissonance reduction. This simply means that a person decides a previous goal is not all that important after all. The person decides other goals are more important and attempts to realize them. Such goals are typically nonwork oriented and provide a rationalization for a person to invest less personal energy on the job. The other possible response is for a person to say, "I am going to be a good craftsman, even if I cannot be a great artisan." This response recognizes personal assets and liabilities and allows the individual to feel good about his or her investment in the job.

In this vignette, Sherman attempted to help John by utilizing this second type of response. Sherman's goal was to defuse John's anger and help him accept his position and contribution as meaningful even though it did not satisfy all of his aspirations. People with no hope are the most likely to become desperate. Sherman neither made promises of future advancement when John indicated his dissatisfaction, nor did he dash all hope of advancement. Instead, he provided John with a rationalization for not advancing more than he had and Sherman reoriented John's thinking in a way that he could still see himself as a very capable engineer.

Unit **5**

Boss / Subordinate Relations

He Doesn't Like Anyone Questioning His Authority

Situation

Almost without exception Tim Walsh was highly regarded by employees and co-workers alike. In his short time as production supervisor he had done much to win the respect and loyalty of those who worked with him. When he appeared at the office of Dan Marston, a good friend and personnel specialist for the company, it initially appeared to be a social call.

Dan: *Hey, Tim, how are things going?*
Tim: *Fine, fine. I played an enjoyable round of golf yesterday. It sure felt good to break 90.*
Dan: *Glad to hear it. You seem to be on your way to breaking some production and safety records, too. You've done well in the six months you've been production supervisor.*
Tim: *I wish I could get my boss to say that. I had heard about Max's reputation before I came to this position. He certainly lives up to his image.*

Dan: *You find him difficult to deal with, eh?*

Tim: *Yeah. How do you deal with a guy who is as autocratic as he is? There seems almost no way to please him. And he especially doesn't like anyone questioning his authority. There's just his way and the wrong way.*

Dan: *What did Bob, your predecessor, say about his relationship with Max? Did he give you any hints?*

Tim: *You know what he said? He told me the less you see of the s.o.b., the better you'll get along. Not much advice of value there. But, of course, Max and Bob never did get along very well.*

Dan: *What have you tried so far?*

Tim: *Nothing particularly novel or new. Basically, I've tried to work with him the same way that I've worked with every other boss I've had. I've tried to work a problem through as thoroughly as I could before taking it to him, thus respecting his time. I've proposed several changes on how productivity might be improved and provided cost justification for purchases that such changes would necessitate. But he always comes up with some screwball reason why my ideas won't work.*

Dan: *You've said two things which taken separately don't mean much. But when you put them together they may suggest the reason for your difficulties. First, you said if something isn't his idea he doesn't think much of it. Then, you said you take your ideas to him once you've worked them through, expecting his approval.*

Tim: *Are you saying I should make my ideas seem like they were his ideas? That sounds manipulative and hokey to me.*

Dan: *Well, manipulative is not a dirty word. I do suspect that any time we try to influence someone else we could always be accused of being manipulative. However, just having the boss believe he thought up your ideas isn't what I was suggesting. Basically, what I see is your taking ideas to him that are worked out so completely that all he can say is "yea" or "nay." He doesn't have a chance to shape them before they are in final form. Since he didn't contribute, he doesn't like it.*

Tim: *But I've never had a boss who wanted to be involved in the formative details.*

Dan: *You also said you've never had a boss like Max before, either.*

Tim: *That's right. Hmmm.*

Dan: *Do you think you can take this idea and implement it?*

Tim: *I guess by getting Max involved early on in working through either my problems or my plans for improving things. That way, not only will he be less surprised by the action steps I propose, but he will also have ample opportunity to insert his input. I could do that by presenting a problem in stages—just enough for him to see there is a problem, but not enough for him to see a solution. That way I can get his agreement that action is necessary, and then I can come with an analysis on what should be done about it.*

Dan: *I like it. Prepare the ground first—get him receptive. Tell him the problem in stages. Avoid presenting the problem and a solution at the same time. Get him involved in defining the problem so that he will plainly see that some action is necessary. How are you going to try this out?*

Tim: *I've already got something in mind. Bob had tried for quite some time to convince Max to buy a new reprocessing unit. The one we have is inadequate since the plant has grown. It is old and constantly needs maintenance repair work. It is also slow and creates problems since materials have to be stockpiled and fed in by hand. Units awaiting reprocessing are simply stacked near the machine awaiting their turn. One thing I could do instead of submitting a proposal to Max outlining the nature of the problem and describing the benefits of a new reprocessing machine is to invite him out to the shop floor. I could spend some time with him that way, and he could look over the situation himself. I could point out the problem, but leave him to draw his own conclusions.*

Dan: *Sounds like a plan. You may want to be ready with a proposal of what to do. He just might ask you. Wouldn't that be a switch, you'd be turning Max into a participative manager.*

Tim: *He may not go that far, but this is a way for me to have*
       more freedom plus get needed changes made.
Dan: *Let me know how things work out. I'm interested in seeing*
       how successfully you implement your plan.

Critique

Every supervisor has a personal syle and particular preferences
regarding working relations with subordinates. Peter Drucker noted
that some are "readers" and some are "listeners" and prefer to
make decisions based on either oral or written information.[1] Some
bosses want to know everything a subordinate does, while others
want "exception reporting" to be the rule. It is important for a
subordinate to know what his or her boss's preferences are in these
matters as well as others. What is "taking initiative" to one supervisor may be seen as "going off on a tangent" by another.

Subordinates can improve relations with their bosses by working
with their supervisors' preferences. In this discussion, Dan helps
Tim come to this conclusion. Dan deals in a rather directive,
information-oriented way with Tim. By asking probing questions,
the nature of Tim's relationship with his boss was discovered. Since
Dan did not agree with Tim's assessment of his boss, the discussion
was able to remain problem-oriented. If Dan had taken up Tim's
position at that point, the discussion would likely have ended up
blaming and describing the faults of Tim's boss without resulting in
productive thinking. On the other hand, if Dan would have suggested ways for Tim to handle his boss at this point, it is likely that
Tim would have listened politely but dismissed Dan as not
understanding the nature of this particular situation.

By pointing out the type of decisions Tim was taking to his boss
as well as recalling his description of the boss as preferring a different decision-making style, Dan was able to help Tim reorient his
thinking. Dan presented a *dilemma* based on what he had heard, and
Tim reached his own *conclusions* about why the situation existed as
it did despite Tim's efforts to gain the confidence of his boss. Like a
good storyteller, Dan described incidences but left the moral to the
listener. This strategy is similar in nature to the one that Tim
decides to use to improve his batting average with his boss.

[1] Peter Drucker film series "Effective Executive" distributed by BNA Communications, Inc.

She Takes Everything So Personally That No One Can Ever Please Her

Situation

Jerry Reeths has worked in the budget section of a small company for about five years. He received a promotion coming into the budget section and has done well in his career. He's considered to be an important asset to the company and definitely someone with additional management potential. About six months ago a new budget director was appointed. She was the first woman budget director in the company. Glenda is bright, capable, and very aggressive. She expects people to perform and has a reputation for accepting no excuses. Susan Fields, a personnel specialist of the company, is a good friend of Jerry's. In fact, they car pooled together for about a year before Jerry accepted his new assignment.

Jerry: *Susan, I was just in the area and thought I would stop and chat.*

Susan: *Well, I'm glad you could, Jerry. How are things going?*

Jerry: *Oh, pretty well. I'm glad we're through with the primary budget cycle. Now we will be able to relax for a couple of weeks.*

Susan: *Oh, that's good to hear. Say, how do you like your new boss, Glenda?*

Jerry: *Oh, she's all right.*

Susan: *You don't sound very enthusiastic about it.*

Jerry: *She is fine. She's just fine. It's just a matter of getting over a few rough spots right now.*

Susan: *Oh, like what?*

Jerry: *Oh, nothing that is really significant. It is just, well, it's just that she's so demanding of everyone.*

Susan: *Demanding? In what way?*

Jerry: *Well, I don't know if it's because she's a woman or not, but she seems so intense. She's such a perfectionist. It doesn't seem like anyone can ever please her.*

Susan: *She doesn't seem satisfied with your efforts?*

Jerry: *That's right. Regardless of what I do, she is never satisfied. She always wants something more, something additional.*

Susan: *And you think it's because she is a woman?*

Jerry: *I don't want to stereotype her, but I've never seen anybody who is such a perfectionist. It's just that she doesn't want to let anything go. Now, if it's a mistake, I can understand that. But she doesn't want to let anything go, even an undotted "i" or an uncrossed "t". Consequently, she is always looking over everyone's shoulder. She seems to be watching everybody like a hawk.*

Susan: *Is this true of everyone or just you in particular?*

Jerry: *Oh, I don't know that I'm any worse or any better than anyone else. I don't think she is any more careful with me or scrutinizes my work any more than she does anyone else's, but I am not used to having a boss supervise me so carefully.*

Susan: *I see. What have you done or considered doing to improve your relationship?*

Jerry: *What do you mean?*

Susan: *I mean every boss has a different style, different expectations, different orientations. What have you done or considered doing to meet your boss's expectations, to establish a boss/subordinate relationship that both of you could find satisfying?*

Jerry: *Oh, I don't know. I hadn't really thought about it in those terms. I guess all I've done is worked as hard as I could.*

Susan: *It is certainly important to try and work as hard as you can, but I think it is also important to ask your supervisor what her position demands, and how you, as a subordinate, can help her with those demands.*

Jerry: *I'm not sure I understand what you are driving at.*

Susan: *Well, let me put it this way. If you're going to take a proposal to Tom Brandon, would you have a different focus than if you took it to Steve Fernez?*

Jerry: *Sure, they have different orientations. With Tom, I'd want to show the market potential of the proposal and let him know that I had discussed it and gotten approval from those who would be involved; but for Steve, I would want to be very quantitative and show him what the numbers indicated.*

Susan: *Just as you have different approaches to different people, I think you also need to recognize different bosses have different styles and different demands. I think you need to look at the demands placed on those bosses in order to decide how you are going to effectively work with a particular boss.*

Jerry: *Now I see what you are getting at. You're saying that all I've done is looked at Glenda as if she were another boss without considering the demands placed on her.*

Susan: *Right. In fact, it seems to me you've looked at your relationship and it's been pretty one-sided. You've looked at only what you wish she would do differently without looking at what you may need to do differently to improve your relationship with her.*

Jerry: *Oh, I guess that's to the point.*

Susan: *I don't mean to come on too strong, Jerry. It's just that any new boss is dependent on the people who work for him or her. I think what Glenda is trying to do is set up some firm standards and let people know what she expects. Then she can see for herself who she can trust and who she can depend on.*

Jerry: *Well, don't you think that working hard and doing well will be the basis for her developing trust in me?*

Susan: *Yes, I do, and I think that is a necessary condition, but it's not sufficient. It's not enough. There are other things you need to do as well.*

Jerry: *Well, like what?*

Susan: *I think there are several things that could help develop a mutual trust between you and Glenda. Trust is dependent on several factors, including being accessible, being dependable, being predictable in doing your work and doing it on time. Then, of course, there is abiding in confidences and being loyal to your boss, not gossiping, sharing organizational secrets with your boss, letting him or her know such things as your observations about working with people like Tom and Steve. These things will let Glenda know that you support her, that you're behind her, that she can trust you without actually going up to her and saying, "Hey, I'm OK, I can be trusted."*

You can deliver the same message in a more convincing
way by doing these kinds of things.

Jerry: *I think I see what you mean. You're saying that this is*
similar to sales proposals, that I need to know the
customers and their needs, and I need to know the kind
of approach that will work with this customer.

Susan: *I think that's a good analogy, a good way to think about*
it.

Jerry: *Well, you've given me something to think about, including*
some things I hadn't even considered before. Maybe it's
not all her fault.

Critique

Every supervisor has a preferred way of doing things. Understanding a particular supervisor's style is important in order to know how to work with him or her. Peter Drucker, for instance, maintains that every manager is either a reader or a listener. Readers prefer written reports and updates, while listeners would rather be told verbally with a follow-up note submitted later if necessary. It may also be useful to clarify initiative with each supervisor and appropriate areas in which to exercise it. Some prefer strict adherence to certain policies which others consider as obstacles to go around or over.

There are several management observers who have described the importance of specifically managing the joining process by firmly establishing a psychological contract between supervisor and supervised. This contract would simply clarify some of the preferences both the supervisor and the employee have in a working relationship. One employee established this contract by requesting an interview with his boss and then supplying him with the following responses:

- Here's how I can be a resource to you...
- Here's how you can be a resource to me...
- Here are some projects I think would be productive...
- Here is a status report on current and recent activities in my work area...

In this case, Susan described the importance of explicitly defining working procedures. It quickly became apparent that the problem was one of supervisor-subordinate interaction rather than a male-female issue. By asking questions, listening, confronting irrelevant perceptions, and reorienting the definition of the problem, Susan helped Jerry see an acceptable method for dealing with this situation.

He's Always Testing My Limits

Joan: *Hey, Ben, got a minute to talk?*

Ben: *Sure, Joan. Come in and close the door.*

Joan: *Fine. Say, I want you to know how much I really enjoyed that supervisory training program we had last week. That's part of the reason I'm here. I have a situation that I'd like to discuss with you.*

Ben: *OK.*

Joan: *You see, I've got an employee that I don't know how to handle exactly. He's a hard worker and has some good ability, but he's always testing the limits, trying to see just how much he can get away with. He's a design engineer and shows great technical promise, but he won't go anywhere in the company if he doesn't get rid of that chip that's on his shoulder.*

Ben: *I see. Can you give me some examples of things he does?*

Joan: *Lots of little things, all of the time, not always overt. He doesn't usually come out and openly rebel against things that I've said or done. It's more subtle than that. But he does make a lot of sarcastic remarks in group meetings about company policies. Like the time I explained the Conflict of Interest policy to the group. He wanted to know if the company thought that most employees were crooks. But that's just one example. It's usually not the things he says but what he doesn't say. If I try and give him some advice on a project he just stares into space. If I correct something he's done, he glares.*

Ben: *Is he a fairly new employee?*

Joan: He's been with the company about a year and a half and in my group about three months.

Ben: Has he ever talked about how he feels about his work?

Joan: Yes, a couple of times. He likes the work and the technical challenge it provides. But I'm not sure about the work relationships. He doesn't seem to have any close friends at work, and he doesn't fit in too well with most of our other engineers.

Ben: It sounds like a general pattern of nonconformity to me.

Joan: I think that's right. I don't think anything he does is directed at me personally; rather it's focused at me, the boss.

Ben: Joan, the boss/subordinate relationship is characterized by mutual dependence. However, subordinates generally are more aware of their dependence on the boss than vice versa. Most of us learn to sort through our feelings of dependence and cope with them in positive ways. I think when a person exercises initiative, he or she is just trying to deal positively with his or her feelings of dependence. But I know I've been in situations where I felt over-controlled and one down relative to my boss and my peers. My own "misfit" feelings that I was not a part of the group seemed to push me towards doing things to try and show the others up. I'm sure others saw me as rebellious.

Joan: So you think the cause of his acting this way is because he doesn't fit in?

Ben: I don't know if it's the cause or not, although I think based on what you've said it is a contributing factor. I think his own feelings about authority that have been created during his lifetime have a large impact. You said earlier that you thought his actions were directed against you as the boss not you as a person, didn't you?

Joan: Yes, I did. Some of his actions are so impulsive that it seems like he is reacting without thinking first.

Ben: I think your responses reveal a really positive perspective. You don't seem to be taking it personally, which probably diminishes some of his feelings of dependency. Based on what you know about the fellow and your work *requirements, what else do you think you can do to reduce his feelings of dependency?*

Joan: *I don't really know. I've already tried talking to him casually and finding out some of his personal interests. It just hasn't seemed to help.*

Ben: *Maybe not visibly yet. But what have you tried or what could you try that would give him the feeling of being more in control of his work life and less dependent on you and others? For instance, could he be given responsibility for planning a project and then reviewing progress with you at specified dates?*

Joan: *I usually do that with my senior engineers, but I guess I have supervised him closer than others because I didn't think he could handle it. Maybe my extra supervision increased his resentment instead of improving things.*

Ben: *I think that the more you give responsibility and let him take initiative, the more he will feel in control and less dependent.*

Joan: *This has been a good discussion. Now, I think I have a better understanding of what's been going on, and I have some ideas about what to do about it.*

Critique

Many employees struggle with the dependency they feel in a hierarchical relationship with their boss. They want to do well and speak their minds freely, but they are also aware that the boss is the key to salary increases and advancement opportunities. Some people overreact to such dependency in one of two ways: they either become organizational "yes men" or they become somewhat rebellious as a sign of their independence. Both complete conformity and counter-dependency are undesirable.

It is often difficult for an individual to see a pattern in his or her own reactions. Observers are much more aware of an employee's typical responses to the boss's authority. In this particular case, Ben attempted to provide Joan with a different *perspective* on what Joan thought was a personality problem inherent in an employee. The basis of a perspective intervention, or method for creating a change in someone else, is to provide the other person with enough additional information that they come to look upon a set of facts differently. Like a good dramatic play, a perspective intervention should tell a story with a purpose but let the listener decide the moral for himself or herself.

Ben utilized the perspective method well. He listened and asked probing questions until he had enough information to see the real problem. Then he described some of his own reactions to authority and how they made him feel. He continued to remind Joan of her rebellious employee's insecurity but left it up to her to work out a final solution. By helping Joan define what she wanted to do (an objective), he could leave the definition of methods up to Joan's own good sense and know that the outcome would be positive.

Are You Saying That I Feel Threatened By Her?

Situation

Ralph Obenshaw is a first line supervisor in a large retail store operation. He is in his early thirties and has worked several years for the company. The company recently transferred a fairly short service employee to Ralph's group. Ralph's supervisor has presented the situation to him as, "Here's a bright young person who someday may be the boss of both of us." Ralph has been working with this employee, a woman, for several months, but it is now growing rather rough. He has worked with Mel Renfro on several employee relations matters over the years and so decided to take advantage of an opportunity to discuss with Mel any ideas he may have had on working with this female employee.

Ralph: *Hey, Mel, got time to talk for a few minutes?*
Mel: *Sure, Ralph, come on in. What's on your mind?*
Ralph: *Well, to get right to the point, it's about the new woman they brought in to work with me. It seems that we've got nothing but problems.*
Mel: *What have some of the problems been, Ralph?*
Ralph: *It's almost impossible to work with her. She's created chaos in our group as we tried to work together.*

Mel: *Chaos?*

Ralph: *Well, she's just a young upstart. She has all these ideas and wants to try everything and it's created lots of problems. It's hard to handle.*

Mel: *Like what? Can you give me an example of what's happening? Either some of the things she's done or some of the outcomes or problems that have been created because of her intiations.*

Ralph: *Mainly, it's her "pie in the sky" ideas. She has some of the wildest ideas I have ever heard. Impractical, every last one of them. She just seems to completely get out of hand. She thinks that she knows it all; she's a real prima donna, and it causes confusion. It seems like we never get our actual business accomplished, because she's got so many ideas that she's trying to throw in to do things differently.*

Mel: *Do other people see the disruptions that she's causing?*

Ralph: *Well, they just seem to be blind to it. I don't know why, but it seems like she's got them all won over. I don't know what she does on her extra time but she seems to have them all on her side.*

Mel: *I see. Have you talked with her about this at all?*

Ralph: *Oh, she's just impossible to talk to. You can't sit down and have a decent conversation with her at all. She's always trying to tell me all the things we could be doing. One think I can say, she's got enthusiasm but it's uncontrollable.*

Mel: *That's interesting. You have given me an idea of how you see her and her impact on the work group. Do you have any idea of how she sees you or how she sees herself fitting in with the group?*

Ralph: *Well, she just ignores the fact that I'm her boss. She feels like she can just go over my head and she seems to do whatever she pleases.*

Mel: *Has she ever said anything to you about how she feels about working in the work group or about you as a supervisor?*

Ralph: *No, she's never talked to me directly about anything. She seems to like the group, I haven't heard any complaints.*

Mel: *How do you think she sees herself in the work group? Does she see herself as fitting in or not? Does she feel accepted?*

Ralph: *Oh, I think she thinks she fits in and is accepted. Yes, she thinks she is. No one else seems to complain too much. I don't think she feels uncomfortable at all. She just says and does whatever she feels like.*

Mel: *The way you see the situation is probably different from the way she sees it. You're probably seeing it as, "I need to hold on and I need to make an example and make sure that other people don't see me as treating her unfairly." She's trying hard, looking for a signal to be accepted, probably needing some support, if our experience with other women in the company is right. How do you think she perceives her relationship with you? You have said some things about how you see your relationship with her. How about the flip side of that?*

Ralph: *Well, I don't know. She probably doesn't know what her relationship is with me.*

Mel: *Could that ambiguity be a problem source for her?*

Ralph: *Yes, it probably could be. I never thought of it that way.*

Mel: *As you think about your relationship with her and how you see her, maybe you will see that there is some reason to believe that she has some concerns about this ambiguity in relation to how she sees her relationship with you. What do you think would have to happen for either one of you to change your perceptions?*

Ralph: *I don't know. I guess we could talk about it.*

Mel: *Would that do any good?*

Ralph: *I don't know.*

Mel: *When you give out work assignments, do you give them out directly? Do you talk to her about what you expect from a project?*

Ralph: *Oh, no. I try and stay away from her as much as I can.*

Mel: *You know, one of the things I have noticed a lot even in my own family, when we try and get together and talk about something, is that we can talk a lot about things in the abstract and nothing seems to really happen to improve them. But when I can structure and experience where we can talk about what we are doing, it seems like the family members learn a lot more. Having a common experience creates a bond. It seems to go a lot smoother if you share a common experience rather than if you just talk about it in the abstract. If that same kind of idea is analogous to your work situation, is there a common experience that you think you two have that would allow either of you to break through and begin to share your perceptions of how you see each other? Not that those perceptions have to change, but by talking about them, you can at least understand each other better.*

Ralph: *I guess I could work out something like that. But I'm not sure I want to do that, Mel.*

Mel: *Do you have some reservations about doing that?*

Ralph: *Yeah.*

Mel: *Like what?*

Ralph: *I don't particularly like working with her.*

Mel: *Is it her personality or the fact that she's a woman?*

Ralph: *I don't know. I guess I shouldn't say anything about her being a woman. I just don't know exactly what to do with her.*

Mel: *You know, maybe a good starting place would be to express to her that you haven't worked with a woman before and that you're not exactly sure how to work with her, if you ought to be doing things differently with her than you would with the men. This way you could discuss the performance you expect as a supervisor and get from her some of the things she expects and hopes for as a subordinate. I noticed you furrowed your eyebrow when I said that. Do you have some apprehensions about that?*

Ralph: *I don't particularly like laying my cards down on the table in front of her. I guess I could find out what she expects of me and tell her what I expect of her, though.*

Mel: *Would that be a good place to begin?*

Ralph: *Yeah, that would probably be all right.*

Mel: *I think it would be a useful activity for you to be clear and explicit about some of the things you expect of her and to likewise allow her to express some of the things that she expects. I don't know if "expects" is the right word, but rather "wants" from you as a supervisor. That way she'll be better able to identify her own needs and requirements, and you can, with that position, say a lot or a little, depending on how the conversation goes. You may want to lay everything on the table, or you may want to hold back, but that will become apparent in the course of the discussion. I think, however, that unless you share something—kind of priming the pump—share something that is more than just conversation and include some of your thoughts, your beliefs and your feelings, she's probably not going to be inclined to say much about how she feels. She'll probably be careful as well. I don't think you have to tell everything, but I do think you need to go far enough to establish a mutual confidence.*

Ralph: *OK. I can see where that might help a little bit. I could try it.*

Mel: *That's good. Why don't you let me know how it goes after you have had the conversation. I'm interested. I'm glad that you talked with me, and I'm interested in the results of your conversation.*

Ralph: *OK. I'll let you know.*

Critique

In this vignette, Mel quickly realized that Ralph's problem was more Ralph than it was anyone or anything else. He did not confront Ralph with this observation directly, but tried instead to get Ralph to look at the situation from his subordinate's point of view. Such role reversal methods as this are often as useful as confrontation because they help someone realize there may be reasons why the other person acts as he or she does.

It is not unusual for people to be threatened by highly motivated subordinates. To think that a subordinate could someday have a higher position in the organization than they can cause even those who have few insecurities some reflection. It is not easy to accept being upstaged.

The key to helping supervisors like Ralph is to realize the value of the teacher/mentor function and assume some responsibility for the development of others who have considerable potential. In order to perform that function, however, supervisors must see it as justified. The concept of "justification" is a common one in theatrical drama. An actor or actress is more likely to play the inconspicuous part of a role well if he or she has a function or purpose for being onstage even though not directly a part of a conversation at the moment. Justification can be applied just as well to counseling at the workplace. By giving a supervisor a challenge, he or she is more likely to do something positive. It creates its own incentive to take action. This is the principle that underlies Mel's counseling approach in this situation.

Unit **6**

Performance Problems

You Guys Want More But You're Not Willing To Pay More Money

Situation

Bill Jackson is a machinist with almost 15 years of experience working for a non-union, medium-sized manufacturing plant. Because of his seniority and outspoken manner, he is looked to as an informal leader by many of his co-workers. The industrial engineer in the plant recently recommended some new re-tooling procedures that Bill's boss, Steve Ramon, has decided to implement. Shortly after an announcement of the changed procedures was made, Bill appeared in the doorway of Steve's office.

Bill: *I don't understand you guys.*
Steve: *Come in. Sit down. What do you mean?*
Bill: *I just don't understand you. You always want more work. Increased production. But you don't want to pay for it. You're just like those people on welfare. You want something for nothing.*
Steve: *Are you referring to the new re-tooling procedures?*
Bill: *You bet I am. Those new procedures are going to mean more work for everyone in the shop. They aren't going to be easy, you know.*

Steve: Are they a better way of doing it? Are they an improvement on the old way?

Bill: Oh, I guess so. But that's not the point. The point is the company's going to benefit, but the employees are not.

Steve: You feel the procedures are good, but they should include something that passes on the benefits to employees?

Bill: That's right. Why not raise our pay by a nickel an hour? The company can afford it.

Steve: Are you sure productivity will be improved enough to justify an hourly increase?

Bill: You bet! The company ought to do something. It's not fair for them to benefit and not us.

Steve: I guess I see the company as us, Bill. There isn't some "them" somewhere. There's just people like you and me who work here and who try to do what's best for everyone involved: employees, customers, stockholders.

Bill: You know what I mean. Don't give me that stuff about "we're all in this together." You know as well as I do that some people get more from this company than they deserve. I don't see some of those management types working very hard, but I'll bet they get paid a lot more than I do. Don't they?

Steve: I don't know what others make in the company, Bill. Nor do I care. I think that I'm being fairly paid because I know what people with my background make in our city. I feel good about that. I think you are being fairly paid too, because I know what people with your background make in our city. It's always been our policy to pay competitively as well as to provide a competitive benefits package. To help determine a fair pay scale.

Bill: But when the company benefits from a new procedure, why aren't those benefits passed on?

Steve: They are passed on, but not immediately. It takes time to see the effects of changes. Would you like the company to reduce your pay if quarterly earnings declined?

Bill: You can't cut wages just like that. A person has to be able to plan so that he can pay his bills.

Steve: Companies have to plan so that they can pay their bills, too. Wages can't be adjusted every time a new procedure is *implemented. Maybe it will be a cost-saving device and maybe not. Being able to try something and plan future improvements based on current trends can be beneficial and important to the company.*

Bill: *Well, I don't know about all this. The company always seems to benefit, but the employees never do. I've half a mind not to work so hard just to balance out the benefits the company's going to get with the increased effort this new procedure will require.*

Steve: *I'm not too worried about your doing that, Bill. I know you enjoy your work as much as I like mine, and you take pride from the fact that everyone pulls their own weight around here. You were the one who suggested several changes last year that allowed us to improve our operations. Your own pride in being a craftsman will not let you do a sloppy job. I'm not worried.*

Bill: *Listen, Steve, I want to do a good job. It's important to me to earn my pay. But I don't want to be taken advantage of. I don't want you guys not giving us a pay raise just because we aren't raising hell to get one.*

Steve: *Bill, we give pay increases based on pay surveys we do in the community. If our products are going to be competitive, then their price and quality must be comparable to similar products in the marketplace. That means we must pay well enough to attract, retain and motivate high quality people. It also means we can't overpay or our prices will be overpriced; unless, of course, we can make productivity improvements like this new procedure that allows us to pay a little more.*

Bill: *Let me ask you, Steve. You've been around here a while, you're in on management discussions, is the company really paying us a fair wage?*

Steve: *I really believe the company does a lot to ensure that employees receive a fair competitive wage. I believe it's important, Bill, to think of fairness in terms of competitive practices rather than just as a general term. I don't know what fairness means as a general term when it comes to pay practices. But when fairness is used in the context of competitive pay rates, it's easy measuring*

*it against what others pay for the same skills. That's
why I feel confident in saying the company does pay
fairly.*

Bill: *That's good. That's good.*

Critique

Everyone wants to receive a fair day's pay for a fair day's work.
The problem is, what is a fair day's pay? Fairness is an abstraction
when it comes to pay practices. In order for employees to know that
they are fairly paid, organizations should conduct regular salary
surveys and equip supervisors and managers to discuss their results
with employees. This quantitative approach to a fair day's pay is
the key to convincing employees that they are fairly paid. Without
this data, supervisors may be less effective in discussions such as
the one contained in this vignette.

While many studies have been conducted on satisfaction with pay,
fewer investigations have been made on the effects of pay on
performance. The work of Frederick Herzberg[1] is often cited as
supporting the notion that pay may affect satisfaction, but has little
effect on motivation or performance. Herzberg's own research,
however, shows some relationship between pay and performance and
a strong relationship between advancement recognition.

How satisfied people are with their pay and its effect on their
performance does seem to vary. However, the effect of extrinsic
monetary rewards and intrinsic personal rewards (recognition,
achievement, competence, etc.) does seem to have an additive impact
in influencing performance. The noted psychologist B.F. Skinner
maintains that both of these objectives can be met. He notes:

> It is important to remember that an incentive system isn't
> the only factor to take into account. How pleasant work
> conditions are, how easy or awkward a job is, how good or
> bad tools are—many things of that sort make an enormous
> difference in what a worker will do for what he receives.[2]

In this vignette, Steve utilizes both Bill's desire to be paid well
and his prior knowledge of Bill's positive work ethic to reassure Bill
that he is being well rewarded.

[1] Frederick Herzberg,, "One More Time: How Do You Motivate Employees," *Harvard Business
Reviews*, 46, (1968), pp. 53-62.

Nobody Told Me To Do That

Situation

Lynn has worked as an administrative assistant in the claims department for only four months, although she has eight years of company service. Her boss, Carol, considers her a hard worker who is generally very dependable. However, when Lynn rushes, there is a tendency to overlook a procedure or practice that is necessary to follow in processing a claim. Thus, when Carol noticed that industrial fire investigation reports had been improperly reported, she saw this as a good opportunity to talk with Lynn.

Carol: *Lynn, can you come into my office for a few minutes?*

Lynn: *Sure. What have I done now?*

Carol: *(Closing the door behind her) Now, don't get overly concerned. You're doing a fine job here, and I'm very pleased overall with the work you're doing. You've adjusted well to the kind of work we have here, but there is something I'd like to talk to you about.*

Lynn: *Here it comes.*

Carol: *You're apprehensive?*

Lynn: *Oh, a little. What's the matter?*

Carol: *Before we discuss it, I want you to know that it's not that earth-shattering. It's something that needs to be improved upon, that's all.*

Lynn: *OK. What is it?*

Carol: *We need to be certain that we properly post and process industrial fire investigation reports. There are different procedures for industrial fires than home fires, you know. You must post them with the Arson Committee before doing anything else.*

Lynn: *Nobody told me to do that.*

Carol: *No one told you that was a necessary first step?*

Lynn: *No. This is the first I've ever heard of it. Gee, how about that, I get blamed for something I didn't even know that I was supposed to do.*

Carol: I'm not blaming you, Lynn. I am glad I brought it up so that I could get the procedure clarified, but I'm not accusing you. Are you unfamiliar with the procedure?

Lynn: No, I know how to handle it. When I saw a description of it in the Policy Manual, I asked Carolyn about it. I just didn't know that I was supposed to do anything about it. I thought it was something you would handle.

Carol: Me?

Lynn: Yeah, but I guess I was wrong about that, too.

Carol: Lynn, I can sense that this bothers you. I wish you would see that I'm not blaming you. I'm honestly surprised that we haven't talked about this before, but now I see this as an opportunity to clarify other things that may be ambiguous. First of all, though, I would like you to post and process all industrial fire reports and not wait for me to initiate them. Okay?

Lynn: Sure, I know how to do it. No problem.

Carol: In addition, I'd like you to make a list about any gray areas which you see in your job. If you are unsure whether or not you need to initiate paperwork on some matter, talk to me about it. Also, include on your list ideas you may have for improving any of the procedures. I want to know what you think since you bring a fresh perspective.

Lynn: Well, thanks. I'm glad you're interested in my ideas. But do I have to make a list? It seems so formal to do it that way.

Carol: I don't want to create another policy manual with the list, but writing things down can help. It can help both of us know what we discussed and thus minimize the type of confusion we had over the industrial fire reports. Writing things down also helps to focus attention. I find that I'm more likely to say what I really mean when I write it down.

Lynn: I can see that.

Carol: What you might want to do is think of an effective boss/employee relationship as well as try to identify the specific characteristics of that relationship. We can then

> *use those characteristics as guides for developing our own*
> *relationship. I'll make a list with both of these items on*
> *it, too.*

Lynn: *Oh, okay. I'm glad you're developing a list too. I'll feel*
         less self-conscious about it that way.

Carol: *Good. Can we get together at the end of the week to*
          discuss our lists?

Lynn: *Sure.*

Carol: *Fine.*

Critique

People who are perfectionists have a difficult time dealing with
their own mistakes. They want to do well so badly that any mistake
that is brought to their attention goes all the way to the core. This
may produce apprehension or a generalized feeling of expectant
foreboding. Such people are overly sensitive to criticism and are
likely to take a discussion of a mistake personally. Lynn, in this
situation, fits into this category.

Carol was perceptive enough to pick up Lynn's reaction to her
criticism and see that Lynn felt badly about her mistake. The
function of correction, however, is not to exact penitence or levy
punishment but instead to obtain improvement. Consequently, Carol
did not drop the topic altogether when she saw that Lynn felt badly,
but instead implemented a working procedure that would avoid
similar mistakes occurring in the future. By writing down each
other's perceptions, Lynn and Carol are more likely to clarify who
should be doing what. In addition, this formal method would provide
a forum that was less personal and thus lessened the likelihood that
Lynn would take criticism personally.

How Do I Overcome People's Resistance To Change?

Situation

Kelly had spent months planning and modifying the installation of
some computer hardware for the data processing group. When she

transferred into the unit, she was eager to show Tom Garrett, her new boss, that she could improve the efficiency of the work group and reduce the delays regularly experienced when the existing system went down. She knew that her plans were workable if she could just get the cooperation of the employees she supervised. So far, she wasn't doing very well in that area. In fact, just this morning she had overheard two programmers complaining: "They're always changing things around here. Maybe if we don't work very hard on implementing this system they'll think twice about changing things so often." Although she talked to these two people about helping make the changes work, she had the uneasy feeling that the eight people in her work group would rather see the change fail instead of succeed. Thus, she decided to talk to Tom Garrett about the situation.

Kelly: (Knocking on Tom's office door) Is this a good time to interrupt you? I've got a problem.

Tom: This is as good a time as any; come in and tell me about it.

Kelly: Well, you know I've been working on the conversion to a new input system for our data processing unit.

Tom: I know that. How's it going?

Kelly: Not too well. That's what I'd like to talk about. The change has been in effect for five weeks now, but the programmers still haven't adjusted to it. They keep coming up with reasons why it won't work and cost projections on work requests we've received in the last few weeks have all been very high. My people seem bent on forcing me back down and reverting back to the old system. But I know this new method will work and will prove beneficial in the long run if I can get enough cooperation from my employees. How do I do that? Tell me, Tom, you're more experienced at this than I am and a lot of people respect your ability to get others to pull together.

Tom: I don't know that there are any magic answers, Kelly. But I am willing to talk through the situation with you to see if there is something we can think of together which might work.

Kelly: I would really appreciate that. Right now I'm at my wit's end.

Tom: Tell me, when did you first involve your employees in your plans to reorganize the input process and add some new hardware to our current capabilities?

Kelly: Not until I had worked all the bugs out myself. I suspected that there might be some trouble implementing the new procedures, so I didn't tell anyone about the changes I intended to propose until I had worked the bugs out. I guess my suspicions about these folks being resistant to change have been borne out.

Tom: I think it is wise to work out as many bugs as possible in any new procedure as early as possible, but I'm not sure if doing it alone is the most efficient way to go.

Kelly: What do you mean by that?

Tom: I mean it is never possible to completely eliminate all complications in a new procedure before it is actually installed. Usually, there are some initial problems. Those who are closest to the potential problems are most likely to see them and give their input if their suggestions are sought when an idea is still in the development stage.

Kelly: But I did ask for their ideas after I told them about my reorganization plans.

Tom: By then it was clear to most of them that this was to be your idea and no one else's. The way this undoubtedly came across to your employees is, "Help me with my idea." Even though your words may have been sincere, most people would have interpreted your actions as suggesting you really didn't need any help. So that's what you've been getting for the past five weeks—no help.

Kelly: I can see what you're saying. Even though my intentions were to get help from my group, because my plans were so complete when I introduced them, no one thought I really wanted or needed help in making the change work.

Tom: How do you think people reacted to this?

Kelly: They were probably resentful. I've had a boss myself who never consulted anyone before telling us about a change, and we resented being kept in the dark until he unveiled his plans.

Tom: Since you are new in the work group, this may also have contributed to the lack of acceptance of your plans by *your employees. By making such a significant change so soon after becoming their supervisor and doing it without consulting them, you implicitly sent a message that things are really messed up and you have come to save the day. For employees like yours who take pride in their work, that's a difficult message to accept. However, it is important to recognize that these are the feelings and concerns they have so that you can now plan an activity that will get them working with you instead of against you.*

Kelly: *I'm eager to do that. How do I turn the situation around?*

Tom: *I could tell you, but you know the answer to that as well as I do, don't you?*

Kelly: *I guess I do. What I need to do is to get my people involved in completing the changes I've already started. I need to convey to them that I really do want their ideas and plan to consult with them frequently in order to debug the system.*

Tom: *I think that's the right direction. Participation is not just a technique for improving morale and gaining cooperation, but also a means of uncovering new information and working through problems. Since your employees know firsthand some of the problems caused by the new system, if you have a means for them to share their thoughts and observations on its implementation, you can more easily separate complaints about technical defects from complaints about interpersonal problems caused by the change.*

Kelly: *Yes, I see that now. Unless my group feels like they are consulted, they are going to be less likely to cooperate on making the change work. Without a means of including them and getting their feedback, I won't be able to sort out whether a complaint is actually a technical problem or a disguised interpersonal one.*

Tom: *One suggestion you may find useful when you do seek out this kind of feedback is to keep the situation problem-focused. Blaming won't help anyone.*

Kelly: *You're right. I need to show that I'm interested in moving forward, in getting on with it, and that a forward-looking perspective of "how can we make this work" is the only one I possess. Hey, I think I know what to do now. Thanks for listening.*

Critique

The problem with most ideas is that they are difficult to implement. This is true not because they are impractical or unworkable, but because they require changes. Change disrupts routines and creates uncertainties; anxieties are aroused; patterns are altered; predictability is exchanged for unpredictability. But in addition to the interpersonal problems created, the implementation of ideas also creates technical problems. It is unlikely that any new piece of equipment or procedure would not need to be fine-tuned once implemented. It is rare that all details could be accurately taken into account prior to the implementation of an idea. Thus, both technical and interpersonal factors make the implementation of new ideas difficult.

As revealed by the dialogue in this situation, Kelly found out that it is difficult to sort out technical complaints from interpersonal ones. They interact with each other and make change difficult. Eventually, Tom is able to help Kelly see the importance of involving employees in implementation of decisions in order to facilitate the change process. How Tom did this is instructive. Tom helped Kelly see the difference between her *intentions* and her *actions*. He noted that Kelly really intended for the programmers to offer their suggestions, but her actions seemed to say, "I don't need your help." Consequently, other people didn't offer suggestions because they resented what appeared to be Kelly's self-sufficiency. By distinguishing between her intentions and her actions, Tom was able to help Kelly see the impact of her decisions on others.

Tom avoided dependency-inducing offers made by Kelly as well. At two separate times when Kelly asked Tom what he would do, Tom turned the question back to her. This was very appropriate for this situation. Kelly was new as a supervisor and on the verge of implementing her first major change in her work group. If Tom had told her what to do, she may have further doubted her own ability and even lost confidence in her judgment. As it was, she left not only with an action plan, but also with self-insight. Tom was useful to test ideas and redirect her thinking, but he also reinforced her ability to derive solutions for her own problems.

How Do I Develop A Sense Of Teamwork With My People?

Situation

Phil Grant is the new staff manager in a large corporation. He has worked for the company for about 15 years and is in a very responsible position, especially given his age and experience. He supervises a group of about 15 professionals. There are two different supervisors who report directly to him, although the group has been fairly unstructured and free flowing because of the nature of the work relationship. Everyone is required to work together in order for the group to function effectively. Phil is concerned about coming in as a manager because he knows that each of the two supervisors had considered themselves potential candidates for the job. Additionally, some of the professionals have a feeling that he doesn't have the necessary experience to be the manager of the work group.

Don Brown is a training specialist for the group and met Phil at a training program that Don put on several months ago. Consequently, when Don was in Phil's area, he decided to drop by and ask him how things were going with the new job.

Don: *Hey, Phil, I was just passing through and thought I'd stop by and chat.*

Phil: *Well, hello, Don. It's good to see you. I'm glad you did come by. I wanted to say thanks for the training program you put on a couple of months ago. I thought it was very well done.*

Don: *Great. I liked your comments and wondered exactly what you thought of it. I am glad to find you enjoyed it.*

Phil: *Yes, I really did. It was something that was very useful for me. It was also very timely.*

Don: *I know that you're in a new job. I guess that's part of the reason for my wanting to stop by. I wondered how the adjustment was going.*

Phil: *Oh, it's going pretty well. I feel like this kind of work isn't completely new to me, and I've been a supervisor before, you know.*

Don: *Yes, I know. This is, I think, a particularly challenging group. A lot of senior professionals are in the group. A lot*

*of people believe they can work almost without a
supervisor.*

Phil: *Yes, I know. I've experienced that already.*

Don: *Do you find any particular challenges that the program
may have been helpful with?*

Phil: *Oh, I don't know. I guess there are several kinds of things.
I did get some new ideas and see more clearly the
challenges of a new supervisory assignment. I am not
exactly sure how to implement and apply all those good
things I learned, but I'm sure it'll come.*

Don: *Well, that's good. I want you to know, Phil, that I'm
always available if you would ever like any private
consultation. I'll be happy to talk and work with you and
hope that you'll feel free to call upon me.*

Phil: *OK, I'll do that. There is one thing that I had in mind. I'd
like to talk with you now if I could, for a minute.*

Don: *Sure, Phil. What is it?*

Phil: *How do I develop a sense of teamwork with my group? It
doesn't seem like we are really working together as a unit.
Have you got any particular ideas?*

Don: *Oh, I have some ideas on that topic. It certainly is an
important question. Can you tell me a little bit more why
you feel that it is a problem?*

Phil: *Well, there is a lot of internal conflict. Things like
backbiting and backstabbing. Unless people are absolutely
required to work together, they don't. I mean not on a
surface level. If something is visible and needs cooperation,
it's given. But if something occurs where no one is clearly
identified as responsible, it seems to fall through the
cracks—no one takes responsibility. Then when a problem
does result from something falling through the cracks,
everybody blames one another. It's just not a good
situation. And I'm not sure exactly what to do about it.*

Don: *Does this seem like something that has been fairly recent,
or have people worked this way for a while?*

Phil: *Well, I think it began before I came here. The kind of
resentment that some people have for one another is
something that wouldn't just develop overnight. I think it
has been fairly long-term.*

Don: Well, your people do seem to need to work together a lot. What have you thought about?

Phil: I have thought about just getting them all together and laying down the law. Letting them know I expect them to cooperate and work together and stop their juvenile way of operating as in the past.

Don: Well, that certainly is one approach. You think it would be effective?

Phil: Well, I think it would help. Don't you?

Don: I don't know. It did come across like an accusation and kind of parental. Like these are the things you should do. People may resent that even more.

Phil: You mean like I'm "big daddy" coming in and telling them what to do, that they haven't been acting as they should.

Don: Yes. In fact, the difference is that you used the word juvenile in saying that you wanted the people to stop acting that way.

Phil: Oh yes, that's true.

Don: Phil, if I were to ask you to describe the best work team that you had ever worked on, do you think you could do it?

Phil: Oh yes, for sure. It would be easy. I think that...

Don: Don't tell me right now, Phil. I was just wondering if you could do it.

Phil: Yes, it would be easy.

Don: Would it be easy to describe the things that people did, the kind of behavior, the way they acted with each other as well?

Phil: It would take a little bit more thought. Yes, I think it is something I could do.

Don: That's good. I think it is something that people on your work team could do as well. If you were to ask them to describe characteristics of the best team they had ever worked on and things that people did to make that a good work team, you'd come up with a lot of their own ideas.

Phil: So you're saying a way to develop teamwork is to have people describe the best team they've worked on?

Don: That's right. You get a chance to participate in that activity as well, and someone isn't just telling them about *it, but they develop ideas from their own experiences, and ideas that they will see as being valid.*

Phil: *That's good. That's a good suggestion and an important way to begin to develop teamwork.*

Don: *I think it's useful to look at a team like a family, if you want to develop teamwork. In a family, everybody has responsibilities, and if there are problems, then all share some degree of responsibility. I guess I'm saying in a family, if there is a wayward child, it's not just because the child is bad or is a bad person, but because things have happened in the family as a result of interaction between that child and other brothers and sisters, friends and others, that the child acts the way he or she does. The same thing is true in a team. If there is conflict, backbiting, blaming, or things falling through the cracks, it's not a matter of identifying individuals, but of saying, "There's something going on in the whole team, something that is not right." When there are problems in work teams, it is usually due to the way the team does or doesn't fit together; looking individually for a source or root of a problem is not going to be as helpful as looking at the whole interaction.*

Phil: *That's an interesting perspective. Comparing a team to a family, looking at the interaction as a focal point, are perspectives I hadn't thought about. But now that you've said it, I can see that it would be important. As much as anything, it would prevent people from blaming each other because there would be no one to blame but themselves; and since everybody shares in responsibility, if something fell through the cracks, we would all feel the same responsibility for it.*

Don: *That's right. The fact that something fell through the cracks is more important than anything else. Everybody shares responsibility to a certain extent. Then you don't begin to look at who or why it happened but rather at what the conditions are that support something falling through the cracks and how we can change those conditions to make sure everything is picked up.*

Phil: *That is a good perspective. One I would like to share with my team as well.*

Don: As much as anything, I think, Phil, sharing experiences and common activities builds teamwork so that people can begin to see that they have a common responsibility to one another. The more you can develop common activities, like having everyone describe the characteristics and actions of the best work team they've been on, the more successful you are going to be in developing teamwork.

Phil: That's a good idea. Tell me, Don, what do you think about this idea of participative decision-making?

Don: What do you think about it, Phil?

Phil: Well, I see some advantage to it, but I also have some reservations about it. I see that it could promote this common activities idea of yours, but I guess I could feel apprehensive about it because it could also cause negativism if people aren't prepared to handle it. It would just promote more backbiting, more infighting.

Don: Well, I think you've identified some of the pluses and minuses, and now you'll have to decide yourself if and when they may be useful. The one thing I think is a key factor to ask yourself is "How much support do people in the work team need to give to implement a particular decision?" When you need their support, you may want to invite their participation. Yet when their collective support is not a necessity, it may not be as useful to have their participation. The thinking I like better than participation is the idea of consent, Phil.

Phil: What do you mean by that?

Don: I mean it's the manager's responsibility to make decisions. But in making those decisions, whatever you decide is only part of the answer. How it is implemented is also important, and until that decision is well-executed, well-implemented, it's not well-made. I think as a manager you may have different perspectives and different information than others on your team, and so it may be important for you to make a lot of decisions on your own; but it is also important to communicate the basis for those decisions and to get people involved in implementing them. Management by consent means you share implementation procedures with other people.

Phil: *I like that notion. That's something that seems to be more direct, more specific. It also fits in with this whole idea of sharing responsibility for achieving collective goals.*
Everyone has different responsibilities in a family. Well, you've certainly given me a lot of ideas. What I'd like to do is think about them.

Don: *Well, if you want to talk about this again, feel free to come and talk.*

Phil: *OK, this has helped me. Thank you for your time.*

Critique

Every organization possesses two conditions. One has to do with organizational output or consequences and the other with organizational dynamics or methods. Most of the time the performance of organizational units is measured strictly in terms of output: production, costs, turnover, absenteeism, and the like. But these outputs are affected by various organizational dynamics that, although measured less frequently, are also important. Commitment, involvement, and satisfaction are just some of the possible ways to measure organizational dynamics.

The distinction between organizational output and dynamics can be highlighted by comparing an organizational unit to a complex piece of machinery. The piece of machinery is designed to produce some output, such as loaves of bread, aluminum cans, or cardboard boxes. But to achieve that output it must be lubricated, have worn parts replaced, and have all gears meshed. This is directly analogous to organizational functioning. In order for people in an organization to achieve output objectives they must share the organization's goals, priorities, and procedures.

One way to get employee commitment, researchers have consistently found, is by getting employees involved in matters that affect their organizational lives. The essence of the involvement principle is that employees are most productive and satisfied when they are included in the establishment of some of their own goals and procedures.

Team development can supplement the usual downward flow of information with some communication moving upward. It can do this by getting all of those who work in an organizational unit involved in the assessment of how well things are going. Managers, with all of the demands inherent in their position, cannot know enough or control enough to run the whole show.

Team building can achieve five primary objectives when conscientiously applied at the supervisory level. These are:

1. increasing employee identification with the organization;
2. increasing employee identification with the work group;
3. increasing employee commitment;
4. expanding the perspective of all workers;
5. assisting the manager in actively managing the work.

During this counseling session, Don avoided giving quick and easy answers to the questions Phil posed. He did this for a very important reason. Phil seemed to be looking for an easy way out of his situation and would clutch at any straw available as long as the solution was neither time-consuming nor demanding of him. He was looking for a way to escape responsibility for solving the problem himself.

By continually asking probing questions, Don was able to help Phil more completely analyze the situation. Don freely expressed his ideas and did not hesitate to join with Phil in evaluating possible options for developing teamwork. Without Don taking this position, Phil might have grabbed the first option that appeared reasonable and ended up with the right solution to the wrong problem. Don shared his thoughts whenever they talked generally about teamwork, but held back and asked questions when Phil began to talk about building teamwork in his own work group.

Work Rules

But I've Never Had An Accident!

Situation

Art is an exceptional worker in most respects: dependable, thorough, experienced. As one of the senior people on his shift, he is looked up to and respected by most of the younger employees. Ben, his supervisor, is appreciative of Art's good example in every aspect of his work except safety awareness. Seeing Art in an area that requires safety glasses, Ben decides to discuss safety with him.

Ben: Hey, Art, how are things going?

Art: Pretty good. What's up? You look like you have something on your mind.

Ben: As a matter of fact, I do, Art. At our safety meeting last week, I stressed the importance of wearing safety glasses whenever you were in the A zone. This is Zone A. Where are your safety glasses, Art?

Art: I don't know if they're home or in my locker. I'm never sure. I'll look for them first chance I get.

Ben: That's good. Meanwhile, here's an extra pair you can wear until the shift's over.

Art: Oh, come off it, Ben. We've known each other for 10 years, and you know that I've never had an accident in that entire period. Why should I wear safety glasses?

Ben: Because you never know what tomorrow may bring. What's more important to you than your eyes? Have you thought about what it would be like if you were blind?

Art: What are you trying to do, play on my emotions?

Ben: Remember when we saw that kid take off from the parking lot on a motorcyle the other day? He had his helmet slung over his sissy bar instead of on his head. And you said, "There goes an accident waiting to happen." You're not much different from that guy, Art, because both of you think you're experienced enough that an accident can't happen to you. But like that biker, you can't predict what mistakes others might make that would affect you.

Art: Yeah, but I do watch out for the other guy. I know he's there.

Ben: Do you also know that all those other guys are watching you? You're one of the senior people in this section. The less experienced employees watch you and learn from your example.

Art: I hadn't thought about that before. But they're so bothersome to keep track of, Ben. It's too much of a nuisance for me.

Ben: I can understand that. What do you think would help not only you but also the others to use your safety glasses more often?

Art: Tie 'em around our necks, maybe.

Ben: We could do that.

Art: I was only kidding, Ben. But seriously, the hassle of carrying them around and only needing them when doing certain jobs during the day is the biggest reason some of us don't wear them. If somehow they would just be there when we needed them, more folks would use them.

Ben: How about that as an idea?

Art: What?

Ben: Keeping safety glasses at hazardous work locations where they are needed. We could build a little box for them and put up a sign. We could even have employees initial a *schedule showing the times when they used a pair of glasses to do a particular task. We could monitor the effectiveness of the effort that way.*

Art: *That would work because it would make safety glasses more accessible and would eliminate each employee keeping track of his or her own pair. This convenience factor would really help. Let's try it.*

Ben: *If we do, can I count on you to set an example by using them and encouraging others to do the same?*

Art: *Yes, you can.*

Ben: *Good. You or someone else may someday be grateful for the emphasis placed on wearing safety glasses.*

Critique

Knowing is not necessarily doing. The profundity of this simple statement is amply illustrated by examining safety behavior. It is not enough that people know how to perform safely on the job, they must also be stimulated to do so. Most efforts at accident prevention focus on training employees to work safely. Developing this job know-how is an important first step to safety achievement. But it is also important to consider the factors in the job environment which either encourage or discourage safe behavior. Since most organizations that utilize machinery of some kind in their production process emphasize safety, understanding why people ignore safety rules and how counseling approaches can be applied to improve behavior seems important.

Ben's approach with Art begins with a direct confrontation. But Ben and Art are friends, and Art is able to use their relationship as well as his accident-free history to defend himself. Art further resists Ben's attempts to rationally convince him to wear safety glasses. Art's logic is suspect because both men know the *outcome* Art is seeking. This is always a detriment to persuasion. When there appears to be a predetermined outcome to a situation or solution to a problem, people will interpret attempts to get them to that outcome or solution as manipulation. They will resist it. In cases like these, it is easy for the boss to simply say, "Do it." But if the boss does fall back on asserting authority, the worker is likely to resent it and comply with this and other rules only when the boss is around to enforce them.

When Ben's attempts at describing the value of wearing safety glasses proved unsuccessful, he switched his focus from Art to the other employees. Art didn't think wearing safety glasses was useless, he just considered them unnecessary for *him*. When Ben pointed out that other employees were watching and taking note of Art's example, a chink of his defensive armor was penetrated. Art stated a reason why he didn't wear his safety glasses: they were bothersome. Then, instead of discounting this, classifying it as merely an excuse, Ben seized upon it as an opportunity to do problem-solving. He used the opportunity to involve Art in developing a solution to this new problem knowing that involvement is a prelude to commitment. After a solution had been identified and plans for implementing it formulated, Ben exacted a specific commitment from Art to improve his safety performance.

I Was Only A Few Minutes Late

Situation

Phil Daniels is a recently hired employee. He is assigned as a clerical assistant, and this is his first real job other than occasional day labor. He is eighteen, and dropped out of high school 2 years ago, but has recently been going to night school to get a high school certificate. When Dottie Moffet, the supervisor, hired him, she knew that she would need to work carefully with Phil to explain the job, answer questions, and generally be a resource to him. His first day on the job, Dottie spent a lot of time with Phil and felt that she had made progress in working with him. All was well for the first few days until Phil Daniels came into work about an hour late.

Dottie: *Phil, I'd like to talk with you for a few minutes if I could.*
Phil: *Sure, Dottie. What's on your mind?*
Dottie: *I am really pleased to have you working for us, Phil. I feel like the first few days you made a good impression on several people and tried hard to hold your job.*

Phil: Well thanks, Dottie. Uh, what else is on your mind,
though?

Dottie: I think you had a really good beginning coming in 4
days in a row on time. Today was really your first miss.
Phil, it is important for everyone to come to work on
time. We all depend on one another.

Phil: I know that, Dottie. I don't want to let anybody down.
Actually, I intended to come to work on time, but I had
car trouble.

Dottie: I know things come up from time to time. If you know
you are going to be late for some reason, though, it is
important to call your supervisor. You knew that, didn't
you?

Phil: Yes, I guess I did. I just forgot to call. I thought it
would be easier if I worked on the car and came in as
soon as I could.

Dottie: I am glad that you are here, and that you came in as
soon as you could. But I do want to stress the
importance of calling if you're going to be late or not
going to be here at all. I also think it is important to
come to work on time everyday. And as I say, things do
come up, but we do expect everybody to be at work on
time everyday, unless there is some extenuating
circumstance.

Phil: I know that, and I will be at work on time from now on.

Dottie: I know you will be able to do it too, Phil, if you work on
it. Sometimes it's not easy to get up in the morning and
plan a day. Especially when the night before you may
have had other things to do and couldn't check on things,
or maybe unexpected things come up, like car trouble.
But I think it is important to realize that we all have a
responsibility to be at work as well.

Phil: I know that, Dottie, and I don't think this is anything to
get upset about. It only happened once. You said it is
only the first day I've missed.

Dottie: I know it is something that only happened once and I
am really glad for the days that you have come to work
on time. I just want you to know that tardiness and
absenteeism are things we all need to control. There are

procedures that management established as work rules for all of us, so that we all feel like we have the same standards. Probably the thing that can reduce morale in a work group quicker than anything is if the boss is seen by employees as giving one person preferential treatment. I want you to know, Phil, that every time you're late or absent that I want to talk with you about it. That doesn't mean that I don't trust you, or that I think you've done anything wrong, except that I want to treat you the same as every other employee. Any time any other employee in the plant is late on my shift, I talk to them; likewise, any time an employee is absent. I want everybody to know that we have no part-time jobs and also that we all are expected to live up to the same standards. I think it is important to treat everybody the same, don't you, Phil?

Phil: *Yes, I do. I'm glad that you are willing to treat me the same as everyone else, and I'm going to do better.*

Dottie: *That's great. I'm glad. I really am glad to have you as an employee, Phil, and I think you are going to make a good contribution. I'm also glad for our little talk. And please remember to call if you're going to be late or absent for any reason. Establish this precedent, that regardless of the reason for lateness or absenteeism, I'm going to have a little talk with you and with anyone else. I am concerned for your well-being as well as for establishing fairness and uniformity by treating the same. Thanks for the chat. See you later, Phil.*

Phil: *Thanks for talking, Dottie. See you later.*

Critique

Dottie has either learned or knows intuitively about reinforcement and control. It is especially important in dealing with an employee who is new or feels a little insecure to place stress on positive aspects of performance. Discipline or expressed reprisal are likely to have negative effects, produce temper outbursts, or create a desire to get back at the boss in some other way, possibly, even resignation.

A supervisor, who patiently encourages an employee and reminds the employee about what still remains to be done to meet the total job requirements, will most effectively handle problems such as this. It is just as important to be firm on standards as it is to show concern. This takes conscious effort on the part of the supervisor to avoid a more obvious emotional reaction or temptation such as: "He let me down, he's just as I thought he would be—inadequate. The only thing he will ever understand is discipline. I'll show him who's boss here." Such attitudes and perspectives are likely to produce negative rather than positive results. Someone who has never been required to be on time, who never has had the importance of being on time stressed, who feels that excuses can be offered and absenteeism or lateness justified, will continue to be late and develop or make up reasons for doing so. It is natural to expect that a person who is absent or late has done it for a devious purpose and will be both on the offensive and embarrassed when approached. Calling a person on the carpet, questioning their integrity, will not produce desired results. The likelihood is that it will only make the employee mad. It is important in such cases to be supportive, positive and know things the employee has done well in order to build the necessary self-confidence—the feelings of acceptance in the employee. Similarly, it is necessary to let the the employee know that rules or standards must be abided by.

The supervisor, in this vignette, not only was positive in encouraging the employee by noting things the employee had done well during the first few days of work, but also was positive in stressing the importance of being on time and the fact that a supervisory discussion could be expected every time someone came in late or returned from an absence. The reason for the lateness or the absenteeism did not matter. The fact that it occurred was justification for the discussion. The mere fact of having a discussion, of stressing the importance of standards, not acknowledging the validity of whatever reason for absenteeism was given, will serve as an effective reinforcement tool which will let the employee have an opportunity to produce positive results at work. Proper reinforcement requires frequent contact and feedback and prompt response on the part of the supervisor. Unfortunately, it takes time on the supervisor's part. The problem will not go away by itself. It needs to be confronted and dealt with in a positive rather than punitive manner. A supervisor needs to be matter-of-fact rather than vindictive about enforcing rules. If enforcement of rules is consistent and uniform, that is, if truly no one is treated differently, it is rare that the discipline will be resented. Obviously, and with individual differences, the manager must expect to devote extra time and effort if he or she is genuinely interested in improving in these matters.

Are You Saying I'm Abusing the Absenteeism Policy?

Situation

Jean has returned to work after being absent for two days. She has been out quite a bit for various reasons in recent months. She has provided a doctor's statement regarding her illnesses on most occasions. She has never been out for more than four days at a time, and sicknesses have typically been colds or the flu. Her boss, Bob Brown, has just called Jean into his office.

Bob: *How are you feeling today, Jean?*

Jean: *Better. It was nothing very serious, but I did feel under the weather. I think I'm over it now, though.*

Bob: *I'm glad, Jean. I wanted to talk to you about your absenteeism record. I was reviewing it earlier today, and I counted 15 days lost on six different occasions in the last five months. I'm concerned about a record like that, and I want to discuss it with you.*

Jean: *I'm not sure why you want to talk about it. Sure, I've been out a few times, but I haven't stayed home unless I didn't feel well. Surely you wouldn't want me to come to work and make everyone else sick, would you?*

Bob: *No, when you're sick and in bed, I do want you to stay home. But, I think there are times when someone doesn't feel 100% and should still come to work. It is difficult to find a substitute for a day or two to do the work that you can do when you are here.*

Jean: *Are you saying that I'm abusing the absenteeism policy, that I wasn't really sick? Is that what you are accusing me of?*

Bob: I'm not accusing you of anything, Jean. I am concerned about your absences and want to emphasize the importance of coming to work if you just feel a little under the weather.

Jean: I do come to work in those cases, lots of times. Are you saying I really wasn't sick some of those days that I was out?

Bob: I'm not saying that, Jean. If you are sick, no one wants you to come to work. But, I also want you to know that it is difficult to cover for you when you are out. Some days we may want to stay home when we feel under the weather, but we could still do our work without making others sick or feeling much worse ourselves. In the future, I'd like you to think in those terms before deciding to stay home.

Jean: Yeah. Sure.

Bob: I want you to know that you are needed here. I want you to know what I expect in all aspects of your work. I don't want you to feel that you must come to work if you are sick, but likewise, I feel that you can still decide to come to work even when you don't feel very well. At least, that's what I think. How about you? Tell me what you think about it.

Jean: Oh, I don't know. You're right, I guess.

Bob: I do want you tell me what you think.

Jean: I am. It's just so hard some days to get up and come to work. Get up. Gulp some coffee. Fight the traffic. Sometimes the routine gets me down. I don't feel well, so I stay home.

Bob: I know the feeling. I like my job, but sometimes the hours go slow. When that happens, I try and think of some way to break up the routine, some little thing. It really helps me.

Jean: Oh, yeah? Some little thing, huh?

Bob: Sure. In your case, something different for breakfast, a different route to work, a walk around the building once you get here. What do you think?

Jean: That might help.

Bob: Will you try something? Sometimes getting to work is the worst part of the day.

Jean: *I know. Sure, I'll try some of those things.*
Bob: *Good. I do hope your presenteeism will be the result.*
Jean: *It will. Thanks for your understanding.*

Critique

Absenteeism is a common problem in some organizations. Sometimes job factors such as stress contribute to high absenteeism rates. Sometimes personality factors such as maturity correlate with higher than usual absenteeism. Absenteeism is generally a symptom of some other more basic problem. It is a sign that the person has not adjusted well either to the job or some non-work related event. Moreover, a single absence means far less than a pattern of missed days.

Bob handled this correction discussion well. After some small talk, he came to the point and explicitly described his reason for wanting to talk to Jean. He made no excuses or allegations. He simply presented the facts: Jean's recent history of lost days. As was to be expected, Jean became defensive. Bob, however, avoided talking about Jean's reasons for being out—all of which he did not question. Rather, he stuck with his position that Jean's total missed days were high and emphasized the importance of work attendance.

This approach of Bob's is generally the most beneficial in correction situations such as this. Discussing reasons why an employee was out seldom does any good. He or she will likely see this as a time to defend his or her integrity and will only feel vindicated when a supervisor or someone else is not able to back up any other position. Instead, Bob suggested that a work-related standard of performance was not being met, regardless of the reason, and that something needed to be done about it. Through his persistence, he was able to get Jean to see this point.

Once Bob had gotten Jean to accept the importance of regular attendance, he then became interested in listening to ways that goal might be achieved. He asked for Jean's ideas and found out a primary reason for some of Jean's missed days. Together they then discussed options and action steps. The sequence of these procedures is important. Bob showed no sympathy until Jean seemed convinced that attendance was an important standard of performance that needed to be met. Once the boundaries of the discussion had been defined, only then could a productive problem-solving interview take place.

Unit 8

Coping With Job Demands

There's So Much Stress In This Job

Situation

Harold Bronson is a newly appointed supervisor over a group of engineers. He has worked for the company for about ten years and was promoted less than a year ago to the engineering supervisor. Recently, he was asked to attend a supervisory training course that was conducted and coordinated by Lynn Reece. At that course, Lynn and Harold had a chance to talk about several different topics. Thus, it did not come as a major surprise for Lynn to see Harold one morning in her doorway.

Harold: *Say Lynn, got a few minutes so we could talk?*
Lynn: *Sure do. What's on your mind?*
Harold: *Oh, I thought I'd come by and talk with you a little bit about a problem I'm having.*
Lynn: *Problem?*

Harold: Yes. You know, Lynn, I just can't seem to get my act together and do this job well. There just seems to be so much stress in this job, so much pressure for me to perform, so many demands. I really have a hard time thinking.

Lynn: What kind of demands do you feel, Harold?

Harold: Oh, demands from everybody. Demands on my time from my boss, demands on my time from subordinates, pressure to perform, complete projects and do them to meet all deadlines, pressure to perform well socially. We've recently been invited to several social events that people in the company here sponsored. I even feel pressure to perform there. I take work home every night; I never seem to have enough time to take a vacation day, just take a day off, or even go out for a relaxing lunch. I feel uptight, nervous, and intense a lot. I don't know, I just don't seem to be coping with it all very well.

Lynn: It seems that at least you have identified that you have a problem in this area.

Harold: Yeah, I've got a problem, all right. I've got lots of problems. My problem is not that it's difficult to see, my problem is what to do about it.

Lynn: I think I hear you saying, Harold, that you feel fairly confident that the problem you have is the stress in your life: the demands, the pressures and being able to cope with them.

Harold: Yeah, that's right. What do I do to cope with such stress?

Lynn: Well, I think one of the most popular solutions is to meditate and spend some time relaxing and thinking about something else. There are many courses available on meditation, and a lot of good books as well.

Harold: No, no, I don't want to do that. You know, meditation may be good for some other people, but it's not for me. It seems so hokey to me, something that is faddish, that only somebody who is radical would even consider.

Lynn: You'd be inclined not to try meditation because of other people who are using it?

Harold: That's right. I don't want to be stereotyped by someone else. I want to try something that will work, not something that is off the wall.

Lynn: A number of executives have found relaxation techniques like meditation effective, Harold. I know it's been used by a number of companies and has even been encouraged by some presidents of major corporations.

Harold: Well, it may work in other companies, but it wouldn't work here. No, Lynn, that isn't something for me. I think that would create more stress rather than reduce it. I'd feel I was doing something crazy, something that was not completely acceptable.

Lynn: Another approach that a number of individuals and companies as well have found useful is regular exercise each day. What would you think about working out in a gym or going jogging on a regular basis? What appeal does a planned exercise program have for you?

Harold: No, I don't think that will work for me either. I know it will work for some people, Lynn, but I have tried exercise before. As a matter of fact, I get a lot of exercise. I walk to the bus stop and walk home and I get some good exercise that way. You know, I think exercise is fine for the right people, but I do a lot of exercises and that doesn't seem to have helped me much. It doesn't seem to release any pressure. Most of the time when I go out and play golf or tennis, I feel even more competitive. It induces more pressure and creates more stress, rather then relieving it. No, I don't think that would work either. Besides, I don't have the time to do something that would take more time.

Lynn: Well, I guess another thing that people have tried and found to be useful is to identify stress indicators, things that tend to induce stress in you. For example, you say that sports create more stress rather than relieve it. Are there other job-related actions that create stress? Can you identify those conditions, those factors, and then when you see them on the horizon, use them as early warning signals and realize that you may just need to talk to yourself, to say, "Hey, here's something I need to be *calm about"? Maybe even try some breathing exercises. That has been a useful technique to reduce and cope with stress.*

Harold: *My problem is, Lynn, that everything right now causes and creates stress. Nothing seems to work in my favor, and everything I do seems to add more fuel to the fire. As for breathing exercises, I don't know, I don't see how that could be very effective.*

Lynn: *Have you ever tried breathing exercises as a way to reduce stress and feel more in control?*

Harold: *No, but I don't breathe abnormally. I don't think it's anything that would work very well, that would help me.*

Lynn: *Harold, what do you see as contributing to your own stress, and what do you think could be done about it?*

Harold: *Me?*

Lynn: *Yes. You said several things that you do or encounter in your work add fuel to the fire, but are there some specific things that you think create stress, or do you have some specific ideas on how to deal with it?*

Harold: *Well, I guess I came to you to get some ideas, Lynn. If I already knew what to do, I wouldn't be coming to you to get your advice, would I?*

Lynn: *Gee, I'm not an expert in this area. The only thing that I can do is relate what's worked for other people. And there are some things that have worked for other people. What's worked for somebody else may work for you to a certain extent, but I'm sure that you have some ideas, Harold. Are there things you have thought of that could help you better cope and deal with your own situation?*

Harold: *I don't know, Lynn. I just don't know.*

Lynn: *Are there things you have considered trying or things that you have thought you would like to try?*

Harold: *Oh, I don't know, Lynn. I guess being aware that I have a problem in this area and that I need to do something is a beginning point. At least I know that something has gone wrong in my own system.*

Lynn: *That's right. Recognition is an important first step.*

Harold: *But recognition isn't enough, Lynn. That doesn't solve my problem.*

Lynn: I'm sure that's right. What solutions to the problem can you consider?

Harold: I guess the thing I have considered the most is trying in some way not to let the pressures bother me. Not to let them concern me so much. Not to be so anxious about them.

Lynn: I think realizing that you have some choices and you can choose how to react to the circumstances and events that come to you can be an important first step as a part of that awareness in realizing that you can cope with your stress and anxiety.

Harold: I'm not exactly sure what you mean.

Lynn: I guess what I mean is when you realize that you can make some choices about how to act or react to particular events, anxiety and tension are reduced a lot. It's only when we feel locked in, when we don't feel like we can make choices, that we feel a lot of pressure and anxiety. Recognizing that you can choose how to act and react to the tension and pressure is, in itself, an important tension reliever.

Harold: I can see what you mean. I can choose to let it eat on me, and I can continue to worry if everything is done, if it's done right, and if it's done on time. I can get upset at myself and worry. Or I can handle it another way, and just let things go as they will. But I'm not very good as a "ne'er do well", Lynn, it's too difficult for me and I don't think it's right to say, "Damn the whole thing, I'll just do my job and forget about the consequences."

Lynn: I agree, I don't think that kind of approach would be very successful. Let me ask you, though, how successful are you now?

Harold: I guess not very successful. I imagine other people pick up my tension as well. It's probably not too easy to work with me right now.

Lynn: I'll bet that's right, Harold. That's an important part of realizing how you cope with your own stress. That you look at the impact that your behavior has on other people, the influences it has on other people. And you ask yourself, "How would I react under those circumstances?"

Harold: *That's good, Lynn.*

Lynn: *Well, Harold, I guess what I would suggest is that you do look at your own life and at how you are responding to conditions and that you try some specific technique. Maybe it's meditation or just breathing exercises, or maybe it's some kind of recreation where you're not competing with somebody else. But do something that gives your body and your mind a chance to rest. As much as anything, stress is a reaction from our inability to cope. It's not all the pressure that creates stress, it's our inability to cope with the pressure that creates it. And the way we learn to cope is to give our bodies and our minds a sabbatical to a certain extent. Don't let them go all the time, but rather to consciously do nothing from time to time.*

Harold: *To consciously do nothing, huh?*

Lynn: *Yes, to allow your mind and your body to do something out of the ordinary. That's why I think that things that are a little different can sometimes be effective because they are out of the ordinary, out of the norm, out of the routine. And that gives our minds and bodies a break from the regular action.*

Harold: *Well, that's something to think about. I do appreciate your ideas, Lynn, and the time you have spent with me.*

Critique

Much of this vignette presents a typical dilemma faced by counselors. They want to help and they have some ideas which could be useful to the person they are counseling. But that other person isn't listening. For every suggestion the counselor offers, the employee has a reason why it can't work. This is an interpersonal game known as "Why don't you...", "Yes, but..." because it follows a pattern of counselor hints and employee excuses. People who are avoiding some personal decision and looking for ways to avoid taking responsibility often play this game. Whatever the decision is they are avoiding, they are also trying to reduce their anxiety caused by not making a decision. They want to put the blame for things as they are on someone or something else and thus fill their time with discussions centered on the fact they are not guilty of doing nothing themselves.

This particular interpersonal game is perhaps the most deceptive, and consequently the most common one, in which counselors participate. They want to help and so their good intentions get in the way of being helpful. When a counselor realizes that a counseling opportunity has turned into a "Why don't you ...", "Yes, but ..." game, the following questions might be asked of the other person to generate a more productive mode:

- What do you think you should do?
- What have you already considered doing but rejected?
- What were the pluses and minuses of these options as you saw them?
- I feel as if you came here looking for advice or assistance, but you don't think what I have to say is very helpful. Is there something I can do to be more helpful?

Each of these questions will cause the person to reflect on the discussion and look at the problem from a more personal point of view.

It is easy for a counselor to get entwined in a "Why don't you..." "Yes, but..." game with an employee who feels too much stress in his or her job. There are so many clichés and so many apparent solutions that work that a counselor may slip into this mode without even realizing it. This is because the human tendency is to be overwhelmed by tension and stress, and a counselor may try too hard to give the person techniques to resist it. An effective way of dealing with stress is to avoid what one observer calls "terrible simplifications."[1] Too often we attempt to reduce a situation down to an either/or dilemma and then get cold feet about it. Common simplications may be ones such as a choice for a man to "please my wife or please myself" in deciding on a promotion that would involve a relocation or a choice to "stand up for my rights" versus "turn the other cheek" in deciding how to respond to a racial or sexist joke. Tension increases with the importance of what we perceive as "no win" dilemmas.

Such stress-related concerns can often be reduced by making the dilemmas into objectives. How can I please my wife and myself? What do we really want? What conditions would make this move at-

[1] Karl Weick, "I Can Handle It: The Management of Stress," MBA (October, 1975) pp. 39-40.

tractive to her? What would I be able to do to enjoy my work if I turned the promotion down? Instead, simplifying things, making them move complex can help us see what we really want to do and why, and thereby open a tension relief valve.

I'm Really Not Sure What's Expected Of Me

Situation

Bill is a short-service employee with the company. He graduated about a year ago from a major university with an engineering degree and began working in the Civil Engineering section. He has had several good experiences in work assignments and has gone to several training programs where he has been able to learn more about his job and about company policies and practices. He recently attended a program that was conducted by John Henroten. John is an employee relations professional who has worked for the company for about ten years and is knowledgeable of company policies and practices. John and Bill talked informally for a few minutes and, because of the relationship that was established, Bill feels that he can express himself openly to John. Consequently, Bill has appeared at John's office to talk with him about a question he has.

Bill: *John, can I come in for a minute?*
John: *Sure, come on in, Bill.*
Bill: *Have you got a few spare moments on your agenda today, or are you pretty tied up?*
John: *I've got some things later today, but I've got a few minutes now.*
Bill: *I guess what I'm asking you is for some personal types of information. We had talked before and you indicated that you have had some background in counseling and performance appraisal. I know that that's the kind of thing you do in employee relations for other people, and I guess I'm coming here to pawn some advise from you.*

John: Well, if I can help in any way, I will.

Bill: I don't know if you can specifically help me or not, and maybe I'm just bellyaching, but I have been here a year now and I still don't know exactly what my job is with the company.

John: You say you don't know what your job is? Are there some specific things that you feel unsure about, or is it the nature of your work?

Bill: Well, I know when I come into work there are certain routine tasks that I have to do every day; certain amounts of paperwork, certain amounts of reports that I have to get out and go through. I guess what I'm really asking you is about some of the intangibles that are part of the job. You know, I have worked on a couple of major projects that have been really good; we have gotten them finished on time, and I played what I think is a pretty important part in them. And yet, no one has really sat down with me at any point in this whole year and said, "Bill, here is what we expect of you; these are the things that we would like you to do." It's more than just the job. More than just the things that I have to do each day. It's also things that I should be aspiring to. But there are no formal types of role guidelines laid down for me. There are things I've picked up, but I don't know if I am doing them right or wrong.

John: I guess it sounds like you feel you have done some good things in your work with which you feel satisfied. But you're not sure if that's all that's expected, or if there are other little things that you ought to be doing.

Bill: That's right.

John: Bill, is this something that somebody may have suggested to you, that you ought to be looking at other things, or is this just your own reflection?

Bill: I think it's mostly me, but I guess you can't always know for sure. Unless you have a straight set of standards by which to compare yourself, you always keep wondering, "Is there more that I should be doing? Should I have been doing this? Should I have stayed a little longer?" Yet, all I can do is watch those around me. And everybody's different, so I don't know what is right and what is wrong,

what's normal and what's above normal. I don't know into
which category I fall.

John: *Those are a lot of different questions. I think that they are*
all good questions. Some of them are questions that only
you yourself can answer. But some of them I think are
questions for you to be addressing with your supervisor.
How do you feel about your relationship with your boss?
Could you go to him and talk to him about these things?

Bill: *I guess I could. Maybe I'm naive, but I was hoping that*
sometime within this year he would sit down with me and
more or less say, "Bill, you know, you have been here so
long, three months, six months, nine months, a year, and
you have done these things and we think those are fine.
Let me sit down with you and give you some ideas of
your future and some acceptable standards that we would
like you to judge yourself against, some standards that you
can aspire to." I would have expected him to initiate that.
Maybe I'm wrong. In college it was a lot easier. I knew
what was expected to get an A, what was expected to get
a B, what would happen if I didn't turn a report in on
time. But here there are all kinds of deadlines—you meet a
lot of them, but you miss a few. And I kind of wonder,
"Where do I stand in terms of my performance, in terms
of my overall behavior in the job?" I think that my boss
should have done that and, since he hasn't, I guess I feel
that maybe he doesn't feel comfortable in that kind of role.

John: *Do you see it as your boss thinking that it's not*
important, that he doesn't have the skills, or that he feels
that you may already know how he feels about your
performance?

Bill: *Well, I don't know. It could be a combination of all three.*
Maybe he doesn't feel really confident about his ability to
get those kinds of things across to me. And then again, I
sometimes think maybe he thinks that since no one told
him any of these things and he had to pick them up
through the school of hard knocks, that's how everyone
should learn. You know, I'm not sure.

John: *I think everybody is different. I don't know your boss well*
enough to assess his perspective on the situation. I think a

big difference between college and work is the amount of feedback that we get. Oftentimes people like yourself don't get the feedback they seek and desire. I think, just as you asked the questions, about looking around and seeing everybody doing things a little bit differently, the same kind of thing is true about the amount of feedback people seek and the amount they want. How would you think your boss would respond if you went to him and said, "Here are some of the things that I am doing in my job. Here are some questions that I have about whether or not I should be doing other things." Have specific other things so that you don't just ask him in the abstract. Do you think he would be receptive to that or do you think he would feel you were being too aggressive, or would he see that as something that would be useful? This is from your boss's point of view.

Bill: *Yeah, I think he probably would find questioning useful. There has to be a middle ground; there has to be something that is a general type of thing, yet specific enough to suffice as a frame of reference for the information or feedback that I want. Yes, I am apprehensive that he might think that I'm looking for some praise or that I'm in there to brown-nose him or something by saying, "Hey, look, how do you think I'm doing?" I don't want to come off that way. I think that if I approach it in the right way, from a fairly objective standpoint, that might make his feelings such that our time talking together might be a little more beneficial.*

John: *I think that's a legitimate concern. Is there anything you think specifically would reduce your concern about brown-nosing, about coming on as just seeking praise?*

Bill: *I guess it would depend a lot on how I preface the situation.*

John: *You might ask him before you even go in how he would feel about a session like that.*

Bill: *Right.*

John: *You could tell him what is forthcoming.*

Bill: *You know, honesty is really the best policy. So if I were able to sit down with him and say, "Look, Bob, I really would like to talk to you very straightforwardly. I feel there are a couple of gray areas, things that I have some concerns about. Maybe then he might take it a little better and be able to handle it, too.*

John: *I would think as well that if you were up front about your concerns and said, "Listen, I'm not interested in just seeking praise. In fact, what I'd like to do is to write down some of my own weaknesses, some areas where I think I could develop." That way you go in with a kind of description of yourself, where you feel like you have not done as well as you could. If you can identify some of your areas of needed improvement, that may be more helpful for him. He probably sees you as someone who is eager, who wants to do well; he doesn't want to give you negative feedback if he does see your work going well. That may be a concern on his part.*

Bill: *It could definitely help me. I guess I am kind of jokingly thinking that maybe I'll point out some negative things that he hasn't seen in me. I guess I have nothing to lose, you know.*

John: *I guess at this point you have to ask yourself a question: Is it more important to look good or is it more important to learn? My own feeling, Bill, is that a lot of times I myself get too concerned about looking good. What I'm really interested in is improving. Especially at this point in time, the most important thing you can do is sort out the system, learn how things work, learn about the areas where you need to improve and get that kind of needed feedback. That's something that in the long run will be really valuable; I don't think in the short run it is going to hurt you either.*

Bill: *Do you think in the learning process, if I don't bring up the negative side, if I just kind of let things slide and try to look good on the outside, that policy might carry on and I might keep looking good. But if I approach it from, "I want to learn," and then maybe didn't look so well, do you think that would carry over in other peoples' minds? Would they think, "Hey, this guy is probably not as good as we thought he was." Do you think it would be kind of* a *"halo effect" and other people would see me that way too?*

John: *You sound a bit like you think it might.*

Bill: *I guess without knowing, without having experience in an organization or a lot of supervisors down the road, my only experiences are from classes. If you have a lot of professors in one department and one tabs you as a good student, it's likely to carry over. And it works the other way too. I guess I'm just wondering if, in my learning process, I don't come across as looking so good because I took the time to learn, maybe I was a little slower, maybe I asked more questions, or whatever. I'm just hoping I don't get tabbed as somebody that's a slow learner, not as sharp as they thought I was. I hope it doesn't carry on. I know how valuable this first impression is.*

John: *Let me ask you, Bill, relating back to the college's engineering department, people who asked a lot of questions, students who really sought to learn, to clarify, how were they viewed? Were they viewed generally as positive or did you see professors getting impatient with them?*

Bill: *Well, I guess the ones who asked a lot of questions basically asked them because they needed to know and wanted to learn more. I guess you're right. It all depends on the kinds of questions you asked. There was always somebody in the class who looked like he or she was asking questions just to be heard or to hear his or her own voice.*

John: *To show off.*

Bill: *Right.*

John: *I think this same kind of process is something that can be a means for you to show your boss how eager you are to learn and can likely be a very positive experience for you. Go in and see your boss, say some things like, "I'm working on my job, and I'm not sure how you see it. Here's how I see my performance. Here are areas where I want to do something else." And attempt to clarify and specify some things. I would think that could be a positive experience.*

Bill: I guess I'll just have to give it a try. It can't hurt. I'm kind of in the dark now, and I know if I don't do something fairly soon I'll either lie dormant or become too negative about even trying.

John: Again, I think it could be a useful experience. I think you have identified some concerns that are legitimate: concerns about having your boss wonder about your intentions, is it just to look good; concerns about learning, concerns about whether or not your boss sees this whole area as your needing more feedback. I think those are all concerns. You have addressed some ways to deal with them either by identifying your intentions early on, trying to objectively say how you think you have done in your work with reference to improvement or learning more. The whole process of initiating, if I were a boss, would come across to me as something very positive. Here's an employee who took initiative, who sought an area where he needed to get more feedback, where he wanted to learn more, and initiated this with me. I would think that would be positive.

Bill: Do you think that would make it easier for him to give me not just favorable feedback, since I would initiate it?

John: How do you feel about it?

Bill: I think it probably would. I haven't ever been in a supervisory position, but I would think that if someone came soliciting feedback and criticism, it would be a lot easier to give them the bad with the good, rather than to come and kind of dump it on them.

John: I would think so too.

Bill: I guess all I have to do is give it a try.

John: Let me know how it goes, Bill.

Bill: OK, I sure will. Thank you.

Critique

A common complaint voiced by short service employees or those recently transferred to a newly created job, is they do not understand what is expected of them. They indicate they get little direction and less feedback, and they are wandering from pillar to post in their assignment doing things that seem to need doing but not knowing if they are working on important matters or not. The lack of structure in their jobs, the limited supervisory interaction in most cases, and their own newness in a job all combine to promote a concern about doing accceptable work.

Managers and supervisors need to be aware of these conditions and take appropriate action to reassure those who are doing well and discuss standards of acceptable performance for those who are not. But the job should not be left to them. Individual employees need to take responsibility for their own development and request feedback from their bosses. Appraisal discussions and structured feedback need not be left up to the supervisor. In fact, such sessions should more appropriately be thought of as a tool for "managing the boss" since a subordinate finds out what the boss expects and learns how the boss sees the subordinate's development period. This process can be more productive, in fact, the more a subordinate is willing to assess his or her own strengths and weaknesses, describe what he or she has learned on the job in the last six months or year, and knows what he or she wants to learn in the next six months or year. In this counseling situation, John urged Bill to do some of this "spade work" and not expect his boss to take the initiative.

My Job Is So Boring

Situation

Carol showed a lot of promise during her first year with the company. She seemed so eager to learn and so willing to accept any new assignment that she was included on several key projects. Mid-level managers, when talking among themselves, often used her as an example of someone who had the personal traits plus the engineering know-how to really advance up the corporate ladder. Lately, however, several people had noticed that she wasn't as outspoken as she had been and her work was showing an unusual inattention to detail. Thus, when she finished talking with Mary Davis, a personnel specialist with the company, about another matter, Mary decided to talk to Carol about her job and her working relationships.

Mary: Now that we have that other project out of the way, tell me, how are things going in your job?

Carol: Oh, not too badly. I'm getting along okay. Why do you ask?

Mary: No particular reason, I'm just interested in seeing you do well. It is not an easy transition from graduate courses in engineering to a full-time engineering job. I'm simply interested in what things various people do to make the transition and what problems they experience in the process.

Carol: I'm not so sure that I'm a good example to use in either respect.

Mary: Oh, why is that?

Carol: Well, because just when I thought I had made the transition, I find myself dissatisfied. It's as if I've made it over the first hurdle and found that it's all downhill from there.

Mary: Your words suggest that's positive, but I get the feeling that you think it's not.

Carol: My job seems so boring to me now, I wish it were more challenging. I feel that everything is more of the same, that I may get better at what I'm doing or that some phase of a project will be unique, but I feel that basically I've learned all there is to learn in my current job. I know that sounds presumptuous, but it's how I feel.

Mary: Well, it's good to feel a sense of competence in your job.

Carol: It is, and I feel competent now. But I haven't always. I guess that's basically the reason why I don't feel my work is as challenging any more. Even though it was scary when I first started here, I realized there was so much that I didn't know and needed to learn just to survive. But survival isn't an issue anymore. I know I can make it, I'm just not sure if I want to . . . I've thought about going back to school and taking some courses in something else—maybe that would help.

Mary: More schooling might help, but you may not want to get locked into a solution until you have a better idea of the problem.

Carol: Oh, what do you mean?

Mary: Taking classes can give you information on topics, but once you master the information available in a given topic area, you are right back where you started from.

Carol: I see what you mean.

Mary: What I'd suggest instead of courses is self-analysis. Look inward instead of outside yourself for answers. For instance, since you have liked what you have been doing and have done well at it, why not discover what it was that made your job seem so challenging for six months and then try to orient your work and your day in such a way that you build these conditions into your activities.

Carol: What you are saying makes sense, but I'm not sure I even know where to begin.

Mary: Let me give you some suggestions, then. First of all, write down somewhere some recent experiences or activities that have been particularly satisfying. Select both some work and nonwork events. Then, analyze the situation and record why it was so satisfying. Was it because it was something out-of-the-ordinary? Did you get some particular recognition for doing it? Did you feel a part of a grand plan? Or feel included in a select group? Asking yourself questions like this can help you identify what makes something interesting to you. Then, you can examine your job and build into it some of these conditions, either through your own actions or by discussing them with your boss. The way I see it, any staff job has enough intrinsic flexibility in it that you can make it challenging by actions you take. First, though, you need to identify what challenges you.

Carol: I can see what you're saying. And you're right about my boss, too. He will allow me enough latitude to do things my way as long as things continue to get done.

Mary: If you'd like, Carol, I'd be happy to talk to you about translating your interest into job components once you have identified why the satisfying experiences you've recalled were so enjoyable.

Carol: I'd like that. It would help me do some good reality testing.

Mary: Fine. Call me later in the week whenever you're ready.

Critique

In 1970 the U.S. Department of Labor surveyed a broad sample of the American workforce regarding what they wanted from their jobs. Blue and white collar workers, managers, professionals and others were questioned. Eight separate factors were identified as important in a job and are listed below in priority ranking:

1. Interesting work
2. Enough equipment and help to get the job done
3. Enough information
4. Enough authority
5. Good pay
6. Opportunity to develop special abilities
7. Job security
8. Seeing the results of one's work

It is instructive to note that interesting work was seen as the most important job factor by this representative sample. It seems clear from this data that most people want more from their jobs than a paycheck. They also want work that is challenging and meaningful.

In recent years, much has been written and discussed about how jobs can be made more satisfying. Five characteristics of a satisfying job have been consistently documented by Richard Hackman of Yale.[2] These factors include:

- Task variety: Being able to work on several different kinds of tasks and use a variety of skills on the job
- Task identity: Being able to work on whole projects or tasks instead of bits and pieces of them
- Task significance: Working on things that really matter, that contribute to the goals of the organization
- Autonomy: Having some discretion about how or what things will be done
- Feedback: Knowing how well one is doing, both from verbal reports of others and seeing the results of one's work.

[2] A classic presentation of this research is reported in J. Richard Hackman and Edward E. Lawler, III, "Employee Reactions to Job Characteristics," *Journal of Applied Psychology* (1971) Vol. 55, pp. 259-286.

The responsibility for ensuring these job characteristics is usually thought of as resting with supervisors and managers. Although management definitely has a certain amount of control over these conditions, their influence is not all-encompassing, especially in staff jobs. Any job can be made more challenging and interesting by actions which the job incumbent takes. Making others responsible for one's satisfaction, either on the job or in other aspects of life, is a cop-out. People can and do have influence on how they do their work.

Is the direct and simple approach the best one? If someone feels under-utilized, should he or she approach a supervisor and state the case? In some situations, this method will work. In other situations, however, a boss would not know what to do with this information. He or she might by sympathetic, but what can be done about it? The work must still get done. A better approach than stating dissatisfaction would be for a subordinate to describe ways to be better utilized personally and to suggest tasks or goals that the unit might consider to achieve overall organizational goals better. This approach does two things. First, it puts the onus on the subordinate for stating ways and activities to be utilized better. Second, it is pragmatic and allows a supervisor to respond to specific suggestions instead of abstract feelings and perceptions.

In this situation, Mary was able to help Carol appreciate that she had primary responsibility for making her job challenging and interesting. A key reason Mary was able to reorient Carol's thinking towards self-analysis was that she did not overreact to Carol's statements regarding her job mastery. When Carol said she felt she had learned all she could in her job, Mary gave a neutral response. Then, Carol said more about why she felt bored, and Mary was able to point out that this could happen again if Carol decided to change fields just to relieve her boredom. By pointing out the likely consequences of her solution, Mary was able to redirect Carol. This is an important and useful counseling device. It is nonthreatening and nonevaluative. It helps the other person re-evaluate previous assumptions and remain open to other options. Once this receptivity is established, it may be appropriate to be directive and assist the other person in problem-solving. The sequencing, however, is critical.

Personal/Work Problems

I'm Not Sure I Can Handle Moving Again

Situation

Don walked slowly back to his office from his boss's office. He closed the door, propped his feet on his desk, rolled a pencil over and over in his hand, and studied the rain spots on his window. Finally, he picked up the phone and called Judd, a senior accountant in the company and a close friend. Judd had taken a special interest in Don when he first transferred into the home office and Don had often confided in him about personal problems as well as work-related problems.

Don: *Judd? Do you have some time right now to talk? I need your advice.*

Judd: *Sure, come on over.*

Don: *(After a few minutes Don arrived and closed the door behind him as he walked into Judd's office.) Well, they're about to do it to me again.*

Judd: *Who? What?*

Don: *The suckers are about to transfer me again. After only 19 months here, they're about to do it to me again. I can't believe it! I have told practically everyone that I wanted to stay here for a while, to establish some roots in the community, to give my wife a chance to know her neighbors. Fine, they all said. This job needs someone in it for a while, they said. Besides, we could move you into another section in the building when you're ready for something else so you wouldn't need to move again, they said. I just can't believe they would do this to me again!*

Judd: *Another move, eh?*

Don: *Yes, and to Los Angeles of all places. I just can't believe our enlightened management. They talk about being sensitive to employee needs and then do something like this to me.*

Judd: *Well, Don, if you really feel that strongly about it, don't go. I've known people who've turned down transfers and lived to tell about it.*

Don: *Oh, I know that. But I know the way those guys think, too. They'll say, I'm not loyal, not willing to make some personal sacrifices in order to advance myself professionally. Listen, if I thought I wasn't going anywhere in the company I'd turn down this transfer in a minute without any qualms. But I've been given a lot of encouragement in the last few years by people up the line. Unless they're just leading me on, they think I could go somewhere in the company.*

Judd: *Like Los Angeles? (Laughter)*

Don: *Yeah, I guess—like Los Angeles. And what would you do, Judd?*

Judd: *I'm not sure I even understand all your feelings about the situation yet, Don, let alone have enough information to give any advice. Tell me, what would your new job be?*

Don: *I'd be the Accounting Supervisor in the Budget Planning Section for the regional office there in L.A.*

Judd: *Mmmm. That would be a nice promotion for you.*

Don: *I know that. And I know some of the people out there and think highly of them. But I don't know anything about budget planning. As you know, all my experience has been in financial analysis. I know that kind of work and know I can do well in it. Budget planning is an unknown quantity.*

Judd: *Do you feel that you can do that kind of work? Is part of your concern about branching out into a new area?*

Don: *Partly, though I think it would be a good experience for me. Sure, I've some apprehension about doing well in the job, but what upsets me the most about this whole damn thing is the arbitrariness of it. I've told everyone I could that I didn't want to move again for a while. I think 5 moves in 9 years with the company is enough. I didn't want to be placed in a position like this of being forced to choose between my personal preferences and professional advancement. The thing is, Judd, I don't want to be possessed by my job, but I don't want to be left behind while others advance, either.*

Judd: *I can understand that. Have you talked to your wife about this yet?*

Don: *Not yet. I wanted to think about it for a while by myself first.*

Judd: *How do you think she would feel about the move?*

Don: *If I felt strongly about it, she would go. She has gotten used to the moving game maybe even more than I have. She cares about me and wants me to be happy in what I do. Likewise, I care about her and want what's best for her. I don't want her to feel guilty about encouraging me to remain here if we decide to stay. Until I'm less confused about what I want, though, I don't think we can discuss the situation very well.*

Judd: *I agree that you need to decide what you want, but I think talking it out with your wife and others is the best way to decide. Most of us think better when we do it out loud.*

Don: *Okay. So where do I begin?*

Judd: *First of all, I think you need to come to grips with your feelings about how the move was presented to you. Part of what I heard you say you were feeling was resentment due to what you see as the arbitrariness of the whole thing, is that right?*

Don: Yes. I know they think they know what's best for me, but I don't need their paternalism. I want to decide what's best for myself.

Judd: Sure you do. But don't let the way the situation was presented to you, or simply the fact that you were offered it, overwhelm you one way or another when you make your decision. Decide on the basis of whether or not the job and the move are what you want for you and your family.

Don: All right. I'll calm down and try and get a better perspective before I make a decision.

Judd: Do you have some time before you need to tell your boss your decision?

Don: He wants to know as soon as possible, of course. But he'll give me as much time as I need.

Judd: Do this, then. Weigh the advantages and disadvantages of accepting the move and then of not accepting the move with your wife. Write them down. Then, see what you can do to compensate for any of the disadvantages you list either in connection with going or staying. After you've done that, make a decision for a day. Think what things will be like if you followed through in the situation in the way you decided. Project yourself into that situation, for some things will be different whether you decide to go or to stay.

Don: That makes a lot of sense to me. And you're right, things will be different either way.

Judd: One other thing. The apprehension, the anxiety, the butterflies in your stomach, aren't likely to go away even after you've decided what to do. They'll probably stay with you for a while. Most big decisions have left me limp, tired, still a little worried even though I feel I've done the right thing and made the best choice for me. You may have the same experience. I think important decisions, once made, don't leave us exhilarated.

Don: You're right.

Judd: I'll be interested to know how you finally come out. I've had to make the same decision a few times myself, and maybe your choice would enlighten me some.

Don: *I know. Thanks for listening. I think I can approach the situation better now. I may want to talk to you again once I've talked things over with my wife.*

Judd: *Good. I respect and value our friendship and am always available to talk.*

Don: *Thanks. Thanks a lot.*

Critique

The personal and emotional costs of relocating are increasingly being documented. Diane Margolis has written an important new book on this topic entitled, *The Managers: Corporate Life In America.* The book is somewhat mistitled since it primarily discusses the feelings and perceptions of wives of corporate managers who participated in detailed interviews conducted by Margolis. The theme of this book is the benign tyranny of the organization that employs their husbands, a tyranny that is manifest primarily in the requirement that employees move house and household upon demand.[1]

Those who run corporations maintain that there are good reasons for periodically relocating employees: to avoid parochialism in decentralized locations, to provide visibility to those who are on their way to the top, and to encourage the dissemination of ideas and techniques. Yet, whether or not the frequency of such moves matches the benefits obtained, is often an unasked question. It is a question that those who are faced with relocation, however, ask themselves. It is an important personal question that should be both asked and answered.

In this situation, Don confides in a personal friend in order to sort out his own feelings about relocating again. He is angry and resentful about even being asked to move. He feels betrayed in a no-win situation. He believes that he must sacrifice either his career aspirations with the corporation or his family's well-being.

Judd's basic approach is to calm Don down so that they can look at the dilemma in a more rational way. Instead of paraphrasing and active listening, which would likely only cement Don's resentment, Judd provides humor. By doing this, the situation begins to look

---

[1] Diane Rothbard Margolis, *The Managers: Corporate Life In America* (New York: Morrow, 1979).

less bleak to Don. Once Don has expressed his feelings and been listened to by a friend, he has experienced the emotional equivalent of grieving. He is ready now to accept the situation as given and realistically evaluate his options.

Judd's approach emphasizes helping Don make a good decision about the choice that confronts him. Instead of focusing on problem definition, through his questions and counsel, Judd prompts Don to assess his options. An important bit of information that Judd provides is for Don to consider how he might compensate for the disadvantages that would be part of either moving ar staying. In decision-making, it is important, to move beyond *identifying* limitations inherent in a particular course of action and plan ways to *compensate* for them. Making a decision for a day and imagining the likely consequences (both positive and negative) also minimizes some of the finality of decision-making. Judd's approach helped Don to identify and decide in a more rational way—by counting the varied costs of both relocating and remaining where he was.

Who Says I Have A Drinking Problem?

Max: *You wanted to see me?*
Tom: *Yes, Max, I do. Come in and sit down.*
Max: *Okay, thanks. What's up?*
Tom: *How are things going, Max? Have things settled down anymore at home?*
Max: *Oh, yeah, sure. Why do you ask?*
Tom: *Mainly because I'm interested in you. I recall several months ago that you were having some problems adjusting to your separation from your wife.*
Max: *Things are going okay, I said. What's the big deal? (taking a deep breath) Sorry, I guess I am a little on edge. I've been sick the last few days and haven't fully gotten over it. Nothing serious, I just haven't slept well.*

Tom: There is something I would like to talk to you about, Max. You've been absent eight times and late almost a dozen times in the last four months. Your work hasn't been up to par either. You've made a lot more than your share of mistakes lately.

Max: I've been sick, I told you. What is it, a federal offense to take off when you're sick?

Tom: Not when you're sick and get better. You seem to get sick and get worse. Sloppy work, sloppy attendance, sloppy mistakes. I know you've got personal problems, Max, but you've also got a job to do here. I don't mean to be adding more pressure to you, but things have got to change.

Max: (suddenly mellow) Things are rough, Tom. I'm having a difficult time adjusting to Janet being gone. I'll work it out, though. Thanks for understanding.

Tom: I don't think you can work it out by yourself any more, Max. One of the bartenders at Joe's told me that you come in almost every night, sit alone, and drink a lot.

Max: Are you saying that I have a drinking problem?

Tom: I'm saying that you've got a performance problem. Whether or not you have a drinking problem, I'm not qualified to tell. I would like to refer you to a friend I have at the alcoholism center in town, though, to see what she thinks.

Max: I can hold my liquor. I don't know what you're talking about. I don't need to go to an alcoholism center.

Tom: Whether you hold your liquor or not is best determined by others. But I'm saying you're not going to be holding a job unless you use some professional help to prevent your personal problems from spilling over and interferring with your job.

Max: Are you serious, Tom? I thought you were my friend.

Tom: I am your friend, and that is why I'm very serious.

Max: You've always given me a chance before.

Tom: I'm giving you a chance now.

Max: But what about the positives in my work?

Tom: Lately, they've been few and far between.

Max: What if I don't go?

Tom: *You may soon be out of a job.*
Max: *Pretty grim choice you've given me.*
Tom: *Pretty grim work performance lately.*
Max: *Okay, tell me where I go.*
Tom: *Here's the phone number. Call and make an appointment.*

Critique

The key to a successful counseling session with someone who may have a drinking problem is a willingness on the part of the supervisor or manager to confront the troubled employee with the fact of his or her unacceptable performance. Confrontation is not easy. To be done well, it must convince the employee that he or she must choose between continued employment and professional help.

When confronted with documentation regarding poor performance, an employee with a drinking problem is likely to deny any responsibility for mistakes that have been made. Supervisors should anticipate that such an employee will attempt to deny responsibility for mistakes and be prepared for dealing with the employee's shifting the blame to others or promising to do better in the future.

The following sequence of actions provides a useful confrontation guide. The supervisor will be the most effective by:

- sticking to documented job performance;
- remaining detached emotionally when the employee attempts to deny that a problem exists;
- indicating that others are not going to cover for the employee's poor performance;
- insisting that things change immediately;
- offering an alcoholism treatment center as an available option; and
- avoiding moralizing or judging the employee.

Confrontation is seldom easy, but it is essential. Things will rarely improve or change without something specific happening. It is all the more difficult if the employee has been a good performer or is a friend of the supervisor. The supervisor must remember that even though it is difficult to do, it is clearly the best course of action available.

How Do I Satisfy
Both My Wife And Myself?

Situation

Al Rosen, in his mid-thirties, is a mid-level manager in a major corporation. He is seen as a "fair-haired boy" by those who have worked with him because of the apparent ease he has had in climbing the organizational hierarchy. He is respected by those who work with and for him and is viewed as able and competent. A good friend and peer, Vernon Stancil, who is 10 years his senior, has just invited Al into his office.

Al: *I'd like to talk to you for a while if you have time, Vernon. This is not a two-minute conversation.*

Vernon: *Sure, I've got time. What is it?*

Al: *I've got troubles at home, Vernon, and I'm looking for advice. How do you and Peggy do it?*

Vernon: *I think you meant that as a compliment, but I'm not sure I understand it fully. Do what?*

Al: *Oh, come on. You know what I mean. Get along so well. What's the secret of your success?*

Vernon: *Gee, I don't know. We talk a lot about what's important to each of us and we like each other. Other than that, I don't think we do anything all that special.*

Al: *I see. You've either got it or you don't.*

Vernon: *I'm not sure it's all that cut and dried. Is something in particular bothering you, Al?*

Al: *It just seems that Cathy and I are growing further apart. I've been working pretty hard lately and she can't seem to understand why it's necessary for me to do so. I'm trying to do a good job and be in a position to live comfortably. I know she wants that, too, but she's not willing to sacrifice to get it as I know I have to.*

Vernon: *Has she complained about money problems?*

Al: *No, not exactly. It's just that financial security, real long-term security, seems just around the corner if we both sacrifice a little to get it.*

Vernon: *And you're saying she's not willing to sacrifice?*

Al: That's right.

Vernon: What are you sacrificing?

Al: You sound like Cathy!

Vernon: Sensitive subject, huh?

Al: Yeah. (Pause) You know what I'm sacrificing. Time, energy, worry, commitment. All those things, just like you.

Vernon: It's not a sacrifice if I like to do it. If I like my work, it's not a sacrifice for me to put in long hours, go to company parties, and all that.

Al: It's the same with me. I like my job, and I don't mind the hours because I know the rewards that I'll get.

Vernon: Does Cathy see it the same way?

Al: No, that's why things aren't quite right at home. She wants a career, too. She wants to do something else and wants me to spend more time at home. And it's not that I don't want to do that. Listen, I love my wife and kids. They are more important to me than anything else in the world. I wouldn't want to lose them. It's just that I want to really get established in my career. In two to four years I think I'll be where I want to be and can relax and spend more time with my family. Right now Cathy can take care of them and in a couple of years she can pursue a career.

Vernon: She must not like that idea or you wouldn't be concerned about things right now.

Al: No, she doesn't like it. She can't seem to see things from my point of view. She says if she waits any longer to start a career it will be too late. She thinks it's almost too late now.

Vernon: What options have you considered already?

Al: Well, none really. We've had some suppressed discussions but that's about all. What do you suggest? How can I satisfy both my wife and myself?

Vernon: Listen, I said I didn't have a secret formula and I don't. But I do know that people experience different conflicts at home or within themselves and at different times in their careers. Right now your career is exciting to you, and so naturally you want to follow where it leads. But *the dilemma you face is that with your kids being 11 and 7, they probably need you now as much as they ever will. When they get to be teenagers, they won't even want to talk to you all that much even if you do have a good relationship with them. They will want to develop stronger peer ties. How do you meet these two demands on your time? I don't know exactly. What do you do now when you get home from work? Do you have any kind of routine?*

Al: *Nothing special. Read the paper. Eat. Maybe watch some TV and the evening news before going to bed. I like to relax and unwind when I come home from work.*

Vernon: *Sounds somewhat passive.*

Al: *It is a little. I just like to take it easy when I come home. It's nice not to have things as hectic as at the office.*

Vernon: *When did you last suggest a family activity?*

Al: *What do you mean?*

Vernon: *When was the last time—and I mean this sincerely, I'm not laying a trap for you—you said, "Let's do something together?"*

Al: *I can't remember, why?*

Vernon: *The nonparticipation in family affairs may be hurting your relationship with Cathy as much as anything. You want to relax when you come home, but she's ready to do something else. She's ready for you to take over so she can do something for herself. Being an absentee landlord may be part of the source of the problems.*

Al: *You're saying I need to take a more active part in family matters and my passivity is the problem?*

Vernon: *It may be part of the problem. I don't know. I think you know how to find out whether it is or not.*

Al: *Talk to Cathy, huh?*

Vernon: *Yes. But don't just talk to her. Decide what you want to do about it. Your own awareness of your sentiments as well as hers is a good first step.*

Al: *What's the second step?*

Vernon: *Make a list of goals. Write down what you want from your career, your family, and for yourself. Then write*

>*down what you think Cathy wants in those same areas. Have her do the same thing. When you've done that, write down what you're willing to do to achieve those goals and allow her to achieve hers. Then, take a weekend off, just the two of you, and share your lists. Set annual goals and review them on a monthly basis. Set aside a specific time each month to review your progress.*

Al: *Isn't that a bit structured?*

Vernon: *It is structured, but all good planning requires some structure, otherwise things don't get done. It puts you in an active role in your family relations and gives Cathy some input in planning your time so she can know what to expect for herself.*

Al: *These are some good ideas. I'll think about them. Thanks.*

Critique

The way in which the relationship between personal and professional life is experienced is largely a function of the way work itself is experienced. Whereas the pressures and tensions, or achievements and satisfactions, of the job tend to spill over into one's personal life, the inverse does not seem to hold true. People who do professional work, at least, appear to have highly developed skills in switching their personal problems off when they arrive at work. Perhaps because the job occupies so much of a person's waking hours, spillover tends to be only one-way from work time to personal time.

The term "workaholic" has become a familiar one in recent years. Popular books and articles have described overworked professionals and managers who drag their spouses from one assignment to another and remind them how much the company has done for them. Although the connotation of a workaholic is negative, the observation of a large number of successful people is that they seem to have tremendous energy for off-the-job activities as well. In fact, the term itself appears to be somewhat misleading. People who enjoy their work find it energizing and are buoyed up in some cases by decisions others would find as burdensome, time-committing and onerous. The key factor in determining the true impact of work time on personal time is not the *amount* of time spent working but the *quality* of satisfaction derived from it. However, because many professionals find such fulfillment in their work, they become *unaware* that they may be withdrawing from personal aspects of their lives.

In this vignette, Vernon successfully did several things:

1. He listened to Al's concerns without being surprised that Al was having problems at home. (If Vernon had expressed surprise, Al would have been less likely to continue.)
2. He paraphrased by keying off a phrase or word used by Al.
3. He avoided giving his opinion until he had some confidence that he knew what was troubling Al.
4. He gave advice by describing a general process that Al fit into loosely, thus giving Al freedom to draw his own conclusions.

It is not easy for many people to manage all of the activities and interests they have. Most of us want to do many things at once and must choose between competing goals and values. Writing down what we want, why it is important to us, making goals over areas where we exercise primary control, and reviewing our progress toward goal attainment is a process that is more likely to result in the realization of the goals we most desire and the interests that are the most important.

Postscript

Counseling employees at the workplace pays off. It pays off in dollars and sense. It pays off in dollars because people get solutions to their problems and become more adept at problem-solving. It makes sense to effectively counsel employees so they will view the counselor as a resource and be more committed to the organization that employs them. Effective counseling pays off because people increase their competence and are better able to deal with the frustrations and conflicts they encounter in their lives.

Counseling is not merely a skill or even a set of skills, although there certainly are important counseling skills to be mastered. It is also a perspective which suggests that through one-to-one interaction, many problems can be started on the road to resolution. This does not mean that implicit in counseling is the assumption that most problems are communication problems. Too often a failure to communicate is attributed to a particular problem without recognizing other factors that affect the situation. In the movie, *Cool Hand Luke,* a chain gang prisoner who is popular with the other inmates because he champions "causes" others are afraid to support, collides with a tyrannical prison warden. The warden repeatedly subjects the prisoners to harsh treatment and indicates there seems to be a failure to communicate between the two. Although on the surface this is a correct statement, it says little about the basic difference in values, goals, and methods which the warden and the prisoner see as appropriate in running the prison.

Changing people is not often easy, but it is not always difficult. Counseling employees often takes time, but it is not necessarily time consuming. Problems can often be avoided or averted when an organization equips managers and others to effectively counsel with employees.

THE HUMAN RESOURCE CHALLENGE

"People problems" are increasing in intensity as well as in volume. Surveys of top executives by consulting firms and private employment agencies reveal some surprising trends.

Managers and personnel specialists are increasingly being forced to spend a large portion of their time in setting rules and establishing policies to protect their organizations from being taken advantage of by employees or from being attacked by unions or sued by the government. This drain on their time has meant that there is generally insufficient time left over to develop relationships of trust with direct subordinates and other employees. As a result of this lack of interaction, employees are increasingly complaining that their bosses are unaware of their problems. First line supervisors are saying that managers are insulated from pressing operating problems while managers are saying that top executives just don't seem to care what happens to ordinary employees. The result is that employees are turning more and more to the courts or governmental agencies to solve problems which were once handled within the organization.

Organizations seem to be responding to these conditions with demands for tighter controls and more information. A proliferation of data sources and cross checks have resulted which are intended to streamline procedures and make executives more aware of internal operations. However, much of the data is of marginal relevance and nearly all of it has to be interpreted for the executive by a staff expert. Thus, the executive becomes even further removed from the people who actually produce the company's product. In today's organization, there is more information and more efficiency than in the past, but there is less human interaction and less overall effectiveness.

There is truly an array of human resource problems that confront managers and others. The implications of legislative and regulatory mandates such as Executive Order 11246, the Age Discrimination

Act, The Employee Retirement Income Security Act, Title VII, Equal Employment Opportunity decrees, and Occupational Safety and Health Act orders are apparent to anyone who is involved in a management position.

Among the new problems to be solved is effectively motivating and directing a better educated work force. This observation is given substance by a revealing statistic. According to the Bureau of Labor Statistics, only 20% of the jobs in the United States require more than a high school education. Although in 1970 only one out of eight workers had a college degree, by 1980 one out of every four entering the labor market had one. This more highly educated labor force, with increased aspirations, presents its own challenges of providing both satisfying work and advancement opportunities.

A more educated work force wants more interesting jobs and more participation in matters which affect them at work. Interesting jobs are more in demand and secure jobs less in demand. Jobs generally have been getting better in many ways: higher incomes, more leisure, more security, better working conditions. However, as the post-war baby boom moves toward middle age, competition for advancement opportunities will intensify. For those who do not obtain all that they wish, the challenge of dealing with unfulfilled expectations and disappointments and the resultant impact on morale and performance is obvious.

These challenges and opportunities are all too real and all too apparent to many who manage in organizations today. The problem is not noticing them but rather deciding what to do about them. The formula for good employee relations through counseling at the workplace is so simple that it may appear either naive or obvious. Counseling is so effective because it not only solves specific problems, but also establishes a *systematic mechanism* for solving problems. It is an evergreen method for knowing and deciding how to improve employees' competence. This observation prompts the obvious rejoinder: "If it is all so simple and easy as that, why have so few managers mastered it?" Recognizing that simplicity is often wisdom and obvious mistakes are the easiest to overlook, provides the beginning of an answer.

Counseling:
Resources

A list of resources available to assist counselors in maintaining desired changes is included at this point. If there is any message that is a part of this book, it is that many problems are more easily solved when they are shared with someone else. We often see things more clearly ourselves just by explaining our beliefs, sentiments, or feelings with someone else. There are resources available all around us if we will but reach out and use them.

These resources are organized according to the material included in the chapters and application units. Pertinent data relating to the process of counseling and problem-solving are included together, while resources that may be useful in exploring a particular topic in the applications units are identified separately. This list of resources is kept purposely brief, and only the most relevant materials are cited.

COUNSELING AND PROBLEM-SOLVING

James Adams, *Conceptual Blockbusting* (San Francisco: San Francisco Book Co., 1976).

Richard N. Bolles, *The Three Boxes of Life* (Berkeley, California: Ten Speed Press, 1978).

Edward de Bono, *Lateral Thinking* (New York: Harper and Row, 1972).

Irving Janis and Leon Mann, *Decision-Making: A Psychological Analysis of Conflict, Choice and Commitment* (New York: Free Press, 1977).

Dorothy E. Johnson and Mary J. Vestermark, *Barriers and Hazards in Counseling* (New York: Houghton Mifflin, 1970).

John Krumboltz and Carl Thoreson, *Behavioral Counseling: Cases and Techniques* (New York: Holt, Rinehart, and Winston, 1972).

David C. McClelland, "A Competency Model for Human Resource Management Specialists To Be Used in the Delivery of the Human Resource Management Cycle." (Unpublished manuscript, available from McBer and Company, Boston, Massachusetts).

Barbara Okun, *Effective Helping: Interviewing and Counseling Techniques* (Belmont, California: Wadsworth Press, 1976).

Eugene Ranseppand and George P. Hough, *Creative Growth Games* (New York: Harcourt Brace Jovanovich, 1977).

Len Sperry and Lee R. Hess, *Contact Counseling* (Reading, Massachusetts: Addison-Wesley, 1974).

PAY, PROMOTIONS, AND APPRAISALS

Robert E. Boynton, "How Employees Measure Their Pay," *Compensation Review* (Summer, 1970).

W. Clay Hammer, "How to Ruin Motivation with Pay," *Compensation Review* (Fall, 1975).

Edward E. Lawler, *Pay and Organizational Effectiveness: A Psychological Review* (New York: McGraw-Hill, 1971).

Michael Maccoby, *The Gamesman* (New York: Simon and Schuster, 1977).

Herbert H. Meyer, Emanuel Kay, and John R. P. French, Jr., "Split Roles in Performance Appraisal," *Harvard Business Review* (Jan-Feb, 1965) pp. 21-29.

Harold P. Smith and Paul J. Brouwer, *Performance Appraisal and Human Development* (Reading, Massachusetts: Addison-Wesley, 1977).

William Foote Whyte, *Money and Motivation* (New York: Harper and Row, 1955).

CAREER COUNSELING

Gene W. Dalton, Paul H. Thompson, and Ray W. Price, "Four Stages of a Professional Career," *Organizational Dynamics* (Summer, 1977) pp. 19-42.

Douglas T. Hall, *Careers in Organizations* (Santa Monica, California: Goodyear Publishing Co., 1976).

Eugene E. Jennings, *Routes to the Executive Suite* (New York: McGraw-Hill, 1971).

Arthur G. Kirn and Marie O'Donahoe Kirn, *Life Work Planning* (New York: McGraw-Hill, 1978).

Daniel Levinson, *The Seasons of a Man's Life* (New York: Knopf, 1978).

Donald B. Miller, *Personal Vitality* (Reading, Massachusetts: Addison-Wesley, 1977).

David Moment and Dalmar Fisher, *Autonomy in Organizational Life* (Cambridge, Massachusetts: Schenkman, 1975).

Herbert A. Shepard and J. A. Hawley, *Life Planning* (Washington, D.C.: National Training and Development Service, 1974).

Cyril Sofer, *Men in Mid-Career* (Cambridge, England: Cambridge University Press, 1970).

Nicholas W. Weiler, *Reality and Career Planning* (Reading, Massachusetts: Addison-Wesley, 1977).

MALE-FEMALE ISSUES

Cynthia Fuchs Epstein, *Woman's Place: Options and Limits in Professional Careers* (Berkeley, California: University of California Press, 1971).

Margaret Hennig and Anne Jardim, *The Managerial Woman* (New York: Doubleday, 1977).

Rosabeth Moss Kantor, *The Men and Women of the Corporation* (New York: Basic Books, 1977).

Ruth Kundsin (ed.), *Women and Success: The Anatomy of Achievement* (New York: Morrow, 1973).

Rosalind Loring and Herbert Otto, *New Life Options: The Working Woman's Resource Book* (New York: McGraw-Hill, 1976).

Rosalind Loring and Theodora Wells, *Breakthrough: Women Into Management* (New York: Van Nostrand, 1972).

Ruth Helen Osborn, *Developing New Horizons for Women* (New York: McGraw-Hill, 1977).

Alice G. Sargent, *Beyond Sex Roles* (St. Paul, Minnesota: West Publishing Co., 1977).

EEO PROBLEMS

Affirmative Action and Equal Employment: A Guide Book for Employers (Washington, D.C.: United States Equal Employment Opportunity Commission, 1974).

Richard I. America and Bernard E. Anderson, *Moving Ahead: Black Managers in American Business,* (New York: McGraw-Hill, 1978).

Phillip T. Crotty and Jeffrey A. Timmons, "Older Minorities—Roadblocked in the Organization," *Business Horizons* (June 1974) pp. 27-34.

John Fernandez, *Black Managers in White Corporations,* (New York: Wiley and Sons, 1974).

Oscar A. Ornati and Anthony Pisano, "Affirmative Action: Why Isn't it Working?" *The Personnel Administrator* (Sept./Oct., 1972) pp. 50-52.

Richard Peres, *Preventing Discrimination Complaints: A Guide for Supervisors* (New York: McGraw-Hill, 1979)

BOSS-SUBORDINATE RELATIONS

William F. Dowling and Leonard R. Sayles, *How Managers Motivate* (New York: McGraw-Hill, 1978).

Norman C. Hill and Paul H. Thompson, "Managing Your Manager: The Effective Subordinate" *Management Digest* (June, 1979) pp. 23-27.

Henry Mintzberg, *The Nature of Managerial Work* (New York: Harper and Row, 1973).

Eric H. Neilsen and Jan Gypen, "The Subordinate's Predicaments" *Harvard Business Review* (Sept-Oct., 1979) pp. 133-143.

Victor Vroom and Philip Yelton, *Leadership and Decision-Making* (Pittsburgh: University of Pittsburgh Press, 1973).

William Foote Whyte, "Taking Initiative with the Boss," Sayles (ed), *Individualism and Big Business* (New York: McGraw-Hill, 1963).

PERFORMANCE PROBLEMS

James Black, *Positive Discipline* (New York: AMACOM, 1970).

Thomas K. Connellan, *How to Improve Human Performance: Behaviorism in Business and Industry* (New York: Harper and Row, 1978).

Alan C. Filley, *Interpersonal Conflict Resolution* (New York: Scott, Foresman, 1975).

Ferdinand F. Fournies, *Coaching For Improved Work Performance* (Van Nostrand, 1978).

Thomas F. Gilbert, *Human Competence: Engineering Worthy Performance* (New York: McGraw-Hill, 1978).

John B. Miner, *The Management of Ineffective Performance* (New York: McGraw-Hill, 1963).

Lawrence L. Steinmetz, *Managing the Marginal and Unsatisfactory Performer* (Reading, Massachusetts: Addison-Wesley, 1969).

WORK RULES

George S. Booker, "Behavioral Aspects of Disciplinary Action," *Personnel Journal* (August, 1969) pp. 525-529.

Darrel R. Brown, "Do Personnel Policies Alienate Employees?" *The Personnel Administrator* (Jan-Feb., 1970) pp. 29-37.

Arthur Gerstenfeld, "Employee Absenteeism: New Insights" *Business Horizons* (Sept-Oct, 1969), pp. 51-60.

John H. Goldthorpe, et al., *The Affluent Worker: Industrial Attitudes and Behavior* (Cambridge University Press, 1968).

John B. Miner, *The Challenge of Managing* (Philadelphia, W. B. Saunders, 1975).

COPING WITH JOB DEMANDS

Don Gowler and Karen Legge (eds), *Managerial Stress,* (New York: John Wiley and Sons, 1975).

Alan McLean, *Work Stress* (Reading, Massachusetts: Addison-Wesley, 1979).

Alan N. Schoonmaker, *Anxiety and the Executive* (New York: AMACOM, 1969).

Waino Suojanen and Donald Hudson, "Coping with Stress and Addictive Work Behavior," *Atlanta Economic Review* (Mar-Apr, 1977) pp. 4-9.

Studs Terkel, *Working* (New York: Avon Books, 1975).

Karl Weick, "I Can Handle It: The Management of Stress," *MBA* (Oct 1975) pp. 37-40.

PERSONAL/WORK ISSUES

Ralph L. Blankenship, *Colleagues in Organizations: The Social Construction of Professional Work* (New York: Wiley and Sons, 1977).

Samuel A. Culbert and Jean R. Renshaw, "Coping with the Stresses of Travel as an Opportunity for Improving the Quality of Work and Family Life," *Family Process* (Sept. 1972) pp. 331-332.

Paul A. L. Evans and Fernando Bartolomé, "Professional and Private Life: Three Stages in the Lives of Managers," *Organizational Dynamics,* (Spring 1979).

Abraham Kornhauser, *Mental Health of the Industrial Worker* (New York: Wiley and Sons, 1965).

Diane Rothbard Margolis, *The Managers: Corporate Life in America* (New York: Morrow and Company, 1979).

J. M. Pahl and R. E. Pahl, *Managers and Their Wives* (London: Penguin, 1971).

Robert Seidenberg, *Corporate Wives—Corporate Casualties?* (New York: AMACOM, 1973).

Harrison N. Trice, "Identifying the Problem Drinker on the Job," *Personnel* (May, 1957).

Index